PENGUIN BOOKS

T0354176

Garry Linnell is the author of six books, including the bestselling *Buckley's Chance* and *Moonlite: The tragic love story of Captain Moonlite and the bloody end of the bushrangers*. One of Australia's most experienced journalists, Linnell is a Walkley Award winner for feature writing and has been editor-in-chief of *The Bulletin*, editor of *The Daily Telegraph*, director of news and current affairs for the Nine Network and editorial director of Fairfax. He spent four years as co-host of the Breakfast Show on 2UE.

The DEVIL'S WORK

GARRY LINNELL

PENGUIN BOOKS

PENGUIN BOOKS

UK | USA | Canada | Ireland | Australia
India | New Zealand | South Africa | China

Viking is part of the Penguin Random House group of companies
whose addresses can be found at global.penguinrandomhouse.com

Penguin
Random House
Australia

First published by Viking in 2021

This edition published by Penguin Books in 2022

Copyright © Garry Linnell 2021

The moral right of the author has been asserted.

Front cover images by Shutterstock; back cover image courtesy of the State Library of Victoria
Cover design by Alex Ross © Penguin Random House Australia Pty Ltd
Typeset in 11.5/15.5 pt Adobe Garamond Pro by Midland Typesetters, Australia

Printed and bound in Australia by Griffin Press, an accredited
ISO AS/NZS 14001 Environmental Management Systems printer

A catalogue record for this
book is available from the
NATIONAL LIBRARY   National Library of Australia
OF AUSTRALIA

ISBN 978 1 76104 176 1

penguin.com.au

MIX
Paper from
responsible sources
FSC® C009448

We at Penguin Random House Australia acknowledge that Aboriginal and Torres Strait
Islander peoples are the Traditional Custodians and the first storytellers of the lands
on which we live and work. We honour Aboriginal and Torres Strait Islander peoples'
continuous connection to Country, waters, skies and communities. We celebrate
Aboriginal and Torres Strait Islander stories, traditions and living cultures;
and we pay our respects to Elders past and present.

Hell is empty and all the devils are here.
William Shakespeare, The Tempest

DEVILS, DEMONS
AND DOUBTERS:
A NOTE FOR READERS

This is a story about a gruesome and macabre series of murders in the nineteenth century and the twisted and damaged man who committed them. Despite its claims of demonic possession, hauntings and incidents defying the laws of physics, it is not a work of fiction but a true tale that reflects the beliefs held by millions of people in the Victorian era. Anything that appears in quotation marks has been sourced from memoirs, court affidavits and contemporary reports of the time.

CONTENTS

PART I.

'She ain't pretty to look at'

I.

He cradled the dead body in his hands.

It was such a beautiful thing. Death was a brazen thief that stole the warmth from his victims while he watched. But it never took everything. It still left enough to touch and gently stroke and remind him how majestic a corpse could be, long after its heart had stopped pounding and its limbs had stiffened and its blood had clotted and turned cold.

Besides, he was skilled in removing all traces of death's touch, for he was a man who took pride in restoring his victims to life.

So patient was he, so precise. He could take a body twisted and frozen and bent out of shape, all matted with blood and bone fragments. Within a short time it would be cleaned and propped up so lifelike, so *alive*, you were sure its eyes were gleaming and its chest about to rise with newly found breath.

Who knew why he enjoyed doing this so much or why it had become such a passion. Perhaps it offered a kind of redemption, a way to pay back the universe for all the killing. Perhaps that is why he took so much care, for once the grisly business of extinguishing life was over he became gentle with his victims, almost loving.

He put the body down carefully and picked up a knife from his bench. It was sharp and his hand was steady. He had done this many

3

times in many parts of the world. He knew exactly where to make the first incision. He knew how to flay the skin, to peel it to one side, to expertly cut through all the bone and cartilage and tendons before removing the eyes and cleverly adjusting the head to a more pleasing angle.

There were other things he could be doing, of course. There was always more work to be done. But the body in front of him had been dead for more than twelve hours and he never liked it decaying for too long.

There was also no point going outside. It was just after breakfast on Saturday morning, 21 May 1892. A storm had come roaring across Port Phillip Bay in the southern Australian city of Melbourne. He could hear the wild banshee scream of the wind hammering on doors and slamming against windows. Gobs of rain – heavy, leaden – pounded the roof. His rented home, perched on a corner lot on an exposed hilltop, was almost sobbing, its timber frame groaning and sighing like an arthritic old man.

In the front yard two pomegranate trees had surrendered the last of their fruit. No real loss. He did not care for their red seeds and crimson pulp. He was a man of simple tastes and thought the pomegranate's edible qualities overrated. He preferred something less flamboyant, like the orchard in the backyard with its promise – sadly unfulfilled in recent months – of fragrant lemons and plump pears and twisted ropey vines sagging with grapes.

He concentrated on the task before him. He squinted through small wire frame spectacles perched high on his nose. His forehead, ringed by a receding hairline, was furrowed. He could have been a bank clerk methodically counting pennies. He made his first incision, a preliminary cut next to the breast. But as he pulled the knife away to study his progress he heard a bell, its faint ringing almost suffocated by the ferocity of the storm.

Someone was at the front door. In this weather?

Sidney Dickinson put his knife down, his concentration broken. He wiped his hands, stood up and walked down the hallway to the front of the house. Behind those spectacles were eyes that hinted at sadness. He had a thick black moustache and goatee that only partly disguised a gaunt, weary face. He had turned forty-one a few weeks earlier and while there had been much wonder and excitement in recent years, there had also been stress.

He had travelled the world, relentlessly it seemed, on ships, trains and bumpy horse-drawn carriages that jarred a man's bones no matter his age. He had endured typhoid, his body racked by abdominal pains and drenched in feverish sweats. Then, just as he began regaining his strength – the doctors had warned a full recovery might take years – a drunken thug had wrenched his glasses away and hurled him to the floor of a hotel lobby, kicking and beating him almost senseless.

It was enough to make a man feel old. But the incessant travel, the sickness and the bruises from that beating were nothing compared to what Dickinson had confronted in recent months. He was hardly a squeamish man. He never blanched when it came to cutting flesh or scooping warm guts with cupped hands. But he had seen and heard things over the past eight weeks – hideous, revolting *things* – that had given him new insights into the depravity and evil that lurked in some men's hearts.

It had left him horrified and saddened. For days he had felt a heavy weight pressing upon his spirit.

He walked past the parlour to his left with its fine piano and open fireplace. Several excellent paintings adorned the walls. He had closely studied those works of art soon after renting the house. They had met with his approval, which was no small thing, for Sidney Dickinson was a man who had spent much of his life scrutinising the brush strokes of the masters, delighting in the way they captured a fleeting moment to convey so much meaning and feeling.

Dickinson had stood behind podiums around the world and lectured on art to hushed and appreciative audiences. He had only recently completed an extensive tour of New Zealand and Australia. Reviewers had admired Dickinson's 'attractive voice', his 'rich fund of dry humour', his 'witty and terse' style of delivery. They often referred to him as 'Professor Dickinson', which was perhaps a little of an exaggeration, although he never minded. He had mesmerised crowds in Sydney, Melbourne, London, Paris and across his native America with his stereopticon magic lantern, a dazzling contraption with two lenses that projected colourful scenes on to large screens, dissolving one and replacing it with another image.

An American newspaper had hailed him for inventing 'a new form of entertainment for intelligent people . . . any showman can throw pictures on a screen, but it takes a scholar and a critic to select the pictures and draw the value from them'. Dickinson had written critiques of the French Impressionists and once informed readers of *The Boston Daily Journal* that Renoir's 'Luncheon of the Boating Party', while 'at first sight a preposterous jumble of colour and form . . . is found on examination to achieve a certain out-of-door and atmospheric effect which is recognizable as very true to atmospheric conditions'.

He was a man of cultural and intellectual pursuits who enjoyed bushwalking with a loaded revolver and shotgun by his side. Nature's silence offered serenity and new colours and shapes to admire, a welcome change from the drab stone and muted pastels of the city. Australia was still a new country to him and there was something about its strange and often desolate landscape – that sheer expanse of *nothing* – which appealed to him. The light was stark and, in summer, almost blinding. He thought it would be 'quite impossible to find, in any part of the world, more striking effects than are found ready to the artist's hand in the Australian landscape'.

But that Saturday morning when he opened the front door all he could see was a washed-out sky, a gloomy canvas stained with nothing but swirls of black and grey. And in the corner of the front verandah, huddled against the driving sheets of rain, stood a drenched and wretched figure with a faint glimmer of hope in his eyes.

Sidney Dickinson, art critic, correspondent for *The New York Times* and, because one needed a reliable source of income, local representative of the Mutual Life Insurance Company of New York, was impatient.

There was a body on his workbench at the rear of his house that required his attention. It was a purple lorikeet, one of a 'fine assortment of cockatoos, parrots and other brilliantly plumaged or curious birds' he had shot while on a collecting trip in the countryside the day before. Dickinson loved his taxidermy and had several hours of 'congenial labour' ahead of him that day, removing and preserving their skins before stuffing and mounting them so well a visitor would swear he had brought them back to life.

But first he had to listen to that stranger on the porch, a man with wet dark hair plastered to his scalp, clothes sodden and hanging heavy, face ashen and almost jaundiced.

The bedraggled visitor, a salesman for a local publishing company, was offering him a gruesome confession of lust, betrayal, murder and demonic possession. For a mere sixpence Sidney Dickinson could thumb through the damp pages of a just-published pamphlet and read about a man so wicked and morally bankrupt the world now knew him as 'the criminal of the century'.

That man, that creature called Frederick Deeming, was rumoured to be Jack the Ripper, the unidentified serial killer who had murdered and mutilated at least five women in London's Whitechapel district several years earlier. Deeming, a serial bigamist, conman and swindler, had slaughtered two of his wives and all four of his children, slicing their throats and burying their bodies in shallow cement tombs on opposite sides of the world. He had roamed the planet for years under various aliases, preying on the innocent, the gullible and the desperate. In just a few days' time the colony of Victoria intended to put a rope around his neck and send him back to the hell that had spawned him.

Sidney Dickinson put his hand in his pocket and handed the salesman his sixpence, more out of charity than curiosity. He didn't expect to learn anything new. He had already heard this story before, in all its stomach-turning detail.

Two days earlier he had stood in front of the killer and spoken to him. The aftermath of that visit with Frederick Deeming would leave him shocked and sleepless for a long time to come.

It would also confirm what Sidney had long suspected. Reality was nothing more than a carefully crafted stage. Behind it lurked a realm of shadows where demons and monsters like Frederick Deeming dwelled and preyed on the living.

II.

The doomed man stood in his death cell in the Melbourne Gaol. He was alone except for a bucket, a small flimsy cot and his dead mother crouching in the corner. As usual she was screeching at him, telling him he was worthless, that he would be dead before he turned forty.

Frederick Deeming had heard it all before. The old hag never had anything new to say. She was always spitting the same gobfuls of hate and spite. You would think he would have been used to the death and decay on her breath and all those horrible insults she hurled his way. You would think he could have summoned one of his well-known callous sneers and made her cower and shake with fear, too.

But he cringed every time. Mother's voice never lost its sting. She knew her boy too well. She didn't need a belt to make him cry and beg her to leave him be. This son of hers disgusted her. He was an abomination, the spawn of the devil himself, a twisted, evil *thing* she should never have pushed from her womb.

Mother had always been right and the entire world agreed with her.

Hadn't everyone known little Freddy wouldn't amount to much? He had spent most of his life trying to prove them wrong, to show them Frederick Bailey Deeming was not a man to underestimate. Hadn't he escaped from that dull Merseyside life as soon as he could? Please, Mother. Give him some credit. He wasn't like the rest of them back in Birkenhead, those unimaginative brothers of his content to endure their miserable lives in the noise and filth of the Laird Brothers shipyard, who came home to endless rows of tiny houses where kids played on grimy streets and every day – *every day* – was the same.

Saw the world, he had. Sailed its oceans and crossed its continents. Was it any wonder that whenever he returned from one of his overseas odysseys he couldn't help but boast about his achievements? Old Lancashire folk who stubbornly clung to the old words called it *braggarting* and once Freddy got himself all wound up he would find it hard to stop. If you disagreed with him or – far worse – ridiculed him, he'd start a decent *fratching*, a loud quarrel that would see him get so worked up his voice would climb higher and become more frantic until it was almost a squeak.

He had been a right strutter with his fancy clothes and diamond rings and awkward airs and graces. Sometimes he had hung a heavy gold watch from a chain attached to the breast pocket of an expensive frock coat. On other days he replaced it with military medals he claimed to have won in torrid battles in foreign lands. He had scars to prove it, too, and he wasn't shy when it came to showing them off. He would quickly roll up a trouser leg and show you the wound on his leg, or open his shirt to expose where an enemy's knife had slashed his chest. If he was really out to impress there was always the small hole at the back of his head he was only too willing to allow the curious to examine. Put your finger in there, he would say. See how it fits? Bullet did that.

Big little man was Frederick Deeming. If he pulled himself up straight in a pair of well-heeled boots he might have been described, somewhat generously, as being of *average* height. Nothing more. But the way he swaggered? Everyone agreed that, for all his strangeness, he was a cocky one. He was like one of those bantam roosters that dwelled in many of Birkenhead's tiny backyards; scrawny, defensive things scratching in the dirt below clotheslines sagging with stained overalls, always preening and fluffing their feathers to make themselves look bigger and more important.

If he was conscious of his height he would have you know it never stopped him from cleaving the heads of angry savages in deepest Africa or entering a darkened cave and launching a battle to the death with a pride of ferocious lions. Every story bigger, every tale more outlandish, every lie more unbelievable.

So many lies. The doctors who had examined him, the police who had interviewed him and the priests who had tended to his soul no longer knew what to believe. He had told them all about his dead mother's abusive visits and how, over the years, she had woken him at night and urged him to kill. He had resisted for as long as he could. But Mother could be awfully persuasive when she was in a mood.

But was Mother really there? Or was she just another of his many deceptions? The question had dominated his trial. Was the man genuinely insane? Or was his claim about his dead mother's murderous orders just another of his crude ploys, a way to feign madness in a bid to avoid the noose? If that was the case you had to give him credit for keeping up the pretence, because Frederick Deeming had run out of chances. There would be no more appeals. In a few days they would lead him to the gallows.

He was thirty-nine years old. He would be dead before he was forty.

Bloody Mother. Right again.

Ann Deeming must have sensed during her pregnancy that this fourth child of hers would be different to the rest of her brood. Her sullen husband, Thomas Deeming, certainly had.

The way Frederick's oldest brother told it, Thomas Deeming had turned real nasty when Ann fell pregnant with Freddy. Cruel, like. Father would criticise everything she did. If Mother dared open her mouth and express an opinion her husband would respond with a stinging rebuke or the back of his hand.

He was, said the brother, a man whose moods swung even faster than his fists.

'He was a most passionate man and when out of temper had no control over himself,' Edward Deeming, the oldest child of the clan, had declared in a sworn affidavit not long after Frederick's arrest.

It was as if Thomas Deeming, a whitesmith who shaped metal into kitchen goods and was a tortured soul at the best of times, had sensed the baby was not his. One day not long after Freddy was born in 1853 Thomas went to work and never came home. According to Edward, he simply took off and left Ann on her own with four young children and no way to feed them. Humiliated, embarrassed and no doubt afraid, she had trekked all over the English countryside, knocking on doors, asking questions of strangers, visiting all his old haunts until she tracked him down and he took her back in.

But the father's sins were nothing compared to the crimes committed by Frederick. Was it any wonder Ann woke her son in the early hours of every morning to tell him he was no good? She had been dead for many years but that hadn't stopped her climbing out of her grave and scaring the life out of her boy. The guards pulling the nightshift outside Frederick Deeming's cell could set their clocks by Mother's visits. Each night at 2am they heard him let out a blood-curdling scream.

Most reasonable folk assumed Frederick was faking it all. But in the late nineteenth century there remained many – an astonishing number of them enjoying prominent and influential roles in society – who were convinced the dead could communicate with the living. And it wasn't as if Ann Deeming was one of those predictable spirits that appeared only at night when the living were at their most vulnerable.

Sometimes she came in the daylight, too, just to keep that son of hers on his toes. Like that day – the nineteenth of May 1892. It was two days before a violent Saturday morning storm, before a ringing doorbell that would distract Sidney Dickinson as he sat hunched over the corpse of a purple lorikeet.

Footsteps echoed down the cold stone hallway of the Melbourne Gaol. Frederick Deeming had visitors and he was eager to introduce them to Mother.

III.

Sidney Dickinson had been forced to do some fast talking to convince his wife Marion to accompany him on his visit to Deeming. The thought of stepping inside a Gothic prison with its rows of caged inmates and reputation for savagery had horrified her. Marion was a highly sensitive woman and Sidney was often taken aback by her uncanny ability to detect *disturbances* in the air around her.

Like millions of other middle and upper class couples around the world who wanted to keep up with the times, the Dickinsons were devotees of spiritualism, a quasi-religious movement that was peaking in popularity toward the close of the nineteenth century. If Sidney remained curious about its claims of an afterlife where the dead could communicate with the living, Marion was a devout believer who sometimes seemed more at home in the shadowy border land separating the two worlds. She barely blinked when material objects appeared to defy the laws of physics. She smiled when apparitions seemed to appear out of walls. Participants at séances she had hosted back home in the United States claimed to have seen tables levitating in her presence. Disembodied voices – usually sad and pleading for help – were said to fill darkened rooms when she entered them.

Spiritualism's critics – many of them reputable scientists – had long dismissed the movement as a hoax perpetrated on the gullible and the vulnerable. Prominent mediums – often patronised by European royalty – had been exposed using secret wires and fake limbs to simulate ghostly visits and apparitions. But what Sidney had experienced in the years since his marriage to Marion had finally convinced him that a realm of disembodied souls existed.

Dickinson's training as a journalist and critic had made him a studious note-taker. All those observations – many of them involving his experiences with Marion and also Frederick Deeming – would, three decades later, contribute to his book, *True Tales of The Weird – a Record of Personal Experiences of the Supernatural*.

Along with a copy of his original manuscript, Sidney provided the American Society for Psychical Research with a cache of references and supporting testimony from eyewitnesses. According to Gertrude Tubby, a senior researcher with the society, 'no more better attested phenomena of the kind have come to our attention . . . they ring true. And they are, in addition, moving human documents, with a strong literary appeal.'

A friend of Sidney's in his later years, Raymond Stetson, the professor of psychology at Oberlin College, would write in the book's introduction that Dickinson 'had an unusual memory, a keen sense of accuracy and he was cool and practical rather than emotional or excitable. No one who was much with him in the later days could doubt the entire sincerity of the man . . . the narrative was written because he felt that it might well be a contribution of some scientific interest.'

By the time he completed the book Dickinson had spent decades dwelling on what he had seen. 'These stories are not "founded upon fact",' he wrote. 'They *are* fact.'

One of the strangest had taken place in the 1880s when he travelled to Europe to study the art of the masters. Marion, God bless her, had remained in Boston to care for Sidney's seven-year-old daughter from his first marriage. She and the girl had moved into a suite in Winthrop House on Bowdoin Street. How fortunate a man was he? Marion had immediately bonded with Sidney's daughter and the pair quickly became inseparable. This closeness between stepmother and stepdaughter – surely another example of Marion's grace and empathy – had been a constant source of comfort for him during his overseas journeys.

Sidney's travels had taken him across the Continent and deep into southern Italy. One day he caught a boat from the Bay of Naples to the island of Capri where, being Sidney, he couldn't help but explore the hills behind the port with their fields of long grass 'spangled with delicate white flowers bearing a yellow centre'.

Knowing how bleak the weather would be back in New England, he collected these blossoms because they reminded him of the daisies that lined the streets at home during spring. He then placed them gently to dry between the pages of his much-prized guidebook, the German publisher Karl Baedeker's *Southern Italy*. One never travelled without Mr Baedeker's comprehensive tourist manuals. Their attention to detail was astonishing. Before his sudden death in 1859, Mr Baedeker had been spied climbing the stairs to the roof of the Milan Cathedral with a pocket filled with peas. After every twenty steps he had placed one of the peas in another pocket to ensure he had faithfully counted every step for his readers.

When Sidney returned to Rome he had placed several letters to Marion and his daughter in envelopes and included the newly dried flowers from Capri. For good measure he added a scattering of fragrant violets he had found strewn across the grassy floor of the tomb of Caecilia Metella.

Ten days later Marion claimed to have woken to find the ghost of Sidney's first wife, Minnie, standing at the foot of her bed.

Minnie Stockwell had married Sidney in 1876 and died after giving birth to their daughter less than a year later. Marion, who wed Sidney two years later, felt no fear. It all happened so quickly. Minnie's spirit – 'so serene and gracious' – shimmered in the darkened bedroom. Before it vanished it told Marion: 'I have brought you some flowers from Sidney.'

Marion, according to what she later told Sidney, got out of bed, lit a small gas lamp, glanced around the room and, finding nothing, decided she must have been dreaming. She went back to sleep. At six that morning she woke again and entered the suite's parlour. Scattered across the centre table were violets and small white flowers that reminded her of daisies. She gently nudged Sidney's sleeping daughter and asked her if she knew anything about them.

'Why, no, mamma,' the child said. 'I have never seen them before.'

Later that day several letters arrived from Sidney. One of them referred to the dried flowers he was enclosing. Marion carefully examined every envelope, turning them inside out. But try as she might, there were no blossoms to be found.

Confused, Marion confided in a friend who was renting an apartment on the same floor. Celia Thaxter was a poet and writer on her way to becoming one of America's most popular nineteenth century authors and she and Marion had grown close. Thaxter had attended séances held by Marion and was convinced she had seen and heard things which defied natural explanation. She had watched Marion fall into an unconscious state and believed she was possessed with 'astral qualities' and was 'as true as truth'.

Some of Celia's sceptical acquaintances had warned her that Marion was a fraud, a trickster using spiritualism to make friends among Boston's upper class. But Celia was adamant. She was certain Marion was genuine. Surely the flowers scattered about the woman's parlour were further proof that her new friend had a knack for communing with the dead.

Thaxter, a short woman prone to parting her hair severely down the middle, told Marion she knew a well-known botanist in town who might be able to shed more light on the mystery. He was quickly summoned to Marion's apartment. The two women chose not to tell this learned man about the supernatural events that had led to the appearance of the flowers. But would he mind inspecting them so they might learn where the blossoms might have grown?

The botanist peered at the violets closely. He picked them up by their stems and carefully sniffed them.

'Difficult to say where they grew,' he told the women. 'However, coupled with the scent they still faintly retain . . . incline me to the opinion that they came from part of southern Europe – perhaps France, but more likely Italy.'

And the small white flowers that resemble daisies? 'They must have come from some point about the Bay of Naples, as I am not aware of their occurrence elsewhere.'

The Strange Incident of The Mysterious Flowers was just one of many supernatural events the Dickinsons would experience. Sidney would find no rational explanation for them. He was not blessed, he wrote, with Marion's supernatural vision and could never see the ghosts she did. But he had no doubts that Marion – 'intensely human . . . and in all things womanly' – believed the visitations to be real.

She had accompanied him several times around the globe and allowed him glimpses inside this mysterious spirit world she inhabited. There was the night she felt her shawl being tugged by an unseen hand. Another when a fire spontaneously erupted in a bedroom drawer. She often heard the weary sighs of the dead and their tapping and knocking on walls in empty rooms. At séances Marion had staged, visitors claimed murky figures had emerged from the walls. Sometimes guests had been doused in showers of petals. The dead, it seemed, had a fine appreciation for blossoms of all kinds. Could it be, thought Sidney, that his wife was a human antenna, one of those rare people capable of detecting transmissions from a world beyond this one? He had sought out experts around the world, placed all the evidence before them and been surprised when they, too, could offer no credible explanation.

In the end he would conclude 'that disembodied spirits can at least make their existence known to us appears to me a well-approved fact; that they are "forbid to tell the secrets of their prison-house" is my equally firm conviction'.

He was certain of something else, too. He wanted the reluctant Marion by his side when he came face to face with the prisoner he and many others regarded as 'the criminal of the century' – the most infamous murderer of the Victorian era and a wayward son claiming to be haunted by his dead and disapproving mother.

IV.

Marion Dickinson did not require a séance to summon demons and spirits out of the darkness on the day she went with her husband to the Melbourne Gaol. The prison, regarded as one of the most brutal in the world, was haunted enough by the living. Even on a warm day visitors would feel their skin dimple. The stone walls were scarred and pocked and smelled faintly of earth. Screams and cries echoed down the halls. The cells reeked of despair, of fresh shit and stale piss, of bitter tobacco and uneaten food. The men inside muttered threats and protested their innocence. The mad – and there were many – pressed their faces against the bars, leering and spitting.

Sidney and Marion made their way down the hall surrounded by that menagerie of the damned. With them was the gaol's governor, John Shegog, and behind them walked two armed guards. It was a testament to Sidney's persuasive abilities – and no doubt the reputation of that respectable journal he wrote for, *The New York Times* – that he and Marion had been allowed such unprecedented access.

In a pocket of Sidney's jacket was a letter from the most powerful man in the colony of Victoria, Colonial Secretary William Shiels, granting permission for the couple to meet with Frederick Deeming. Shiels had done so reluctantly. Journalists had been badgering him for weeks to allow them to interview the condemned man. But he had refused them all except Sidney.

When Sidney met with Shiels the man had shown the usual caution and timidity so common in the colony's politicians and bureaucrats. 'The trial has been so sensational,' he told Dickinson, 'the crimes . . . so atrocious . . . popular feeling has risen to such a pitch . . .'

Shiels was a tall man, lean and prematurely balding. He kept his hair tightly cropped and his thick moustache heavily waxed so its fine ends could be turned upward like bent needles. He had a reputation as an orator who littered his speeches with literary references and sprinklings of Greek and Latin. But he also had a chronic heart condition. There was a bulge in his aorta, the major vessel carrying blood to his heart. His doctors had urged him to take things slowly, a warning his critics believed he was also more than happy to apply to affairs of state.

Shiels had told Sidney he wanted 'no new occasion of excitement'. Deeming was to hang in a few days' time and once that was over the notoriety the case had attracted from all over the world would surely fade. Shiels and his teetering administration could then get back to the stressful work of tackling the colony's deepening recession, inflicted by a dramatic slump in the property market and a series of spectacular banking collapses.

But Dickinson's request – so different, so *unusual* – had piqued his interest. Sidney, being a collector of exotic and colourful paraphernalia, had his heart set on securing a plaster cast of Deeming's right hand, the same hand that had ripped open all those throats and made him the most reviled man on the planet.

So Shiels had allowed the Dickinsons to meet Deeming. With one caveat: there could be no public account of the interview.

'At least not at present,' Shiels had told Dickinson. 'You may imagine the position I should find myself in if it became known that I had discriminated in favour of a foreign journalist . . . I rely upon your discretion.'

That suited Dickinson. He was writing a lengthy article about Deeming that would run on the front page of *The New York Times* on the day the man was hanged. He already had more than enough material. He had sat through the initial inquest into the death of Deeming's second wife as well as the long four days of the trial that followed. He had watched Deeming closely as he stood in the dock, staring at his deeply lined face and those 'steely, evil and magnetic' eyes that glistened with so much ferocity and savage bravado. He had observed how Deeming's lips were often 'drawn in a sardonic sneer', how he looked upon most of the proceedings with disdain and how, at various times, he would wink at and flirt with women in the gallery and interrupt the court with his shrill, cackling voice.

Dickinson had found it a distasteful experience. The evidence, so detailed, so grotesque, had repulsed him. The year before in the small English village of Rainhill Deeming had cut the throat of his long-suffering first wife, strangled his eldest daughter and slit the throats of three younger children before burying them in the kitchen beneath a thick slab of cement.

Several months later the serial bigamist had brought a new wife to Australia and, after setting her up in a small house in the Melbourne suburb of Windsor, slashed her throat, too. He had then placed her trussed body in a shallow grave beneath the hearthstone of a bedroom fireplace and covered it with more cement. Within weeks he had proposed marriage to another woman. He had been arrested shortly before she was due to join him in an isolated outback mining town where he had reportedly placed an order for more concrete.

Frederick Deeming was the antithesis of everything the Victorian era stood for. In an age that prized restraint, good manners, modesty and a morality based on sober Christian ideals, Deeming defied every convention. He seemed bereft of any moral core, more a demon than a man. Some scientists had declared him to be a throwback of some kind, a living fossil closer in mind and spirit to primal man.

No wonder millions around the world had followed the case. Madame Tussaud's in London was preparing a wax figure of the man and a replica of one of his killing grounds, complete with broken concrete and bloodied bodies. Sidney Dickinson had been as transfixed as everyone else. During the trial he had found himself unable to look away from the accused man. There had been times when he feared his eyesight was playing tricks because there seemed to be two Frederick Deemings. The first was that bantam rooster, puffed up and always crowing and heckling, a man full of spite and contempt who would gaze across the crowded courtroom with a maniacal grin as if expecting a round of applause whenever he uttered one of his witless one-liners. The other Deeming was a sober, almost dignified figure, who might easily have passed for a polite and mild-mannered clergyman, sipping tea at a church gathering and respectfully listening to a parishioner's interpretation of that morning's sermon.

'It was not as if he made an effort to keep himself in control,' Dickinson would recall years later, 'but rather as if he were a man with two strong opposed and antagonistic sides to his nature, of which one or the other might manifest itself without any conscious exercise of will.'

At least the visit to the gaol offered Sidney an opportunity to take another look at the man whose crimes had shocked the world. A much closer look. He and Marion were now deep inside the Melbourne Gaol and the man Dickinson believed was Jack the Ripper was staring at him.

V.

His face was heavily whiskered. But gone was the prominent ginger moustache that had once tumbled over his thin creased lips like a heavy theatre curtain. He had cut it off shortly after being captured, thinking it might alter his appearance and confuse witnesses. He had used a shard of broken glass and, when he tired of that, pulled out the rest of the whiskers by the roots. One by one. It was an act that had astonished his captors. Such patience. Such attention to detail. It had reminded them – as if they needed any further reminding – that their prisoner could be a clever man. Not smart or overly intelligent, that was for sure. But good with his hands, quick to adapt and clearly destined to a life in crime – what the learned men of science in the late nineteenth century called an *instinctive* criminal.

Sidney could see Deeming's hollowed cheeks and melancholic eyes. His jutting lower jaw – so often thrust out in defiance – suggested an underbite, a man prone to grinding his teeth in moments of stress. The end was near for Frederick Deeming and even he, a man of so many disguises and personalities, could sense it coming for him.

So had Sidney. 'If ever a living man was predestined gallows meat it is the keen, calculating scoundrel who is proved already to have been guilty of the Windsor and Rainhill atrocities,' Dickinson had noted in a recent story for *The New York Times*.

Gone were the chameleon-like qualities Deeming had once boasted in his prime when he thought he could get away with anything. There was the time he had fled the English town of Hull after staging another of his frequent frauds – jewellery, coins, deeds to land and titles; the list was endless. Frederick had also left a young woman he had only just married sitting alone in a hotel room. She would be one of the lucky ones, the 'uncemented bride' as some would later joke. While she waited for him to return from what he told her would be a quick walk down the street, he had taken a train and bought a ticket on a ship bound for Uruguay. On the journey to its capital city, Montevideo, he had passed himself off as a wealthy diamond dealer. He flattered and flirted with almost every woman on board, a real dandy always seeking attention, that little bantam rooster with a desperate need to big note itself.

He had organised a concert on the main deck one evening and made sure every female passenger was handed a personally signed invitation. Everyone was asked to perform a song or recite a favourite poem. When it was his turn he launched into a rendition of 'The Dead Horse', an old sea shanty sung to celebrate the end of a sailor's first month at sea.

Deeming was travelling under his own name, which was unusual given the many aliases he had adopted over the years. He had assumed so many different identities that when the known ones were finally collated, the list resembled a football team with a lengthy number of reserves.

He had so wanted to pass himself off as a man of status and high class on that trip to Uruguay. But the song contained plenty of words beginning with 'h' and Deeming, caught up in the excitement of being centre stage, dropped every one of them. By the time he finished the second verse he was so lacking in self-awareness he never heard the muffled sniggers among some of those in the audience, their wry, knowing smiles hidden behind cupped hands.

On he ploughed, massacring the lyrics and exposing himself as just another untutored working-class Lancashire lad.

'E's as dead as a nail in the lamp-room door
And 'e won't come worrying us no more
We'll use the 'air of his tail to sew our sails
And the iron of 'is shoe to make deck nails!

A chameleon. A monstrous one who could slit the throat of his wife and slash and strangle the life out of his four young children and then – the very next day – wander into Rainhill with a smile on his face, a spring in his step and not even a hint of dirt beneath his fingernails after a night spent burying their bodies in a tomb of wet concrete.

Or, just months later, he might catch your eye on a Melbourne street and instantly recognise you as a fellow passenger on the ship that brought both of you to Australia. What a jolly, welcoming fellow he could be. He would greet you with a broad smile, insist he must buy you a drink and slap you on the back with the same hand that – just a few days before – had bludgeoned another wife's head in with an axe before tearing open her throat and burying her, too, in a slurry of sand and cement.

Those days were over. But at least the curious American journalist and his wife who stood in front of his cell appeared interested in his plight. It made a nice change from Mother.

Sidney Dickinson understood the world's fascination with the man. In Australia he was seen as the devil incarnate. England was still reeling from the discovery of the bodies of his first wife and children. Thousands were still descending on the Merseyside village of Rainhill, trampling gardens and shoving one another aside for a glimpse of the house where the murders had been committed. The speculation that he might be Jack the Ripper continued to be fuelled by the London newspapers. There were claims emerging from South Africa linking him to other grisly killings and large-scale fraud.

The electric telegraph quivered with countless murder allegations – some of them plain wrong or just unprovable – from places as far away as the United States, Canada and New Zealand.

That right hand of Deeming, it seemed, had been dealing death around the globe. It would make a fine addition to Sidney Dickinson's collection of the macabre. It might also shed some light on the motivations of the murderer.

Dickinson told Deeming he would like to make a plaster cast of his right hand. To Sidney's surprise, Deeming eagerly agreed 'with a sort of feverish readiness'. Heavily ironed, the prisoner stood and watched, fascinated, as Marion moistened the plaster and worked it to a soft consistency. When it was ready Deeming extended his right hand and pressed it into the plaster to leave a firm, clear imprint. Within a few minutes the plaster had hardened and it was passed through the bars for him to inspect.

For a brief moment Deeming seemed curious. 'Do those lines mean anything?' he asked.

'Many think so and even profess to read a record from them,' Dickinson replied. 'For myself . . . I am ignorant of the art.'

'They call it palmistry, don't they?' asked Deeming.

Like spiritualism, the reading of palms had become another nineteenth century obsession. Marion, unsurprisingly, claimed expertise in the field and counted the wives of some of the most powerful figures in Melbourne among her palm-reading clients. No-one had summed up its appeal better than Langdon Taylor, the author of a much-consulted tome called *A Handy Guide to Palmistry*. It may have been unclear to some if the book's title was simply a neat play on words. But Taylor was adamant about one thing: 'The lines of the hand,' he wrote, 'being formed by nature, show conclusively and physiologically the temperament and nature of the possessor.'

But for a man condemned to die, further discussion about the lines on his hand was pointless. A plaster cast was one thing. No-one had ever requested that before. Deeming's lawyer had also petitioned the authorities to allow doctors to examine his brain after he was executed. Perhaps they could find an answer – signs of a disease, perhaps – to explain the carnage he had wrought.

Deeming wanted to move on to a more pressing subject. He wanted to know if Dickinson, being a well-connected American newspaper correspondent, had fresh news about his final appeal and whether there might be a stay of execution. Lawyers were due to appear before the Privy Council in London within hours to ask for a postponement, citing the unfairness of his trial and how evidence supporting his plea of insanity had not been properly assessed.

The prospect of his pending death, said Deeming, did not concern him. But he had been shown the gallows where they would hang him in a few days' time and the position of the overhead beam and its narrow trapdoor below had been worrying him. What if, when the latch was pulled, the trap fell open and as he dropped to his death his body hit the side instead of descending straight through? He was not a big man – he had lost more than a stone in weight during his months in prison – but to him that lean, slender hole still didn't look wide enough.

Stories of botched hangings were legendary; men left slowly strangling, a horrible gurgling in their throats, blood gushing from their nose and mouth, a red stain spreading through the weave of their white calico mask like a rich drop of ink on blotting paper. Deeming had pestered the gaol officials to have another look at that beam and that small 'ole below it. Perhaps it should be made larger. Wider. Safer, like.

'I wish you could find out whether they are going to hang me next Monday,' he told Dickinson. 'But they'll do that, right enough. I'm thirty-nine now and my mother always said I would die before forty.

'*She* died a good while ago. But she keeps coming back. She comes every night and of late she comes in the daytime, too. Why does she bother me so? Why can't she leave me alone?'

Deeming cast a worried glance over his shoulder.

'She's here now,' he said to Dickinson, conspiratorially. 'Over there in the corner. You can't see her?'

Dickinson stared. The cell was small, all stone and iron, and the prisoner inside it was clearly alone. He shook his head.

'That's queer,' said Deeming. He seemed disappointed. How could this journalist not see her? *She* was still there, cussing and hissing and carrying on as usual.

Please, Mother. Can't you see I have visitors?

Deeming turned to Governor Shegog. 'Can't *you* see her?'

Shegog also shook his head.

'I thought perhaps you could,' said Deeming. 'But you don't miss much. She ain't pretty to look at, crying all the time and wringing her hands and saying I'm bound to be hanged.

'I don't mind her so much in the daylight. But coming every night at two o'clock and waking me up and tormenting me – that's what I can't stand.'

VI.

Frederick Deeming was never a man to let an opportunity pass. He wanted a favour from the Dickinsons in return for allowing them to take a cast of his hand. There was a woman he was desperate to see before he was executed. Could Sidney and Marion persuade her to visit him?

Deeming had met Kate Rounsefell a few weeks after murdering his most recent wife. As usual, he had found himself falling hopelessly in love. Or falling in love at the prospect of another victim. He couldn't help himself when it came to women. Couldn't stay away from them. They were marvellous things and Frederick had always had a deep-seated need to please them and flatter them with praise and presents.

He had told the constant parade of doctors sent to study him that he understood this desire to be an addiction. But it was a craving that always seemed to end the same way. As quickly as he was drawn to them, he was repulsed by them. None, it seemed, were like Mother, no matter how pious they pretended to be.

Mother had taken him to church when he was a lad. She had read the Bible to him. She had shielded him whenever she could from Father's temper. He had tried so hard to replace Mother after her death. But he was always disappointed. The women he found never matched her standards. Then she had started visiting him at night, her voice shrill, ordering him to kill.

Wives, girlfriends, even the whore in South Africa who had given him syphilis. They all had to go.

When Deeming first met Kate Rounsefell on a ship heading to Sydney he was certain she would be his next bride. He had been on the run at the time using the alias of Baron Swanston. It was a name that hinted at titled nobility and that always suited Frederick Deeming just fine when he was out to impress.

Within a couple of days the debonair Swanston had made his intentions quite clear. Kate had been reluctant at first. Why, she barely knew him. But he insisted on following her to her home town where he had impressed her older sister as a man of substance. Lizzie Rounsefell had asked Kate why she was waiting. A man like Baron Swanston did not come along often. Did Kate want to be a spinster for the rest of her life?

So Kate had agreed and accepted several lavish pieces of jewellery from her English beau. Kate told Baron she wanted to make a new start elsewhere and suggested the colony of Western Australia. It was on the other side of the continent and people were flocking to make fortunes on its newly discovered goldfields. Well, that had been another fortunate turn of events because Baron Swanston, an experienced engineer with an eye for quality diamonds, knew his way around mines. So he had headed west and found a job, with Kate promising she would soon follow.

She had meant to keep that promise, too, until the news came through that a Baron Swanston, who was thought to be Albert Williams, who might have been Harry Lawson, who used to be Fred Dawson, or Duncan, or Drewn, or Dobson, or Ward, had been arrested at a remote gold mine and charged with the murder of his second wife.

Rounsefell had been in Melbourne during Deeming's trial. Her evidence and her experiences with the murderer – *She May Have Been His Next Victim!* – had turned her life into constant newspaper fodder. Deeming remained obsessed with her and wanted to see her one more time. Could the Dickinsons, with all their connections, find a way to convince Kate to visit? He wanted to declare his innocence and his love for her one final time, to read to her another of his awkward poems, to gaze one last time at that magnificent throat, its skin so white, so tender, so ready to be kissed and nuzzled and . . .

Sidney and Marion told him they would do their best. And with that, the meeting reached its end.

Marion must have been relieved. She wanted to go home. She had seen something, an evil *thing*, full of malevolence and hate. Her husband, as usual, had seen nothing out of the ordinary. But Marion had observed it crouching in the corner of Deeming's cell. Perhaps she would tell Sidney when they were alone.

So they made a stiff farewell and began walking back down the prison's long hallway.

'Is this insanity?' Sidney asked Governor Shegog.

It was a question that had dominated Deeming's trial three weeks earlier. Alfred Deakin – his barrister who would go on to become Australia's second Prime Minister – had urged the jury to return a not guilty verdict by reason of insanity. But some of the medical experts had hummed and hawed and said they needed far more time to examine the prisoner. The judge had been dismissive of their evidence and the jury had quickly agreed.

Shegog had seen many strange things during his career in the prison system. He was a down-to-earth Irishman who had eloped with his teenage sweetheart and made his way to Australia as a teenager. He had ended up overseeing some of the toughest prisons in the colonies. He had little patience for prisoners and their constant 'shamming' – feigning illness or madness in order to get better food or earn a holiday in the hospital wing where the food and opportunities to escape were better. When a prisoner once went over the wall it had been Shegog who chased him on foot for several miles through dense bush, collared him and dragged him back to his cell.

'I don't know what it is,' said Shegog. 'We all thought at first it was shamming crazy. The government sent in a lot of doctors to examine him but he seemed sane enough when they talked with him. The only thing "out" about him was when he complained of his mother's visits, just as he did to you.

'It is certainly true that he has a sort of fit about two o'clock every morning and wakes up screaming and crying out that his mother is in the cell with him. [He] talks in a frightful, blood-curdling way to someone that nobody can see and scares the death-watch half out of their wits.'

Shegog shrugged.

'Insanity, hallucination or an uneasy conscience? It might be any of them . . . whatever it is, it seems strange that he always talks about visitations from his mother who, as far as I can learn, died quietly in her bed.'

Why, asked Shegog, would he be haunted by his dead mother and 'never of apparitions of his two wives and four children whose throats he cut with a knife held in the hand whose print you've got there under your arm?'.

Shegog gestured at the plaster imprint of Deeming's hand that Sidney was carefully carrying.

'Perhaps you won't mind me saying it but it strikes me you've got a queer taste for curiosities. I wouldn't be able to sleep with that thing in the house.'

Dickinson laughed. He had another trophy in his hands, a real collector's item, a reward for all those long days spent in courtrooms observing the shifting forms of Frederick Deeming and listening to all the horrible, stomach-turning evidence about his crimes.

Tomorrow Sidney Dickinson would relax. He would venture out into the Australian countryside and hike through the bush. He would stop and admire the gnarled gum trees that stooped and creaked like tired old men. He would pass by bottlebrush plants that looked like they had been daubed by French Impressionists with splashes and streaks of crimson and lemon on a rich green canvas.

He would have his guns with him, too. His eyes may have looked weary behind those thin rimmed spectacles. But he prided himself on his steady hand. In the silence he would take careful aim and pull the trigger. The bush would suddenly explode, the gunshot's echo quickly muffled by the frenzied squawking of birds. And then silence would set in as a shower of feathers fell softly to the ground.

Dickinson would then return home with his dead trophies. The following day that fierce storm with its howling wind and sheets of rain would buffet his home on that hill in a quiet suburban Melbourne street. He would place all those stiff bird corpses on his bench, not far from the plaster cast of Deeming's hand, and set about the task of restoring them to life.

And then he would hear that doorbell ring.

VII.

After handing his sixpence to the soaked wretch on his front verandah, Dickinson locked the front door and returned to the warmth of his study at the end of the hallway.

He glanced at the lurid cover of 'The History and Last Confession of Frederick Bailey Deeming' and flicked through its hastily printed pages. The trial had only finished three weeks earlier. But the endless newspaper accounts and the ongoing speculation that Deeming was Jack the Ripper had failed to quench the public's appetite for more information about the case.

Publishers around the country had scrambled to cash in as quickly as they could. Hack writers – quite often the same poorly paid reporters who had filed under strict deadlines those same breath-less newspaper reports – were hired. They cribbed from the stories of others and wrote furiously because there was always an advantage in being first to publish. When they ran out of facts, they filled the gaps with conjecture. And when they ran out of that, they turned to their imaginations.

Dickinson was impatient to get back to the serious work of stuffing his purple lorikeet. As he had suspected, this latest publi-cation contained nothing new, much less any hint of a confession. There had been claims that Deeming had not only confessed to the murder of at least one of his wives, but had also declared he was guilty of the Whitechapel killings. But Sidney knew all the key players in the case – the lawyers, the gaol officials, even the prison chaplain who had been spending hours each day with the prisoner – and he placed no credence in them. Besides, he had spoken with the condemned prisoner in his death cell two days earlier. The man had shown no desire to discuss any possible involvement in the Jack the Ripper case. He had been far too preoccupied with the presence of his dead mother and whether his execution would be delayed.

Sidney threw the pamphlet into the hearth and it was quickly devoured by a blazing fire he had lit to keep the room warm. Then he returned to his bench, picked up his knife and stared once more at the body in front of him.

That feeling of anticipation, of losing himself in the exciting work of restoring his birds, had gone. He could think of nothing else but Deeming and death. He recalled their meeting in the gaol; the haunted look on the man's face, the despair in his voice. There was also the prospect of attending the execution on Monday. He would be a part of that ghoulish crowd staring at the scaffold as the rope was placed carefully around Deeming's neck. He would have to listen to the prison chaplain's doleful prayers. And then would come that awful rattle of the trapdoor, followed quickly by the dull thud as the rope extinguished the man's life.

It all began weighing heavily on Sidney's mind. Deeming's right hand sat lifelessly near him, all those lines etched in plaster just begging to be examined once more. There was no escaping the fellow.

To make matters worse, a letter from Deeming had arrived for Marion the previous day while Sidney had been at work in the city.

'Dear Madam,' Deeming had written. 'I beg to tender my sincere thanks for your extreme kindness on my behalf, in trying to get Miss Rounsefell to come and see me. I assure you that if she had come I could have died happy, as it is I shall die most unhappy. I am very sorry indeed that you did not find her as kind and as Christian like as yourself. Again thank you. I beg to remain, most respectfully yours,

B. Swanston.' At the bottom of the letter Deeming had added: 'You may show Miss Rounsefell this if you wish. B. S.'

Marion Dickinson had left the gaol after meeting Deeming determined to follow through on her commitment to ask Kate Rounsefell to visit him before his execution.

But she had been unable to convince Rounsefell to do so. When Deeming's letter arrived the following day, Marion was overcome with guilt and decided to try once more. She paid another visit to the woman and while she found Kate 'deeply affected . . . and consented to undertake in person the charitable mission that she had been asked to perform', her advisers had been firm that no such meeting should take place.

The entire matter had dismayed the Dickinsons. Sidney felt he had been dragged 'into this tragical affair much more intimately than I liked'. Despite Deeming's evil acts – and the likelihood that he had planned to also murder Kate – Sidney and Marion were disappointed the man would now go to his death 'without the consolation that he had so simply and eloquently craved'.

But there was something else that had disturbed Marion. She had still not told her husband about it.

That day inside the gaol when she had taken the cast of Deeming's hand? That day when both Sidney and the prison governor had told Deeming they could not see the apparition of his dead mother?

Marion had seen the old hag. She was exactly as Deeming described, a dead woman mocking and taunting the son she wished she had never brought into the world, a dead woman who was about to pay the Dickinsons a visit.

VIII.

The fury of the storm had increased and Sidney could feel the house shake with its violence. He peered through the window and watched shadows cast by black clouds twist across the earth. He would never forget this day. Decades later he would be able to summon every detail; the torrential rain, the crying and whining of the wind, its fierce gusts warping and whipping those shadows until the outside world was nothing more than a gothic landscape of shifting silhouettes.

'If the Powers of darkness ever walk abroad by day, they could hardly find an occasion more eerie and fitting than this,' he recalled. Sidney often wrote like that. It was as though he composed his dramatic sentences while listening to an Italian opera reaching its scratchy climax on one of the new-fangled phonographs; cymbals crashing, bass drums pounding, the soprano's voice soaring until it peaked at a glass-shattering high.

But at least he and Marion were inside, warm and safe.

The storm could not drown out the sounds of everyday life. For all his flair for the dramatic and his love of the macabre, Sidney much preferred the mundane. He could hear the rattle of dishes in the kitchen. He could hear his wife singing joyfully as she went about her chores. All those sounds comforted him. Finally he began to relax.

He lit his pipe and decided it was time to put all the morning's distractions aside and soon he was lost in his world of taxidermy.

He parted feathers and sliced through skin. He cracked bones and trimmed wings. He cleaned cavities but made sure to leave the inner membrane moist and intact. He removed the brain with tweezers and scraped away the stubborn remnants of guts with a spatula. He carefully peeled back the remaining skin, expertly moving around the tendons of the spinal cord and avoiding the large tears often caused by the inexperienced hand. He filled holes and gaps with wadding. He threaded thin wire through talons. He squinted and swallowed and in his careful hands the dead came back to life.

He was sitting with his back to the open door an hour later, still engrossed in his labours, when he heard a long, agonised groan.

He froze.

'I could feel my hair move upon my scalp,' he would recall, 'and a chill, as though I had been dashed with ice-water, ran up and down my spine.'

The groan sounded like the cry of someone in pain.

'For a moment an inexpressible horror possessed me – then I felt my blood, which seemed on the instant to have stopped in its course, flow again in my veins, and with a mighty effort I arose and faced the open door.'

He could see nothing except the long dim hallway in front of him. He removed his slippers and began to creep, slowly and cautiously, from room to room. Everything seemed normal apart from the constant drum roll of rain on the roof and 'the wind that sobbed and muttered around the house'. He saw his wife in the kitchen, still absorbed in her work and apparently unaware of any startling noise. The sight of her comforted him. Perhaps the groan was due to a peculiar gust of wind that had somehow worked its way down the chimney in his study. But still . . . something nagged at him. The sound was far too human and tortured to have been created by nature.

He returned to his work. Moments later he heard the groan again – 'more distinct and lugubrious than before' – and he turned quickly.

He could see nothing. But he could have sworn the moan belonged to an old woman, 'an unutterably sad and plaintive sigh'.

He had not moved, had not even had time to blink, when he heard the groaning and sighing again. This time he could almost feel it – 'so close to my ear that, had any living person uttered them, his face must almost have touched my own'. For one of the few times in his life, Sidney Dickinson, a man long accustomed to his wife's belief in spirits, was so stunned he cried out and fell back, sending his chair sprawling.

He was lying on the floor, his breath coming in short gasps, when he heard Marion scream. He stood and ran to the kitchen. She had her back pressed against the far wall and was staring in horror at something in front of her. He rushed over and grabbed her hands. It struck him how cold they were. But it was Marion's eyes that frightened him most. They were wide and unblinking and fixed on the other side of the room. He looked but could see nothing.

'In heaven's name,' he pleaded. 'What is it?'

She whispered so softly he could barely hear her reply.

'It is Deeming's mother.'

IX.

If Sidney Dickinson was ever sceptical about his wife's claims of seeing dead people, he kept it to himself. He was so grateful, it seemed, to have been blessed with such a talented and intelligent woman so soon after the death of his first wife that, if anything, he was awe-struck and even proud of her talent.

He was also curious. The journalist within the man demanded answers. Which was why, a few years earlier on an unusually warm spring afternoon in London, Sidney had made his way to London's Marylebone district and knocked on the door of an impressive four-storey brick house at 90 Gloucester Place.

Back home in Boston the Dickinsons had regularly socialised with prominent artists and writers and saw no reason to discontinue the practice during their frequent travels abroad. A life not surrounded by intellectuals and their endless creativity was simply unimaginable.

But captivating conversation about world affairs and literary trends was not the reason for Sidney's visit that afternoon to the home of the acclaimed English writer, Wilkie Collins. Dickinson considered himself an intimate acquaintance of Collins. He had earlier sent him a detailed report about several of Marion's experiences with the spirit world, including The Strange Incident of the Mysterious Flowers. He had furnished Collins, a trained lawyer long fascinated with spiritualism, with the names and details of witnesses. In fact, Dickinson had 'placed in his hands all the concurrent data which I could secure . . . equipped with which he carried out a thorough personal investigation'. Now the time had arrived for Collins to reveal his findings.

Wilkie Collins had emerged in the 1850s and 1860s as one of the most exciting voices in English literature. Two of his books – *The Woman in White* and *The Moonstone* – would be hailed as the first modern English detective novels. He had been a close friend of Charles Dickens. He had, until the great man's death in 1870, collaborated with him on many plays and works of fiction and more than once accompanied him to London's finer brothels. But by the time Sidney Dickinson arrived at his home, Collins's career had been in decline for more than a decade. His already precarious health was deteriorating and it was only his private life that now generated interest among London's chattering class.

Collins was a true Bohemian. Suspicious of the institution of marriage, he preferred to divide his time between two devoted women. What made his situation even more fascinating to those scandalised by his conduct was that not even the most imaginative novelist of the era would have described him as an attractive man. He had small hands and feet and a disproportionately large head that boasted a bulge on its right side. Collins was also short and a tendency to stoop made him look even smaller.

By the time Dickinson stepped inside Collins' London house where an etching of Dickens hung on a wall – visitors often found the home's stone stairs and panelled walls dingy and cheerless – he was greeted by a man in the final years of his life.

Wilkie Collins' hair and beard were almost pure white and his eyes would almost definitely have been glazed.

Collins was an opium addict. For years he had battled rheumatic gout. He had tried hypnotism and quinine, submerged himself in electric baths and spent hours in Turkish sweat rooms. But nothing had eased the pain, particularly the severe attacks of arthritic inflammation in his eyes, until he was introduced to laudanum, a tincture containing opium. The drug, widely available in the late nineteenth century, had made life bearable and allowed him to continue living with his long-time partner, the widow Caroline Graves and her daughter Harriet, while sharing time with the other love of his life, Martha Rudd, who had borne him three children.

Collins' opium dependency had quickly spiralled into an addiction that paralleled the decline in his writing fortunes. But if his dependency on the drug had left his dwindling legion of admirers concerned, they had also looked on with incredulity at the small man's capacity to ingest enormous amounts of opium.

Within a few years Collins would be dead from a stroke. One of his closest friends was Edmund Yates, the founder of the British weekly *The World*, a newspaper that specialised in covering the social lives of London's upper class. Two days after Collins' death, Yates penned a glowing but frank obituary, which noted that 'for the greater part of his life Wilkie Collins was in the habit of taking daily, and without apparent noxious effect, more laudanum than would have sufficed to kill an entire ship's crew or a whole company of soldiers'.

But the opium coursing through his veins had not blunted Collins' fascination with the occult. Sidney Dickinson found him in good form. They would have sat in the big double drawing-room on the ground floor, Collins perched behind 'a massive writing table furnished with a small desk of the same design as that used by Charles Dickens'. To his left sat a tin box into which Collins stuffed 'all his plots and schemes for stories and dramas'.

'During my life I have made a considerable study of the supernatural,' Collins reminded Sidney.

He had scrutinised and assessed more than a thousand spooky cases as he sat there dwarfed by that vast table.

'Take the matter of apparitions,' he said. 'I have come to regard these as subjective rather than objective phenomena, projections from an excited or stimulated brain, not actual existences.'

Collins seemed to be laying the ground for disappointment. If he had concluded ghosts were nothing but the result of an overactive imagination, it meant Marion might be, at best, delusional. At worst she could have been an attention-seeking fraud. Her sensitivity to the world around her – real or imagined – was one of her many attributes Sidney loved and admired. But if such an eminent specialist as Wilkie Collins had ruled out the ability of the dead to communicate with the living, Mrs Dickinson might require the attention of doctors.

'Why, I have seen thousands of ghosts myself!' said Collins. 'Many a night, after writing until two o'clock in the morning and fortifying myself for my work with strong coffee, I have had to shoulder them aside as I went upstairs to bed.'

Collins neglected to mention he usually fortified himself with a substance stronger – and far more likely to induce hallucinations – than caffeine. But he was adamant those ghostly forms lurking on his staircase had been 'nothing to me, since I knew perfectly well that their origin was nowhere else than in my overwrought nerves'.

He had, he said, concluded that 'most cases of visions of this sort are to be explained by attributing them to a temporary or permanent disorganisation of the brain of the percipient'.

Most cases.

'Mind, I do not say *all* cases,' said Collins. 'There are many that are not to be set aside so readily.'

Wilkie Collins' literary career might have been stuttering – there were critics who said he had not published anything of note in close to two decades. But he had not lost his ability to weave a tale of suspense.

He was teasing Sidney, guiding him deftly, if slowly, toward his grand conclusion. Collins had studied the witness accounts and considered all the evidence, including those mysterious occurrences with those pretty dried flowers Sidney had collected in Naples and Rome.

It was hard, he said, to arrive at the underlying facts behind any case. He was sure Sidney understood why. Stories, particularly those repeated by one person to another, tended to grow, to take on a life of their own.

'A tendency to exaggerate is common to most of us,' said Collins. 'Now and then, however, I have come upon an account of supernatural visitation which seemed an exception to the general run, and upsets my theories.

'I must say that, having from time to time investigated at least fifteen hundred such instances, the stories you have furnished me are, of them all, the best authenticated.'

That was all Sidney Dickinson needed to hear. He surely would have been aware what people said about his wife back in Boston, that she was just another fraud preying on people's vulnerabilities. But now he was certain his wife was not delusional. Nor was she a liar. She was just a woman with a gift for seeing the dead.

X.

'How do you know it is Deeming's mother?' Sidney asked Marion.

'I saw her with him in his cell at the gaol.'

'Then what he said was true?' asked Sidney. 'His mother comes back to trouble him?'

Oh, it was all true, according to Marion. It would all come spilling out, all the things Marion had seen on that day in the Melbourne Gaol and in the forty-eight hours that had followed; things she had kept to herself because they seemed so bizarre and unbelievable that she had been unwilling to tell even Sidney.

Ann Deeming, dead all these years and certainly not pretty to look at, had not only been huddled near her son in prison but, according to Marion, had followed the Dickinsons home to their rented hilltop house. The day before, when that letter from Frederick Deeming had arrived, the ghost of Ann Deeming had suddenly lurched out of nowhere and scared Marion half to death.

The old woman, explained Marion, could do nothing but moan and cry for help. Marion interpreted those groans as a plea for her son. She might have been hard on her boy but she wanted his last wish fulfilled before he joined her on the other side. It was why Marion had been so determined to convince Kate Rounsefell to visit him before the execution.

Sidney tried to comfort his wife. But Marion wasn't listening. Frederick Deeming's mother remained in the kitchen.

'Go away!' pleaded Marion, who was usually calm and measured in the company of spirits.

Sidney looked again. There was nothing there. His wife appeared to be talking to the wall. But he could not doubt her claims. He had, after all, consulted with experts. Besides, he was sure he had heard the groans of Ann Deeming himself.

'I cannot help you,' said Marion to the spirit only she could see. 'Why do you torment me?'

And then Marion sighed. Sidney heard the relief in her voice.

'She has gone,' announced Marion. She slumped, exhausted, into a chair.

Late that afternoon the storm outside also exhausted itself, its howling reduced to a soft sigh. As the clouds parted to reveal a full moon, the Dickinsons finished dinner quietly and walked down the hill toward the railway station. They had an enjoyable evening ahead of them. The Consul-General of the United States had invited them to his residence for drinks and the Dickinsons were certainly not the type to pass on an opportunity to spend a night in the rarefied company of ambassadors and diplomats.

But it would also give them a chance to forget about the harrowing events of recent days. In less than forty-eight hours Sidney would have to attend Frederick Deeming's execution. Perhaps then they could put this chapter in their lives behind them. They could then return to the United States, be reunited with Sidney's daughter, and start afresh.

When they arrived home that night it was well after midnight and not even the glow of a big moon could dull the glittering carpet of stars in the clear black sky. Finally, after all the madness of the past few days, all was right with the world.

But that feeling never lasted long, not for anyone whose life intersected with Frederick Deeming. For it was only when Sidney and Marion Dickinson stepped back inside the house that their nightmare truly began.

PART II.

'That man will do murder'

The Case of the Placid Lion – A Nightmarish Journey into the Pits of Hell – Extraordinary Encounters with a Razor-Wielding Father – A Man of Poetry, Prose and Poise – The Fiend Commences his Life of Crime – Further Duplicity and an Escape to Wild Africa – Jack the Ripper Makes His Debut – The Fiend's Remorseful Wife – The Bigamist makes an Escape to South America – The Prison Governor Observes a Murderer in the Making

I.

Two months before Sidney and Marion Dickinson's world began turning upside down in May 1892, a lengthy queue began forming one Monday morning long before opening time outside William Cross's Menagerie and Museum on the corner of Rigby and Earle Street in Liverpool.

Word had spread that a lion Frederick Deeming had once captured in Africa and brought back to England was on display. If the claim sounded like an extreme addition to the rapidly growing stories about the man's exploits, many were still eager to see the wild beast he was said to have seized with his bare hands. It was just a few days since the discovery of the bodies of his first wife and four children and the English newspapers were titillating their readers with sensational claims about Deeming's crime spree around the world. He was a man, it seemed, whose hands were capable of anything.

But when the menagerie's gates opened – and William Cross was not a man to keep them locked for long if he could hear the sound of coins jangling in the pockets of potential customers – the pressing crowd was surely disappointed. The lion they expected to find raging at its human captors padded politely about its cage, stopping only to yawn and stare sedately. It was placid and clearly well-trained. Like most of Deeming's stories of derring-do, the reality was far more mundane.

William Cross was one of the most prominent animal impresarios of the nineteenth century. He was an associate and sometimes rival of Phineas Taylor Barnum, the American circus promoter and self-described 'Greatest Showman on Earth'. Cross' Liverpool menagerie housed an array of big cats, gorillas, monkeys and snakes that were constantly arriving at the docks of the Mersey River. Cross, who said he was living 'in the heyday of the naturalist', was in the import and export business, constantly negotiating with the agents, collectors and explorers who drove the era's lucrative worldwide trade in exotic animals.

It was a costly and highly competitive industry and Cross, a pragmatist who understood that the rapidly changing world would soon alter his profession forever, relied on publicity and hyperbole to drive business. Visitors could gape at his rare 'white elephant from Siam', despite reasonable suspicions it was actually an ordinary elephant he had doused with fifty coats of whitewash and wet plaster. Years earlier he had drawn huge crowds to his menagerie with his exhibition of the infamous 'Coola Camba' – a species of 'man monkey' from equatorial Africa which some scientists, still confused by Charles Darwin's evolutionary theories, believed was the missing link between humanity and the apes.

But as Cross counted his earnings from his latest promotion, doubts were soon cast about the authenticity of his 'Deeming Lion'. Further south in a small town on the outskirts of Wolverhampton, Frank Bostock, the manager of Wombwell and Bailey's Travelling Menagerie and Circus, claimed that he had bought the real Deeming lion from Cross three years earlier.

'It has always evinced a very ferocious disposition,' said one report, 'having attacked its trainer no fewer than on five or six occasions.' That trainer, it turned out, had been Wombwell and Bailey's famous 'negro lion tamer' Delhi Montana, who a week earlier had been clawed to death by three bears and a hyena.

Death and injury inflicted by wild animals was a drawback common to the industry. Six months earlier, Cross had received a consignment of several large boxes containing more than 300 pythons his collectors had captured in India. Some specimens were fourteen feet long and could wrap themselves around a man until only a few tufts of his hair were left visible. When one of the coffin-length cases was prised open inside Cross's office, bedlam erupted. The serpents, aroused by their first glimpse of light in months and a rare influx of fresh air, thrashed and squirmed and spilled out of the box. Some wrapped themselves around stair bannisters. Others, their sharp white fangs exposed by snapping jaws, curled around the bodies of several of Cross's assistants and began to squeeze. It took three men to prise one of the pythons from the body of a colleague. One newspaper account of the chaotic scene reported that 'Mr Cross himself had several times to be delivered from the coils of the creatures . . . so large a number of snakes has not been seen before in this country; but the demand for them from zoological societies, snake charmers and others appears to be larger than would be readily imagined.'

By the middle of March 1892 it was unclear just who owned Deeming's lion. But there was no disputing that Frederick had returned to his home in Birkenhead three years earlier with a four-month-old lion cub leashed like a pet dog by his side, claiming he had saved it after killing its parents in a ferocious battle to the death inside a remote cave. He had certainly boarded a steamer in Yemen on his way home to England with a lion cub by his side, most likely purchased from a street dealer somewhere in Africa. But that didn't matter. He would have revelled in the status it gained him around the neighbourhood. For weeks children and adults flocked to the backyard where it remained chained to a stake.

The Deemings had contacted Cross and offered it for sale. But when Frederick and his first wife, Marie, had placed 'a fabulous price' on its head, the naturalist said he was not interested. A few days later, Marie, alone once more because her husband had embarked on another of his frequent and unexplained absences, called on Cross 'and begged him to take it away'. The lion had bitten a child and its screams and resulting injuries had drawn the ire of neighbours.

By then life with Frederick had become an endless and frustrating existence for Marie.

Like so many Deeming women, the front door had come to symbolise their marriage. She never quite knew when, or if, her husband would walk through it again.

II.

It never mattered if they had been born into the clan or married into it; life, it seemed, was always destined to be difficult for women in the Deeming family.

They might have had clothes to wash, meals to fix, floors to scrub and children to raise. But a sense of unease permeated their lives, a foreboding that often assumed a physical presence in the form of their home's front door. A Deeming woman waited by it. She cast glances at it. She might even open it and step outside and, with the sun fading, peer down the street in the hope of seeing a weary shadow shuffling slowly toward her in the evening gloom.

A Deeming woman never knew if her man was coming home. She would send him off to work in the morning with a packed lunch – often a thick slab of bread and cheese because big families never had much in the way of leftovers after all those ravenous mouths had finished their supper. By the time it fell dark her nerves would be frayed.

If she heard a noise at that door – that unmistakeable thud of dirty boots being dropped on the front step, or that familiar rasping cough trying to dislodge another day's worth of black dust – she could relax. But if there was a sudden rapping of knuckles on wood, followed by the reluctant shuffling of feet and the nervous clearing of tightened throats, she would know it was a deputation from the mine, a group of tired men with black-smeared faces mustering the courage to tell another Deeming woman she was now a widow.

There were towns and hamlets deep in Lancashire and further south in Warwickshire – and it was between those two counties that many a Deeming could be found – where they believed the name was cursed. It was certainly an old surname. They had been sending Deemings back to the mud of middle England since well before the seventh century. Some believed the name first appeared as 'domung' – the old word for judgement or doom. If that was true, it was certainly appropriate because the end often came early for Deeming men.

Lancashire's prosperity in the middle of the nineteenth century had been driven by the shipyards of the Mersey and cotton, where its damp climate meant cotton fibres were less likely to break when being spun into cloth. But even greater wealth lay beneath the ground. They called it black gold – rich seams of coal that stretched from the deep south of Wales into the midlands and then north past Lancashire toward Yorkshire. It had been lying beneath the surface for more than 300 million years, so shallow in places it reared out of the ground in jagged shards; the fossilised remnants of the fertile swamps and tropical forests that had once covered the rolling green hills and pasture land.

The Romans had ripped it from the ground to fuel their fires as they tried to tame the tribes of native savages. Once they became civilised the English also used coal to stoke their hearths. But coal's real value lay in its ability to be turned into iron. It was a miraculous transformation that created steam engines and kitchen chairs and giant weapons. It had been the driving force behind the growth of the cities with their massive machines and factories.

It took two tons of coal to make a ton of iron and that meant thousands of callused hands were needed to haul it to the surface. For years it wasn't just men who had done the hauling. Until the early 1840s soot-covered women and children as young as five had also spent up to twelve hours a day working in darkness deep in the pits. The youngest worked as trappers – opening and closing a series of trap doors to increase air circulation. Older children and women, known as hurriers or drawers, would be fitted with a girdle connected to a heavy chain to help them drag heavy tubs and wagons chock full with coal back to the surface.

They were overseen by a butty – a pit manager who ruthlessly drove his workers to meet the ever-increasing quotas set by the wealthy mine owners. But there had been an outcry in 1842 when the Children's Employment Commission completed an inquiry into mining conditions. Its report included candid interviews with dozens of miners, women and children that revealed a subterranean world of horror, cruelty and neglect.

The government banned women and children under the age of ten from working in the collieries. But little else was done to improve safety. Deep in the mines where men chipped at seams with axes and hammers, lying on their backs almost naked because of the stifling heat, there would be no warning when they struck a chunk of coal and firedamp – a build-up of noxious and flammable methane – began spilling silently and deadly from a hidden pocket.

A man's head would begin throbbing. Dizziness would quickly set in. A wave of nausea would follow and he would become disoriented as the black walls closed in on him. All it needed was a small flame, or the spark from a mallet striking rock, for an explosion to engulf the site and roll through the tunnel, the fireball consuming everything in its path.

There were so many different *damps*, so many ways to die. A man might catch a whiff of stinkdamp (hydrogen sulphide) or whitedamp (carbon monoxide) or, far worse, be overcome by blackdamp (a toxic stew of carbon dioxide and other gases and water vapour). You might not even be able to detect them at all. Some men just gave up and called them 'bags of foulness'. And if that foulness didn't fill your lungs and lure you into the long sleep, the earth had crueller methods of keeping you entombed. The local newspapers barely went a week without reporting on a makeshift tunnel that had collapsed, quickly crushing and suffocating those inside.

There had been many Deemings who went to work each day in those mines. Many soon discovered that some of those deep pits led all the way to Hell.

On 1 March 1856, the *Leicester Chronicle* covered a coronial inquest into the death of fifteen-year-old Samuel Deeming who had been killed in an accident at a colliery near the town of Ashby-De-La-Zouch. The surname seemed familiar to one of the reporters, who began digging into the newspaper files.

A week later the *Chronicle* noted that 'the number of accidents that have taken place in this unfortunate family is perfectly appalling'. The grandfather of young Samuel Deeming, it turned out, had been killed in a colliery in Warwickshire many years earlier when a pit rope had snapped. His fourteen-year-old son was killed in Banbury not long after when a roof collapsed. Another son had died in a shower of coal while digging in a pit at Badsley. Henry Deeming, sixteen, had also died the same way in the same colliery.

In 1844 Richard Deeming, who by family standards had made it to the decent old age of twenty-eight, was deep in the Snibston Old Pit at Coalville, lying on his back during a rare rest break, when he was hit by a falling lump of coal. He died instantly.

Was it any wonder that the matriarch of that clan who had lost her husband and so many sons, grandsons and nephews to that ravenous earth had made it to the age of eighty but, according to the *Chronicle*, 'the dreadful occurrences in her family had so far affected her intellect as to render her insane'?

Her own father had also been snatched by the pits. At least she had a couple of sons still living. One had tumbled more than fifty yards into the Ibstock pit but his fall was broken by six feet of water lying at the bottom of the hole. He had survived with severe injuries, including a broken thigh bone.

Her other remaining boy, Thomas, had also experienced a nasty fall in Warwickshire, plummeting more than thirty feet down a shaft. He, too, had been saved by a deep pool of water. Unfortunately the fall and subsequent impact meant 'he was dangerously injured about the head'.

Was he the same Thomas Deeming who was the reluctant father of Frederick? Was he the same Thomas Deeming who declared to the census of 1861 that he was now working as a whitesmith in Bebington, was married to an Ann Deeming and had six sons and a daughter living in their small home in Queen's Place?

The dates roughly matched. Frederick Bailey Deeming was born in 1853 in Ashby-De-La-Zouch. And Thomas Deeming the white-smith certainly wasn't right in the head. His eldest boy could tell you that. His black moods and fierce temper were something to behold. Perhaps he'd had enough sense left after the accident to flee the pits and try a new line of work.

He was certainly a man plagued by demons. Thomas had deserted Ann and the children while living in Ashby-De-La-Zouch. The voices in his head had become a babble. Their house creaked and moaned with supernatural sounds. Ann was pregnant with Frederick, their fourth boy (Deeming men might have been doomed to live short lives but it seemed they produced male heirs just as quickly as they lost them). Thomas believed their home was haunted; someone had once been murdered inside it and the body so mutilated the victim's soul had never escaped to the other side. When Thomas failed to quieten all those voices in his head, he simply got up one morning and, like many a Deeming man, never came home that night. Ann had eventually tracked down her man. But so, too, did the demons.

Which was why there were days when Thomas Deeming decided there was only one way to silence them. By then the family had settled in Birkenhead. The boys would hear him yelling, a rage so frightful the blood would drain from his features and his face would turn granite white. Soon after they would hear the back door flung open or, on other occasions, the heavy thud of his boots on the stairs, as he cursed and vowed to slit his own throat with a sharp razor.

The boys, including little Fred, would hold on to him grimly, grappling with him until their combined strength wrestled the razor from his grasp.

He would calm down after that. But the Deeming children never quite knew when he would erupt again. It turned out that Ann, a God-fearing woman who was always trying to instil Christian values in her children, was just another of those Deeming women forced to endure life on the edge, always waiting for bad news.

As for her sons, there were no doubt times when they thought life would have been so much easier if the earth had simply opened up and swallowed their father, as it had done to so many Deeming men.

III.

Thomas Deeming's tormented soul had not stopped him from siring a brood of boys who looked uncannily alike. They boasted square jutting jaws and high cheekbones and muscled, sloping shoulders. One of the boys, Albert, was three years younger than Frederick but could have been his twin, which was not such a good thing on that day in March 1892 when police had led him inside a ghastly home in Rainhill reeking of decaying flesh to identify the grisly remains of Frederick's first wife and four children. A rumour had quickly rippled through the voyeuristic throng of spectators that Albert was the killer himself. He was identical to Frederick. It had required some nifty work by the officers guarding the front door to prevent the crowd from lynching him.

As Albert stepped shakily into the house – his face was ashen and someone was holding his arm to support him – another brother, Walter, had collapsed and was lying in bed in his home in Birkenhead. The news that Frederick was a killer of the worst kind, that he had slashed the throats of his own children, had broken Walter in the same way the world always seemed to crush the life out of Deeming men.

The only brother who seemed unsurprised was the oldest son, Edward. Throughout their childhood he had tried to keep a protective eye on Fred. But if the boys shared a strong physical resemblance, it was the only trait that united Frederick with his brothers. While the rest of the boys stayed close to home, Frederick Deeming was driven by wanderlust and a need to escape a father who loathed him.

Nine hundred years earlier across the Mersey from Birkenhead, the city of Liverpool had formed as an isolated fishing community. By the middle of the eighteenth century it had emerged as one of England's most important trading ports. Critical to this had been the world's prosperous slave trade and America's increasing appetite for cheap labour. Slave ships regularly anchored in the Mersey and engaged in lucrative deals that saw textiles, weaponry, tobacco and sugar exchanged for slaves, who would then be shipped across the North Atlantic.

When slavery was abolished in Britain at the start of the nineteenth century Liverpool became a key embarkation point for those wanting to flee England for a new life in America. When the flow of emigrants slowed, world demand for ocean-going vessels only increased the importance of the shipyards. The biggest of these was run by the Laird Brothers and by the 1880s William Laird's original iron factory turning out boilers had been transformed into one of the world's biggest shipmaking ventures.

It was there where men like Edward, Walter and Albert Deeming had jobs for life. Even Frederick said he had worked there for a short time as a plumber's apprentice.

Giant frames of iron and wood sat on the river's banks like hollowed-out carcasses of beached whales. Tiny workers moved precariously around the makeshift scaffolding surrounding these skeletons, riveting and welding metal skin on to these bones that rose seven or eight storeys high. It was a noisy, dirty environment that reeked of oil and kerosene. Showers of sparks constantly fell from the sky. The place swarmed day and night with labourers, carpenters, sawyers, caulkers, joiners, boilermakers and riggers. It was hard to find a family in Birkenhead that did not have a father or son trudging off to the yards each day to work long shifts amid the fumes of all those massive furnaces.

The iron and steel leviathans they constructed were turned out with brutal efficiency. Some of the world's most famous vessels began their working lives by slipping out of the North Yard and into the waters of the Mersey. The *CSS Alabama* – a sloop-of-war built for the Confederates in the Civil War in the United States – went on to capture or burn more than sixty Union merchant ships and take several thousand prisoners. In the late 1850s the yard's reputation had been so high that the Scottish explorer David Livingstone, already regarded as one of Britain's most heroic adventurers, ordered construction of the world's first steel ship to help him explore the Zambezi River.

His brothers helped build the ships and Frederick used them as a way to escape Birkenhead and his father's loathing and contempt. By the time he was twelve or thirteen he was disappearing for weeks on fishing trawlers. That soon turned into years. And then one day the front door would open and Frederick would wander in as if he had never been away. During one visit home he mentioned to Edward and his wife that he had been shipwrecked off the coast of Newfoundland and that his clothes and money had been stolen.

Edward had no doubts that his younger brother was unstable. Not long after news broke about Frederick's crimes around the world, Edward and his wife made their way to a solicitor's office in London to make a sworn declaration that Frederick, like their father, had never been right in the head.

'At a very early age he showed great excitability of temper,' Edward said. 'He would lie down on the floor and kick in paroxysms of rage, appear to be hysterical, and to lose all self-control.'

Frederick contracted smallpox and scarlet fever as a four-year-old, said Edward. He grew into a stubborn boy who hated school and 'was always difficult to manage . . . at the age of 13 he commenced stopping out at night, and would go to sea with fishing trawlers for several days and nights at a time.

'Father would thrash him severely for it but it would seem to have little or no effect upon him. When he was about 13 or 14 years old he ran away to Chester for four or five days. He then returned for a few hours and left again and was not seen by any one of us for five years.'

Edward had a theory that their father's cruelty toward their mother shortly before Frederick's birth – 'he, at that time, ill-treating her very frequently' – was to blame for his younger brother's mental issues.

'Father deserted mother within a year of Frederick's birth. This greatly distressed her, and she was left with her children to wander about the country after him. She sold up her home to find the means to do this. Frederick was never a favourite of my father's. He seemed to have taken a dislike to him from his birth.'

It had worried Ann, this inability of her husband to bond with Frederick. She had confided in a friend, a local governess who knew the family well, that Thomas seemed to take out all his frustrations and simmering anger on the boy. 'Mrs Deeming's life was a long one of terrible suffering, borne with Christian fortitude,' the friend would later tell reporters. 'When his mother was gone his father treated him so cruelly that Fred went to sea.'

He had never been like the other boys. He preferred the company of girls and women. Edward thought him immature and childish and Frederick, according to the governess, 'if he had any fault as a youth it was his vanity and great love of dress and as he grew, his uncontrollable affection for these gradually overcame him'.

People started calling him 'Mad Fred' and as the years passed his eccentricities only became more pronounced. Perhaps Thomas Deeming found it hard to disguise his contempt for the boy because whenever he looked at him, he saw a large part of himself staring back.

'Father attempted to commit suicide on four occasions,' Edward recalled. The first attempt had occurred when the family was still living at Ashby-de-la-Zouch, a market town thirty miles north of Birmingham. For once there had been no quarrel, no war of words with his wife or children over some petty incident. Thomas Deeming simply announced he was going to cut his throat.

He rushed out of the house with a razor in his hand 'but was followed and prevented from doing any injury to himself. While living at Birkenhead he made three attempts to take his life. Once Frederick had been out late at night and father was angry with him. Mother interfered and father worked himself up into such a passion that he took a razor to cut his throat, but I took it away from him and prevented him from carrying out his intentions.

'The third attempt was when Frederick was twenty-two years of age. There had been a little unpleasantness at home about business matters and father went upstairs, saying he would take his life. He got a razor and ran downstairs into a closet in the yard and closed the door.'

Edward, the strongest of the brothers, broke the door open and pulled his father out. A couple of years later Edward heard a 'slight quarrel' taking place upstairs. Suddenly his father rushed down the stairs and sprinted into the backyard 'with something in his hand'. Frederick joined Edward outside as they wrestled once more with their father. 'After a severe struggle we succeeded in taking a razor from him. He swore dreadfully at us and we had a great difficulty in controlling him.'

Little wonder that Frederick was always in a rush to escape. But if the turmoil created by his father's violent moods and suicide attempts had driven him to explore the outside world, it was the death of his mother that plunged Deeming deeper into his darkening inner world. Ann had a diseased liver – probably cancer – and died in her Birkenhead home in October 1877 at the age of fifty-one.

According to several accounts Frederick soon fell 'ill' and claimed to have seen his mother floating outside his window.

Not long after, he signed on as a steward on the steamer *Malcolm* and in early 1878 arrived in India. He was soon admitted to the Presidency General Hospital in Calcutta where its surgeon-superintendent, Dr Alexander Crombie, diagnosed tonsillitis and recorded in his notes that his twenty-four-year-old patient regularly suffered from shivering and fevers that might have been malarial. Frederick would remain in hospital for eighty-three days. By the middle of April the nurses caring for him recorded a series of epileptic fits that grew worse by the day. In the following eight weeks he had dozens of seizures, sometimes fourteen or more in a day. He slipped in and out of consciousness and had to be strapped to his bed. Sometimes his right arm and leg would continue twitching for a week or more. At other times his limbs were paralysed.

In June Dr Crombie believed Frederick was well enough to return home and the British Consul organised a berth for him on the steamship *Orion*. When he arrived in Birkenhead Edward was shocked at the change in his younger brother.

'He was at home ill for three months after this and his mind appeared to be affected. He tried to make us believe that he was a member of the Board of Trade and was very conceited. He further represented he was a person of distinction and used to dress in a peculiar manner.'

Some of Edward's other brothers would later dispute his claims about the family's history of mental illness. But these denials had a hollow ring to them and were probably made more out of embarrassment than anything else. Thomas Deeming would die of 'senility' in 1889, an inmate of the Tranmere workhouse, an institution that catered for the poor, the sick and the mentally unwell.

But long before then Edward feared that Frederick was heading down the same path. 'One morning he went for a walk wearing an evening dress and waistcoat and a large bouquet of flowers, patent leather shoes with silver buckles and a large wedding favour,' Edward recalled.

'On other occasions he dressed in the deepest mourning. He would ramble in his conversation so much that at times it was difficult to understand what he was talking about.'

IV.

There was nothing serene about the dead bodies Sidney Dickinson had seen in May 1874. By the time he arrived to report on one of the worst man-made disasters in North America in the nineteenth century, many of them would have been bloated and turning blue. Some had been dumped on hillsides among piles of twisted debris while others were left hanging mangled in the boughs of trees by a gushing, all-consuming torrent of 600 million gallons of water. Searchers would take weeks to uncover all the victims. For the first time in his life – but certainly not the last – Dickinson would have to find the words to describe a miserable scene of human carnage.

Fortunately, as he would prove throughout his career, Dickinson could always rely on his deep vocabulary and his love of colours and scenery to find a way to describe the indescribable. It certainly helped that he came from a family that had always placed great importance on reading, writing and the arts. The poet Emily Dickinson was an eccentric cousin who would emerge at the end of the nineteenth century as one of the most important figures in American literature, despite a decades-long reluctance to leave her bedroom. A nephew, also called Sidney, would go on to become an acclaimed portrait artist.

Sidney's father, Henry Kirk White Dickinson, had been the scion of one of the most well-known families in New England whose fortune had been made in paper manufacturing. Determined that his son should receive the best education possible, he had sent Sidney to study painting, sculpture, Greek and Latin at Amherst, a liberal arts college in Massachusetts.

One of Amherst's directors was Samuel Bowles, the editor of the *Springfield Republican*, a morning newspaper which boasted the highest circulation in New England outside of Boston. Bowles had strong views – the *Republican* had opposed slavery in the lead-up to the American Civil War – and had a reputation for mentoring young journalists. He encouraged them to tell their stories as concisely as possible. 'Put it all in the first paragraph,' he would tell his cub reporters.

Sidney had only just joined the *Republican* when word arrived that a dam had broken twenty miles away in Williamsburg and that more than 100 inhabitants eking out a living in the valley below it had drowned. A decade earlier almost a dozen cloth and silk manufacturing companies had banded together in Williamsburg to dam the Mill River, a fifteen-mile-long stream running into the Connecticut River. Trying to keep costs to a minimum, they designed the dam themselves. The workmanship had been shoddy and the grouting holding together the earthen wall of the reservoir soon began leaking. On the morning of 16 May 1874, a huge slab of that wall began to crumble following a night of heavy rain.

Within an hour a forty-foot-high wall of water crashed through the valley below, submerging towns and ultimately killing 139 people, most of them poor immigrants from Ireland and Canada. The death toll might have been much higher had it not been for Collins Graves – sometimes called Colin – a local farmer who raced his horse and buggy minutes ahead of the deluge to warn those in its path to move to higher ground. Graves was credited with saving several hundred lives and within days his bravery was being reported across the nation.

Bowles sent a team of reporters to cover the tragedy and one of them was the young and inexperienced Sidney Dickinson. Captivated by Graves' heroic act, Sidney ignored his boss's maxim to 'put it all in the first paragraph' and instead filed an epic poem titled 'The Ride of Colin Graves' that appeared in the *Republican* four days after the disaster.

He was only twenty-three years old but Sidney's flair for telling a dramatic story was already finely honed.

> *Down the road into Williamsburg*
> *Comes a horseman, breathless and pale,*
> *Swift as his dripping horse can urge*
> *'Neath blows that are showering like hail.*
> *The horse is panting, his nostrils spread*
> *Display their lining of burning red,*
> *His eyes stand out from their sockets deep,*
> *His breath comes shorter at every leap*
> *And his strength is beginning to fail*

Sidney liked to pace his stories, increasing the tension and piling on the suspense in much the same way as his friend in future years, Wilkie Collins. Not for him the traditional newspaper article told in a flat voice using only facts and quotes gleaned from interviews. That Italian opera – the soundtrack for much of his writing – was evident even then.

> *A minute passes, – a towering wall,*
> *A grinding, sickening roar,*
> *And the muddy waters fiercely fall*
> *Like the boiling surf on the shore.*
> *Down with a moan go stones and bricks,*
> *The strongest braces are snapped like sticks,*
> *And up and down in a devil's dance*
> *The heavy beams in the tumult prance,*
> *Then sink to be seen no more.*

Dickinson moved from the *Republican* to work for the *San Francisco Bulletin* and then spent four years with the *Boston Journal* as its theatre and music reviewer. In 1876 he married Minnie Stockwell, only to lose her the following year as she gave birth to their daughter, also called Minnie. It was the same year Ann Deeming's diseased liver finally claimed her life and triggered Frederick's further descent into madness and eccentricity.

Sidney, too, found himself plunged into despair. 'I have nothing to do but brood over my disappointments and bereavement,' he wrote to his old editor at the *Boston Journal*, Colonel William Warland Clapp Junior, asking for more work because his finances were in 'such a narrowing and unhappy plight'.

But in 1879, two years after Minnie's death, Sidney married Marion Miller and began to seriously pursue a career as an art critic. He returned home after his first trip to Europe in the mid-1880s – that same trip which had triggered The Strange Incident of The Mysterious Flowers – inspired by the works of the Old Masters and determined to carve out a career as a public speaker.

It was a time when gifted orators could earn a lucrative living touring and lecturing in public halls and theatres, often dramatising their speeches with the assistance of a magic lantern – a slide projector that could dissolve one image on a wall with another. It was the nineteenth century precursor to the motion picture. In 1860 John Fallon, a Massachusetts chemist, had rebuilt and dramatically improved a lantern he had imported from England and dubbed it the 'stereopticon'.

With Marion faithfully by his side inserting the slides and operating the stereopticon, Sidney quickly emerged as a polished performer on the speaking circuit. His lectures – he would argue that 'the art of the time is invariably the reflection of that time' – drew appreciative paying audiences and positive newspaper reviews.

Toward the end of the 1880s Sidney and Marion decided to leave eleven-year-old Minnie at home in the care of her grandparents and head to the colonies of Australia and New Zealand. Sidney's mother had recently died after a long sickness and his father, who had squandered much of the family wealth, had just been committed to an asylum for the insane.

They arrived in Sydney in June 1888 and, after being acclaimed as touring celebrities, Sidney and Marion immersed themselves in the cultural worlds of Sydney and Melbourne, lugging their 400 pounds of equipment up and down the east coast and through dozens of regional towns.

'How shall I describe Australia – that country of the strange, the weird, the unaccustomed?' Dickinson would write several years later.

It began with the utter desolation of the landscape and the strangeness of the vegetation and fauna; gum trees that shed their skins instead of their leaves and animals that 'perpetuate types that disappeared from nearly every other part of the globe some millions of years ago'.

'It is a country in which nature has established conditions unknown elsewhere, and where civilisation, encountering novel surroundings, is developing in new and interesting ways. It is the Land of the Great Secret, into which some four million human beings are prying.'

One of those who had gone to Australia years before the Dickinsons arrived was a young Frederick Deeming.

V.

Marie James must have seen something in Frederick Deeming that others could not. Perhaps she saw a glimmer of potential behind all that nervous twitching and mumbling. He certainly seemed ambitious enough. Perhaps she believed all his strutting and the boasts of his global adventures were simply the honest accounts of an excitable fellow driven by an innate curiosity about the world around him.

More likely Marie was simply desperate to find a husband and was prepared to overlook Frederick's eccentric behaviour.

Marie, according to an old friend, was 'one of the best cooks in Britain' when she married Frederick at the age of twenty-six. Born in Wales, she was a short, solidly built woman with dark hair, thick lips, a slightly upturned nose and high cheekbones. Her sister, Martha, had married Albert Deeming – Frederick's younger brother – in 1879 and Marie did not have to look far for a potential suitor when she went to live with Martha and Albert after securing a job as a cook in Liverpool.

In February 1881 Marie became Frederick's first – but definitely not last – officially registered wife. The pair exchanged vows in St Paul's church in Lower Tranmere, a suburb of Birkenhead. Not long after the wedding Frederick told Marie he was leaving for

Australia, a country he had already visited before during his life at sea. He would send for his bride once he was earning enough money to cover her fare.

He soon found a job as a gasfitter in Sydney, a lucrative trade in the 1880s. The arrival of electricity in the home was still years away and the gas that came from burning coal, despite its obnoxious fumes, had usurped kerosene lamps as the preferred way to light a home.

But Deeming was under growing pressure to pay for his wife's sea journey to Australia. In January 1882 an F. Deeming placed an ad in one of the local newspapers trying to sell a 'good corking machine, cheap'. A few weeks later his boss, James Jarvis, noticed eight gas burners were missing from his workshop. Jarvis went to the police, who searched a room Deeming was renting in Castlereagh Street and found two of the burners on the mantelpiece. On Friday 24 February a reporter with Sydney's *Evening News* attended a preliminary hearing at the Water Police Court and found F. B. Deeming to be 'a respectable-looking working man'. In early April he was found guilty of theft and sentenced to six weeks' hard labour in prison.

Just as it had in the wake of his mother's death, stress seemed to trigger another descent into ill health. A day after entering Darlinghurst Gaol, Deeming began experiencing a series of seizures. He was placed in the care of the prison's visiting surgeon, Maurice O'Connor. From 5 April through to his discharge on 16 May, Deeming, according to O'Connor, 'was suffering from undoubted epilepsy, and was in a very bad condition'.

He soon recovered – if, indeed, the fits had been genuine – and two months after his release Marie arrived on the *Samuel Plimsoll* to be reunited with her new husband. But that urge of his to keep moving – spurred, no doubt, by his recent incarceration and a desire to escape Sydney – saw the Deemings head south to Melbourne. There, Deeming worked for a short time with a prominent importer of plumbing parts, John Danks, before leaving for Rockhampton in Queensland where he secured a six-month contract as a foreman with the Williams Brothers plumbing business.

On 20 November 1883 Frederick wrote to Danks in Melbourne to tell him that Rockhampton was a town with unlimited potential. He boasted that he had grown the Williams Brothers business 'and I can see there is plenty of room for another plumber's shop; and a great many of the gentlemen here, and two of the MPs, want me to start for myself'. Deeming asked if Danks would loan him 100 pounds 'and give me about six months to pay the money . . . it is only a little start that I shall want, as I know the business will go ahead well'.

Danks sent him money, which would never be repaid. But it would become a valuable lifeline for Marie and Frederick as they prepared to start a family. On the day he wrote that letter to Danks, Frederick's world was caving in around him. Marie was three months pregnant with their first child, Bertha. Frederick was about to be fired from his job. And he had just been hauled into another courtroom on a charge of breaking the law.

Frederick's boss in Rockhampton, Sidney Williams, had found his English foreman to be a sullen and difficult character. Although Williams conceded he had attracted new business to the firm, Deeming's temperament left him hopelessly ill equipped when it came to managing the team of plumbers beneath him. For two months, Williams would recall later, 'there were continual troubles between them'. It came to a head when *The Morning Bulletin* in Rockhampton reported that Deeming had been charged with discharging firearms in a public street in an apparent dispute with a neighbour and possible work colleague. He pleaded not guilty and the charge was dismissed because the identity of the person who fired the gun was unclear.

By then Sidney Williams was tired of his strange employee. Deeming had admitted to him that he had fired the gun – a breach of the local municipal laws – but that it would be easy to find two witnesses to say he had not. If such a man was prepared to perjure himself, thought Williams, there was no place for him in his business and he sacked him.

By early 1884 the Deemings were back in Sydney, living in a series of rented rooms with their new daughter. Frederick set about establishing his own plumbing and gasfitting business and, within two years, it appeared to be thriving. He had nine employees and his family was also growing. Another daughter, Maria, soon arrived and Frederick and Marie were looking at buying their own home.

But the marriage was far from idyllic. When one of Frederick's apprentices, sixteen-year-old John McKewen, moved in to live with the family – a common enough occurrence for apprentices in the nineteenth century – he found Marie constantly in 'a nervous state as if she feared something was going to happen'.

Frederick was rarely home. He stayed out late and Marie often had to prepare his supper at midnight when he finally came through that front door. Although Deeming seemed fond of his children and always ensured his wife had enough money, McKewen found himself working for a man who was 'very eccentric in his ways – some days he would change his clothes two and three times'.

When Deeming drove his horse and small buggy through Sydney's streets he would suddenly swerve in front of oncoming trams, 'so as to make the public take notice of him'. He liked to drive about at night without lights. He was repeatedly cautioned by the transit commissioners, 'and every time he was accosted he gave a different name'.

Deeming seemed to know little about horses, could barely hold the reins and often handed them to his young apprentice. Some of their late evening excursions involved visits to various women because 'Deeming had a weakness for barmaids, and was often at hotels at night when he had led his wife to believe that he was at work.

'There was one barmaid whom he used to drive about in his buggy and she appeared to have great influence over him,' McKewen would recall. 'He frequently visited another barmaid, and on one occasion he got a valuable diamond brooch from her to put a new pin in it, but she never saw it again.'

McKewen's recollections, given to a Sydney newspaper during the frenzied press coverage following Deeming's arrest in 1892, are among the few detailed and verifiable accounts of his movements and misdeeds during his five years in Sydney.

But McKewen was not the only one struck by Deeming's willingness to romance barmaids. In the years to come, Richard Hedge, an engineer who had briefly lived in the same boarding house as Deeming in the early 1880s, would tell police that Frederick had 'a nervous manner and a great habit of stroking his moustache with his fingers and playing with his watch chain. When in deep thought he invariably overlapped his lower lip with the upper.'

There was also his habitual love for displaying jewellery including a 'very great profusion' of diamond rings on his fingers. 'He never manifested any desire to quarrel, cowardice being a noticeable part of his temperament,' said Hedge. 'His lavish disregard for money made him popular in private bars in Sydney, which were the places of resort he most frequented. He was often in the company of women of attractive appearance.'

Deeming, according to McKewen, claimed he had once been contracted to work at the Garden Palace, an imposing cathedral-style building built to host the Sydney International Exhibition in 1879, and had 'appropriated' several valuable diamonds from one of its displays.

McKewen's boss, it turned out, was not just a cad but a practised thief. When working at a client's house 'he generally brought away more lead and other material than he took with him'. He stripped the valuable lead from the gutters and a series of customers would come to his shop as soon as it rained to complain. He stole other valuables, including plush cases of cutlery, and passed them off as gifts.

For months he enjoyed a supply of fresh gas at his plumbing shop in the city after boring a hole through a wall and fixing a jet to the pipe supplying his neighbour.

According to McKewen, Frederick and Marie used 100 pounds as a deposit to buy a house in Vernon Street in the inner west suburb of Petersham, a short walk from the local train station. Deeming dubbed the home 'St Bride's Cottage' after the small Welsh village where Marie had been born. After ordering his apprentice to dig up much of the backyard and plant a series of fruit trees, Deeming changed his mind and told McKewen he instead planned to concrete the entire area.

He would do the cementing himself, he said, and intended to send Marie and the kids away while he undertook the work. McKewen, he said, should also find somewhere else to live until the concrete had dried.

But Deeming was soon complaining that the cement he wanted to buy was too expensive. By then – no matter what his intentions had been with the planned concrete installation – he had bigger problems. His finances were stretched and creditors were taking him to court.

McKewen would say that Deeming sent him home in the buggy one evening with orders to tell Marie he would be working late at one of the breweries. It must have been Friday 2 September 1887 because in the early hours of the following morning, the Metropolitan Fire Brigade and the Standard Brewery Volunteer Fire Company arrived at his plumbing shop at 91 Phillip Street to answer a fire alarm.

'. . . before the flames could be subdued considerable damage to the property was effected,' the *Evening News* reported later that day. It noted that the premises were insured with the South British Insurance Company for 150 pounds, while the contents were insured for 300 pounds with another insurance company. According to McKewen, Deeming eventually negotiated a 100 pound payout.

Not long after the fire he sold the business back to the building's landlords for a nominal ten pounds. But they soon found enormous discrepancies in the books Deeming had given them and decided to pursue him in the Bankruptcy Court. He was also behind on payments to a rental firm which had provided furniture and a piano for his new home in Petersham. Other creditors were also running out of patience. Days after the fire he appeared in the Metropolitan District Court to answer a charge that he owed a wholesale iron-monger seventy-four pounds. A short hearing found against him and ordered him to pay.

It reached a climax in the Sydney Insolvency Court two months later. On 15 December, after a series of hearings in which Deeming had given vague and evasive answers – he admitted to sloppy book-keeping practices but constantly cited lapses in memory – a judge ordered him to serve fourteen days in Darlinghurst Gaol for contempt. The judge regarded Deeming's evidence 'as gross a case of prevarication and evasion as he had listened to for a considerable time'. He was satisfied that the witness 'had been evading questions almost from the first moment when he entered the witness box' and it would be impossible to even believe half of what he had sworn under oath.

Perhaps by then Marie had had enough. Or perhaps, heavily pregnant once again and with two young children at her feet, the journey to the prison was just too difficult.

On Christmas Day it was Deeming's faithful apprentice, John McKewen, who took Christmas dinner to his boss in prison. Marie stayed at home. She could relax, play with the children and not have to cast anxious glances at the front door.

For one of the few times in their six-year marriage, Marie Deeming knew with certainty just where her husband was.

VI.

He was bankrupt. His business reputation – if anything still remained – was destroyed. His wife was heavily pregnant with a third child. His beloved horse gig – with its 'first class leather hood' he had driven around Sydney on all those late-night assignations – had been auctioned at the city's Horse and Cattle Bazaar five days after he entered Darlinghurst Gaol.

Receivers were also selling his stock of plumbing and gasfitting tools and had advertised the sale of all the household items at his St Bride's home, including an ebony pianola. Frederick Deeming needed cash and from within the walls of Darlinghurst Gaol he hatched his next money-making scam.

He had befriended a dentist in the city and Deeming, once his driving skills had improved, had often taken him on rides in his buggy. According to John McKewen, the dentist had told Frederick he was willing to loan him 2000 pounds if he ever needed it. Deeming, never too proud to accept a loan and never too quick to repay it, decided it was time to take him up on the offer.

'During the time he was in gaol he sent a letter to his wife,' recalled McKewen. 'As he did not want the officials to see it he gave it to a prisoner whose term was up; but as that prisoner would be searched, Deeming split open the sole of one of the man's boots and put in the letter.'

According to McKewen, as soon as Marie received the letter she asked McKewen to take her into the city to the dentist. But the journey proved fruitless. When Frederick returned home in the final week of 1887 after serving his two-week sentence, Marie informed him she had not been able to get the money. Years later Deeming would tell a lawyer he had only seventy or eighty pounds left 'out of the wreck' of his insolvency. Of course, he had taken some precautions before being sentenced to gaol. On the morning of the court hearing he had given McKewen a portmanteau of valuable belongings, and had also hidden other valuables beneath the floorboards of his cottage.

He presumably sold these in the days after his release from prison because in the first week of 1888 the Deemings were on the move again. It was time for a new start and Frederick had decided to take his family to South Africa.

Their first stop was Adelaide, courtesy of the steamer *Konoowarra*, and by 10 January they had taken a room in a hotel in Port Adelaide under the name of Mr and Mrs W. Ward. Also staying at the hotel were two brothers with the surname Howe whom Deeming had apparently befriended on the voyage from Sydney and who also planned on travelling to Cape Town.

Two South Australian detectives would later investigate Deeming's three-week stay in Adelaide and uncover his usual pattern of fraud and deception. Frederick had told the owner of the hotel in Adelaide that he was an engineer who had just finished working as a gas-fitter in Sydney. He was always well dressed, wore several diamond rings and had placed in the hotel's secured storeroom 'a quantity of valuable plates' and a collection of expensive books, including one called *The Ruins of Pompeii*, which he said was worth more than fifty pounds.

If Mr Ward was a sharp dresser, his wife – 'a young woman of dark complexion' – was shabbily dressed. The hotel staff told police Mr Ward 'frequently slighted' her in the presence of others and she was forced to spend her time caring for their two young daughters while her husband accompanied the Howe brothers about town.

The Howes and Wards had booked tickets on the steamer *Barossa*, which was due to leave Adelaide at the end of the month for London. Along the way it would stop at the small British-controlled Atlantic island of St Helena, 1200 miles off the African coast, to drop off supplies of flour and wheat. The berths were presumably cheap. *Barossa* was already packed with bales of wool bound for London and the Wards and Howes would be its only passengers.

Not long before the ship departed, the Howe brothers, accompanied by Mr Ward, withdrew sixty pounds in gold sovereigns from their bank. According to the police investigation, they left the sovereigns in a portmanteau at the hotel and that night went to the theatre. Unusually, Mr Ward, normally their constant companion, declined to accompany them.

The following morning the brothers discovered their savings had been stolen. They suspected Ward – but could not prove it because he, too, claimed to have been travelling with gold sovereigns. They also had no time to report the theft to police. *Barossa* was about to leave and any investigation meant they would miss their opportunity to go to South Africa.

When the passengers boarded *Barossa* its captain was dismayed by the sight of the heavily pregnant Mrs Ward being assisted on deck at the last minute. It was 30 January and the steamer had just been cleared to depart by port authorities. The captain had not been told about her condition and had no doctor or stewardess on board to care for her.

By then it was too late to order his passengers off the ship. Within hours the skipper would hear more disturbing information. As the ship lost sight of the Australian coast, the bitter Howe brothers began whispering to the crew that they suspected Ward of having fleeced them of their savings.

According to one of the *Barossa*'s apprentice stewards, Walter Pearce, Mr Ward was a disgruntled passenger who constantly wore a smoking cap and 'made himself disagreeable to everybody'. Another crew member would recall him complaining about the food. He allowed some of the ship's company a peek inside a small case filled with uncut diamonds and a collection of silver plates. He also spent a lot of his time with the ship's carpenter doing 'little jobs'.

When *Barossa* was only a few days out from St Helena, Mrs Ward went into labour. Another of the ship's stewards, George Heap, along with her husband, helped her deliver a healthy baby boy. The couple named the child Sydney Francis after the city in which he was conceived, and after Cape St Francis, a small village on the southern coast of South Africa whose Seal Point lighthouse had probably been seen from the deck of the *Barossa*.

Mr Ward's mood lightened after the birth of his first son. He rewarded George Heap and the ship's captain by giving both men a diamond. According to Heap, 'on arriving at St Helena, Ward agreed to pay the passage money of the two Howes to Cape Town, and they all went ashore on that understanding'.

But the Howes were about to encounter another instance of Mr Ward's duplicity. He and his family quietly boarded the *Pembroke Castle* just as it was raising its anchor to sail to Cape Town, avoiding having to pay for the Howes' passage and leaving the brothers stranded on shore 'who were left without any means of getting off from St Helena'.

Another year had begun for Marie Deeming in the usual fashion, clouded by deception, uncertainty and the ever-present fear of living with a husband who seemed capable of anything, including murder.

VII.

By the late 1880s London was the largest city the world had known, a sprawling, congested metropolis lying at the heart of the biggest empire in history. With more than a fifth of the earth's land mass in British hands and one in every four of its inhabitants paying allegiance to the Union Jack, London's control and influence over global commerce and culture was unprecedented.

But like any enlarged and overworked heart, the city was also showing the strain. Never before had so many human beings been confined within such a small area. More than 1000 tons of fresh horse dung were dumped on London's streets each day. The incessant burning of all that coal – more than 10 million tons each year – contributed to thick, rolling fogs that crept through damp neighbourhoods and left behind layers of soot and choruses of hacking coughs. As a result, wheezing residents and breathless visitors began calling this city of more than five million souls 'The Big Smoke'.

If London was home to the greatest accumulation of wealth and power on the planet by 1888, its squalid slums and fetid ghettos were also unrivalled in the Western world. Even twenty years later the American writer Jack London would be astonished by the view from his cab as he toured the sordid, poverty-stricken streets of the East End.

'The streets were filled with a new and different race of people, short of stature, and of wretched or beer-sodden appearance,' he wrote in his book *The People of the Abyss*. 'We rolled along through miles of bricks and squalor, and from each cross street and alley flashed long vistas of bricks and misery. Here and there lurched a drunken man or woman, and the air was obscene with sounds of jangling and squabbling. At a market, tottery old men and women were searching in the garbage thrown in the mud for rotten potatoes, beans, and vegetables, while little children clustered like flies around a festering mass of fruit, thrusting their arms to the shoulders into the liquid corruption, and drawing forth morsels but partially decayed, which they devoured on the spot.'

This disparity between rich and poor, between luck and misfortune, would never be greater or more obvious than in the four miles that separated two women in the early hours of 31 August 1888.

One of them, Queen Victoria, lay asleep in Buckingham Palace – the official royal residence from which she had overseen her sprawling empire since 1837. The other, Mary 'Polly' Nichols, a mother of five who years earlier had walked out on an unhappy marriage, lay dead at the entrance to a stable, the first official victim of the reviled serial killer, Jack the Ripper.

Nichols' body had been found shortly after 3.30am in Buck's Row, one of the countless back streets and alleys in the poorly lit Whitechapel district. Nichols had spent her remaining doss house money on a drinking binge the previous day and had last been seen by a friend an hour earlier as she staggered down a road in search of a place to stay. The forty-three-year-old's throat had been cut twice. One slash went so deep only her backbone had prevented the attacker's knife from completely decapitating her. There were wounds across her abdomen and her intestines had been partially removed. The doctor who later examined her body would describe the attack as having been conducted 'deftly and skilfully', sparking speculation the killer was familiar with anatomy and might be a doctor.

Two other women had also died after being attacked in the months before Nichols' death. But the methodology had been different – one died after developing peritonitis when a blunt object was inserted into her vagina during a vicious assault by several men, while another had been stabbed thirty-nine times. Those two would be among eleven women murdered in the Whitechapel district between 1888 and 1891. But Mary Nichols would eventually become known as the first of the 'canonical five' victims of the Ripper, all of them suffering similar injuries within a short distance of one another during a three-month killing spree in the autumn of 1888.

With three women already dead the local press quickly began ridiculing the efforts of the Metropolitan police. *The Star*, the first evening newspaper founded in London and a strident critic of the police leadership, quickly dubbed the killer 'Leather Apron' – a reference to a knife-wielding man known among prostitutes in the area for wearing a bootmaker's protective garment while trying to extort money from them. 'His expression is sinister and seems to be full of terror for the women who describe it,' said a report in *The Star* on 5 September. 'His eyes are small and glittering. His lips are usually parted in a grin which is not only not reassuring, but excessively repellent. He is a slipper maker by trade, but does not work. His business is blackmailing women at night . . . his name nobody knows, but all are united in the belief that he is a Jew or of Jewish parentage, his face being of a marked Hebrew type.'

Fears that a crazed killer was on the loose, partially driven by the anti-Semitism of the era, quickly reached fever pitch three days later with the discovery of another mutilated victim. Annie Chapman was yet another 'fallen woman' whose alcoholism had ripped apart her family and, like Mary Nichols, had been left drifting from one cheap lodging house to another. She was found at dawn in a small yard a short walk from the scene of Nichols' murder. Chapman's abdomen had been slashed open and her intestines removed and draped over her right shoulder. Her uterus and the upper part of her vagina had been removed and her throat cut so severely the incision went all the way to her spine.

On 10 September, two days after Annie Chapman's murder, police arrested the Leather Apron – bootmaker John Pizer, a Polish Jew who had been in hiding for several days for fear of being lynched by mobs of vigilantes. But Pizer, who had become the first of more than a hundred suspects over the following century, was quickly released after providing authorities with ironclad alibis about his whereabouts at the time of the murders.

It would be another three weeks before the true legend of Jack the Ripper began. At 1am on 30 September the body of Swedish-born Elizabeth Stride was found lying in a pool of blood. The forty-four-year-old's throat had been cut deeply from left to right in an attack police believed had been interrupted less than half an hour earlier.

Forty-five minutes later, and a ten-minute walk from the scene of Stride's murder, a police constable came across the disembowelled body of Catherine Eddowes. Her throat, too, had been slashed and her intestines placed over her right shoulder in the same fashion as Annie Chapman. Eddowes' left kidney and uterus had also been removed and part of her right ear sliced through.

Three days before those double killings a letter had been received by the Central News Agency purporting to be written by the murderer. Eventually passed on to the police, its public release in the days after the deaths of Stride and Eddowes sparked an avalanche of similar hoax letters and launched the sobriquet 'Jack the Ripper' as the most infamous moniker in modern crime.

'*Dear Boss,*' began the letter. '*I keep on hearing the police have caught me but they wont fix me just yet. I have laughed when they look so clever and talk about being on the right track. That joke about Leather Apron gave me real fits. I am down on whores and I shant quit ripping them till I do get buckled. Grand work the last job was. I gave the lady no time to squeal.*

How can they catch me now. I love my work and want to start again. You will soon hear of me with my funny little games. I save some of the proper red stuff in a ginger beer bottle over the last job to write with but it went thick like glue and I cant use it. Red ink is fit enough I hope ha ha. The next job I do I shall clip the ladys ears off and send to the police officers just for jolly wouldn't you. Keep this letter back till I do a bit more work, then give it out straight.

My knife's so nice and sharp I want to get to work right away if I get a chance.

Good luck. Yours truly

Jack the Ripper.

Dont mind me giving the trade name. Wasnt good enough to post this before I got all the red ink off my hands curse it. No luck yet. They say I'm a doctor now. Ha ha.'

The letter, it seemed, had correctly predicted the mutilation of Catherine Eddowes' right ear. But police – and future generations of professional and amateur sleuths dedicated to solving the mystery – would dismiss the 'Dear Boss' letter as a hoax, probably written by a local journalist to boost newspaper sales. Its tone was similar to many of the cheap and titillating pamphlets known as 'penny dreadfuls' sold on London's streets. And who, apart from a journalist familiar with the workings of the press, would think to send a letter to a news agency rather than one of the immensely popular newspapers?

For the next six weeks London and the rest of the English-speaking world continued to be transfixed by the Whitechapel killings. The case embodied all the cliches and fears about Victorian London and its gothic underworld. The killer did his evil work at night. He haunted mist-filled, dimly lit streets in run-down neighbourhoods. He preyed on the abandoned and the marginalised. He clearly had a hatred of women. Perhaps he had contracted syphilis from a local prostitute and was now out to gain revenge. Hundreds of hoax letters were sent to police. A portion of a kidney preserved in alcohol – said to belong to Catherine Eddowes – was sent to the head of the newly formed Whitechapel Vigilance Committee with a note from the writer saying '*I send you half the Kidne I took from one women prasarved it for you tother piece I fried and ate it was very nise.*' Frederick Deeming never wrote so badly. Crowds roamed the streets searching for suspects. Psychics and mediums were in great demand, many claiming to have been in touch with the murdered women who, of course, had passed on vital information about their killer's identity.

By the first week of November, despite the enormous interest the case had attracted and after interviewing more than 2000 people and detaining dozens of suspects, the police seemed no closer to solving the case.

Then, in the middle of the morning on 9 November, the body of a popular prostitute, twenty-five-year-old Mary Jane Kelly, was found in a shabby, single rented room at 13 Miller's Court. It was the most savage of all the Whitechapel killings and a grisly finale to the Ripper's killing spree. Unlike the rest of the murders, which had hastily taken place in laneways and public spaces under constant threat of being seen, the killer had spent plenty of time going about his work. Doctors estimated the murderer would have required at least two hours to unleash the carnage found in the room. Kelly's head was almost completely severed from her body and most of her face had been removed. Both breasts had been sliced off. One had been placed beneath her head, along with her uterus and kidneys. The other breast lay by her right foot. A great deal of the contents of her stomach were arranged around her – her liver between her feet, her intestines by her right side and her spleen placed on the left side of her body. Part of her thigh had been lacerated to the bone and a skin flap placed on a nearby table, along with flesh from her abdomen.

Mary Kelly's death would be regarded as the last of the 'official' Jack the Ripper killings that, over the following century, would become the most celebrated cold case in history. The vacuum created by the lack of an outstanding prime suspect would spawn a thriving industry involving hundreds of books and countless plays, films, songs, comic books and even operas.

It seemed remarkable that in the most crowded city on earth the culprit had left so few clues about his true identity. Some senior police at the time believed him to be Aaron Kosminski, a Polish Jew who worked sporadically as a hairdresser in Whitechapel and was said to have homicidal tendencies, a pathological hatred of women and who died in an asylum in 1919.

Others, including Frederick Abberline, who led the detective force working on the case and would later become Chief Inspector of the London Metropolitan Police, were said to favour George Chapman (real name Seweryn Antonowicz Klosowski), who was hanged in 1903 for poisoning three of his wives.

Later, suspicions would centre on Carl Feigenbaum, a psychopathic German merchant sailor who later emigrated to America and was executed in the electric chair in 1896 for murdering an elderly widow. Another name that would not publicly surface until the 1960s was Montague John Druitt, an Oxford-educated barrister and teacher whose body was found floating in the Thames shortly after Mary Kelly's death.

By then the list of potential culprits ranged from the partly credible to the fanciful and included Lewis Carroll, the author of *Alice's Adventures in Wonderland*, and Queen Victoria's physician, Sir William Withey Gull.

But another man with credentials as a Jack the Ripper suspect would emerge just a few years after Mary Kelly's murder. Like the Ripper, Frederick Deeming could be an elusive figure when he wanted to be, disappearing as quickly as he appeared. And the brutal nature of his crimes would remind many of the carnage unleashed in Whitechapel during that autumn of 1888.

VIII.

A month before Jack the Ripper's murder spree began in earnest, Britain's South African colony had also been gripped by a rising body count.

On the evening of 11 July a fire had broken out in the main shaft of the large De Beers diamond mine on the outskirts of Kimberley, the capital city of the Northern Cape province.

More than 200 men – the majority of them natives working under slave-like conditions – were burned alive more than 500 feet below the surface. It would take days before the heat of the inferno cooled enough to allow rescuers using dynamite to recover a few surviving victims and far more of the dead. Most would never be found. The earth, as so many Deeming men knew only too well, had a habit of swallowing those who plundered its riches.

Frederick Deeming would have been familiar with that De Beers mine. He had long been obsessed with jewels and diamonds and how the wealthy brandished them as badges of their status. Diamonds, to Deeming's way of thinking, offered a man prone to dropping his h's a chance to be catapulted out of the drudgery of working class life and into the ranks of the well-heeled.

It would have been one of the main reasons why he took his family to South Africa. By the time the Deemings arrived in those opening months of 1888, Cecil Rhodes, a British imperialist who believed white Europeans were the first human race to have appeared on earth, had amalgamated a series of smaller mining companies and set up the De Beers company, which would go on to monopolise the world's diamond trade for the next century.

The fire at De Beers' main mine in Kimberley would soon be forgotten. Life was cheap and sending slaves deep below the ground even cheaper in the late nineteenth century. The only measure of success was wealth, which in turn led to power – Rhodes would soon become the Cape Colony's seventh prime minister. The exploding worth of gems – it was De Beers' clever marketing that would convince the world an engagement ring required a diamond – had lured fortune seekers from all over the world. With its porous borders and lack of centralised law enforcement, South Africa had become a key destination for men like Deeming with a hankering for an easy fortune and a desire to dispense with chequered pasts by adopting new identities.

Deeming would later tell one of his lawyers that after arriving in South Africa in early 1888 he landed a brief job with the local municipal council on a salary of four pounds a week but left not long after for the diamond fields of Kimberley. This corresponds with later newspaper reports in the Cape of a man named Deeming arriving at the Palmerston Hotel in Plein Street in early 1888 asking for lodgings for himself and his wife and three children.

The landlord of the hotel, Louis Sytner, told reporters he took a liking to the new arrival and arranged work for him with local city contractors, who appointed him chief engineer at four pounds a week. But within a month or two Deeming had quit that role for the Kimberley diamond fields where, he would tell his lawyer, he discovered one of the biggest mines had been swamped with water. Its engineer had no idea how to clear the mess and, of course, it was left to Frederick Deeming to perform another heroic feat. Within seven days he had the mine running again and, as a reward, was paid 100 pounds by Cecil Rhodes before he went to Johannesburg where he made money 'hand over fist'.

If the tale of Frederick Deeming being recognised by the most powerful man in South Africa sounded fanciful, it would become just one of the many uncorroborated stories that would emerge about his exploits in South Africa. His boasts were the stuff of a nineteenth century boy's fantasies, plucked directly from the pages of a penny dreadful. He would brag he had explored the Zambezi and fought battles with savage natives, that he had entered caves and killed a pride of lions with his bare hands, that he had been wounded by a bullet during a battle defending the empire against the restless Blacks. Apart from his own fanciful tales, his time in the Cape would trigger a bewildering array of unsubstantiated allegations and, supported by a maddening lack of official records, would raise the possibility that he, an inveterate traveller who thought nothing about boarding a ship for another country, had slipped into England during that autumn of 1888 and committed the Jack the Ripper murders.

In the late nineteenth century a person could move to another country almost on a whim, as long as they could afford the fare. Border control was rare and most countries did not require a traveller to show a passport or other identifying documents. But one thing was certain. Deeming was constantly on the move in the Cape colony, making appearances in Port Elizabeth, Durban, Klerksdorp and Johannesburg.

One swindle was said to have netted him and a mysterious accomplice more than 6000 pounds using falsified bank documents and selling claims to gold mines that either didn't exist or were no longer of any value. Allegations would follow of various jewellery swindles and another fraud that saw him dupe an overly trusting bank manager who gave him an advance of 3000 pounds. At one stage he was said to have posed as the manager of the New Nooitgedacht Gold Mining Company (he would hand out a business card bearing that title on his return to England) and had adopted his usual array of aliases, posing as a 'Mr Leevy' or 'Leavey' or 'Levi' – nineteenth century newspapers being as prone to poor spelling as Deeming himself.

It was in South Africa that Deeming would tell doctors he contracted syphilis and began receiving nightly visits from his dead mother urging him to kill his wife. For most of this period Marie and the children remained in Cape Town. Her husband would return to the Palmerston Hotel every few weeks with a new bounty of cash and jewellery. Marie surely knew about her husband's crimes. Most likely she was simply a pragmatist. A married woman with children in the late nineteenth century, totally reliant on her husband and with family on the other side of the world, would have had few choices.

There was no doubt, however, that she understood the true character of the man she had married. In the days leading up to her death two years later, Marie would send a letter suggesting she wanted to make amends for some of her husband's crimes.

The letter was kept by Agnes Lemaire, whose husband, John, had once been chief engineer of the steamer *New England*.

In 1882 the *New England* had left the Grafton wharf in northern New South Wales on its way to Sydney down the Clarence River. More than fifty passengers were on board when, in rough weather, it violently struck a sand bar near the mouth of the river and began drifting in heavy seas. As it began to sink many of the passengers were washed overboard by large waves. While other boats in the area refused to launch rescue missions because of the treacherous conditions, three sailors on a small coastal schooner courageously braved the waves to rescue almost half the ship's complement, including its first engineer, John Lemaire.

Lemaire, cold and saturated after nearly drowning, refused to be taken back to safety and instead joined the sailors flinging life buoys to those still clinging to the wreckage. Soon after, he and the three sailors were awarded medals and cash rewards for saving almost a dozen lives. The government gave Lemaire twenty-one pounds and he also received a substantial share of a public subscription set up to reward the act of bravery.

Lemaire and his wife, Agnes, were living in a boarding house in Riley Street, Sydney, at the time. Frederick Deeming, newly arrived from England, was a fellow lodger and, according to the Lemaires, after discovering the couple were flush with cash, began pestering John for a loan of fifty pounds. Lemaire resisted but eventually agreed to give him fifteen pounds. Deeming signed a promissory note which, three months later, was dishonoured although, during his insolvency hearings, he had sent Lemaire a two pound note.

Marie's letter to the Lemaires, written from England in 1891 and made public a year later, said she had just joined her husband in Rainhill. The letter, according to one newspaper report, 'was to the effect that she . . . would pay the 13 pounds herself, seeing that he had failed to do so. She did not write again.'

That letter would be written two years after Marie and the children arrived home in Birkenhead without Frederick in July or August 1889. By then it seems clear Deeming, no doubt fleeing from his latest scam, had decided it was best to travel alone and take a circuitous route back to England via Yemen.

Three years later *The Brisbane Courier* would interview one of the crew of the steamer *Jumna*, which regularly made the journey between its home port of Brisbane and London. The claims by the ship's purser, Robert McNab, would be supported by several shipping records of the time.

McNab said *Jumna* arrived at Yemen's port city of Aden in September and 'a Mr S. M. Leavey came on board . . . bringing with him a lion cub and a gazelle. Mr Leavey made himself conspicuous by always appearing at table in evening dress and wearing what appeared to be genuine diamond rings and studs, the diamonds in which were remarkably large and of fine quality.'

Leavey, who gave the impression to McNab of being a Jewish diamond merchant, told passengers stories of his hunting exploits in South Africa 'and had not been many days on board before he proposed marriage to a lady (a widow), offering to settle 3000 pounds on her, but she repulsed his overtures, and eventually had to appeal to Captain Smith for protection'.

If McNab's claims did not already mirror many of Deeming's eccentricities, they were made more credible by his description of the flamboyant Mr Leavey as someone who was 'evidently not a gentleman, and although he spoke with great care he murdered the Queen's English frequently by dropping his h's'.

Leavey claimed to live in a castle in Chester and had sailed to South Africa on a large yacht. When he mentioned the vessel's name passengers from Liverpool instantly recognised it as a famous ocean yacht. He left the *Jumna* when it arrived in Plymouth on 27 September, taking the lion cub with him but leaving the gazelle behind. The shipping company wrote letters to the man's Chester address about the stranded gazelle, but all were returned marked with 'not known at this address'.

Within a day or two Frederick Deeming was back in Birkenhead with his family, showing off his lion cub and boasting about his successes in South Africa by flaunting wads of cash and diamonds.

If the Deeming marriage had been dysfunctional for a long time – Marie, according to Deeming, was aware that he had contracted syphilis – they continued sleeping together because Marie would soon be pregnant with their fourth child.

But for all her tolerance and longstanding loyalty to Frederick, for all those long nights she spent watching that front door and wondering where her husband was and what he was doing, Marie was never a truly typical Deeming woman, because a Deeming woman usually outlived her husband.

IX.

It was one of his better stories. His parents had been poor and decided to take a chance at improving their position in Australia. It had certainly proved to be a land of opportunity and Harry Lawson had turned out to be the perfect son every parent dreamed about.

He had the golden touch. He went to the goldfields and where others struck rock and heartbreak, he unearthed a fortune large enough to buy his own gold mine. He bought land and when others struggled through drought and flood, he became a wealthy sheep farmer. He dabbled in racehorse breeding and, unlike all those dreamers who found the business of bloodlines mystifying and as chance-ridden as the lotteries, he had made a success of that, too.

Frederick Deeming arrived in Hull in late October 1889 using the alias of Harry Lawson and posing as a rich man happy to display the trappings of his wealth. There were large diamond rings on his fingers. He was sometimes fitted out in the regalia and jewellery of a Freemason, the male-only organisation that traced its origins back to the fourteenth-century fraternities of stonemasons. With its secret handshakes, symbolic rituals and reputation for power and influence among the highest strata of society, it was the sort of institution that appealed to a man desperately craving recognition and approval. But those who took a closer look noticed the black robes were thin and frayed at the edges – stolen, it would transpire, during his time in South Africa.

In Hull Deeming was about to embark on an adventure that, even by his standards, would prove to be a quixotic odyssey that would end in a nine-month stint in prison.

The previous four weeks had been a blur of activity. He had returned to Birkenhead in triumph with his lion cub, pockets loaded with cash and his charitable side on display.

'All my brothers were rather hard up, and I gave them a hundred or so each,' he would tell one of his lawyers. But after moving Marie and the kids into a larger house, he had learned a private detective was on his trail and had left Birkenhead claiming he had business in Europe.

He had reappeared in Hull, checking into a local hotel as Harry Lawson. One morning he was on his way to the market town of Beverley eight miles north when he noticed a sign in the front window of a house on 'a beautiful wide avenue' advertising a room to rent.

'I thought to myself, this is more comfortable than living in lodgings; I will go and see what it is like.'

It is possible he was already familiar with Beverley; reports would later claim he had visited the town some years earlier and proposed marriage to the widowed landlady of The Forester's Arms hotel, Jane Gibson. He had, according to those claims, taken thirty five-pound notes from his purse and laid them out on a table, promising her he would also care for her children. She had declined but when he returned to Hull in 1889 he sought her out again and found her working at the Sloop Inn. This time she agreed to marry. 'All the arrangements were made and the wedding dress provided,' reported the *Western Morning News*. But Jane Gibson suddenly got cold feet. She had done some checking and discovered some of her suitor's claims were untrue and had 'refused to have anything further to do with him'.

When Lawson, fresh from his rebuff by Jane Gibson, knocked on the door of the house advertising a room to let, it was answered by Sarah Matheson, a widow who shared her home with her twenty-one-year-old daughter Helen, known to everyone as 'Nellie'.

The following events would establish a pattern that would later become all too familiar to those in the village of Rainhill: a young woman desperate for marriage, a wealthy suitor promising a lifetime of riches and comfort and a widowed mother unaware of rumours circulating in town that her daughter's intended was a cad and married to someone else.

The man Sarah Matheson found on her doorstep appeared to have 'spent some time abroad in a warm climate, his face being tanned . . . his complexion was naturally fair, his hair was of a chestnut tinge, his eyes blue, and he walked with a peculiar posture of the shoulders, which were drawn up almost close to his ears'.

'He said he had been looking round Beverley for apartments, and he thought he should like to stay at our house. It seemed a nice sort of place, he said, and he rather liked it. His manner was suave and engaging.'

Despite boasting about his wealth, Harry Lawson drove a hard bargain when it came to the rent. They eventually settled on an amount and he quickly moved in. Lawson was not just taken with his new accommodation. He was infatuated with Nellie and was soon taking her for drives around town in a horse gig, apparently now far more skilled at driving than he had been during his time in Sydney.

He soon proposed marriage and Nellie, after consulting her mother, agreed. The wedding was scheduled for February 1890. He was always disappearing for a few days at a time claiming business matters called him to London and the Continent. More likely he was returning to Birkenhead and giving Marie cash.

But in late November Lawson abruptly told the Mathesons he needed to return to Europe on further business and had booked a berth on the liner *Zebra*. Not long after, they received a telegram from Belgium. He was in Antwerp and seriously injured after falling from a horse. Would they come and care for him?

In the years to come several reports would emerge about Deeming's short stay in Antwerp claiming he had regularly visited prostitutes while also fleecing a succession of gullible victims, including an art gallery where he posed as a collector and had several paintings shipped back to England on credit. He had passed himself off as Harry Dunn or, on other occasions, 'Lord Dunn', posing for a photograph with a top hat, velvet scarf and holding an unlit cigar. One man who claimed to have formed a brief association with him said he saw him reach into a black Gladstone bag bulging with sovereigns, pull out two handfuls and announce: 'I think that will be enough for one night's spree.' Within a week or two he had racked up a series of debts and shown his creditors a fake telegram claiming his castle and collection of racehorses had been destroyed in a fire. They would have to wait for the insurance payout.

He had failed to give Sarah and Nellie his address in Antwerp and when mother and daughter arrived it took several days before they tracked him to his hotel room. According to Deeming's later account, 'one day, whilst out riding with the British Consul, my horse fell, and I dislocated my shoulder bone'. There he was again, hob-knobbing with the powerful and influential. The three then took an apartment in the Hotel St Antoine and when Sarah Matheson departed for a short trip to Baden, Nellie was left alone with her recuperating fiancé. 'Our intimacy was of the most affectionate kind,' Deeming would claim later.

Not everyone in the family was convinced Nellie was doing the right thing. Nellie had been partly raised by relatives in Aberdeen, Scotland, and they were far from impressed with her betrothed when they met him following their return from Europe. Nellie's mother was also beginning to have doubts and told her daughter there was something strange about her intended husband and she was sure it would 'end badly'.

But the wedding went ahead in St Mary's Church on 18 February 1890. The groom listed his occupation as 'sheep farmer' while stating his father was a shepherd. Despite her misgivings, Sarah Matheson could not fault the 'great kindness' Harry Lawson showed to her daughter in the weeks that followed their marriage. The pair went south to honeymoon for a fortnight in a series of hotels in Torquay and Southampton until Lawson suggested they return north so he could transfer money into his overdrawn bank account.

They stayed in a hotel in Hull on Saturday 15 March. Early that evening, Lawson showed her a diamond bracelet. He had bought it a few hours earlier at Reynoldson and Son, a local jeweller in Whitefriargate. He had purchased items from the business previously, using either cash or cheques which had always been honoured, although he was still to pay for two diamond rings he had taken with him some weeks before. He told the jewellers his account was overdrawn but would be replenished with funds the following week and the 285 pounds he owed them would then be paid. They had never experienced problems with him before and agreed he could retain the rings and also take the bracelet.

Nellie was delighted by the gift and wanted to try it on. But her husband said he wanted to give it to her the following morning. He called a waiter and asked for tea to be sent to the dining room for his wife. Then he told Nellie he had to go into town for a shave and would be back shortly.

But Harry Lawson had no intention of returning. He had been quietly sending his luggage collection to a storage facility in Southampton. After ordering the pot of tea for his wife he left the hotel and caught a train to London. It appeared he stayed in London overnight before making his way to Southampton, just in time to purchase a berth, under the name of Deeming, on the *S.S. Coleridge*, a steamer bound for Montevideo, the capital city of Uruguay.

It is possible he still believed he was being tracked by detectives over his frauds in South Africa. He may also have spent most of his savings after his marriage to Nellie Matheson and decided it was time to get away and cash in the jewellery. It is also possible Marie, aware of his bigamous marriage, had tracked him down and was threatening to report his whereabouts unless he provided her with more cash – something she would do again the following year when she learned her husband was preparing to marry yet another woman.

Whatever the reason, he was in a rush. The *Coleridge* was due to depart at 4pm. Thirty minutes before it departed a lawyer and budding politician from a wealthy family, Pearce Edgcumbe, arrived in his cabin to discover that someone else's portmanteau and large lounge coat had been placed inside. He summoned a steward and told him to remove the luggage because the cabin had been reserved for his sole use. The steward apologised and said they had been placed there on the orders of the captain. Edgcumbe picked them up and tossed them into the passage outside.

Within moments the captain arrived and explained that a passenger had only just arrived 'and it was of urgent importance for him to travel by that steamer to Montevideo' and the rest of the accommodation was booked out. A heated discussion ensued.

'The captain thereupon said he was the captain of the vessel, and that he must order me to admit this passenger,' a pompous-sounding Edgcumbe would later tell *The London Star*. 'I replied that he might be captain of the vessel, but that I considered myself captain of the cabin, and that I declined to do anything of the kind.'

The captain backed down. The new passenger, a round-shouldered short man with a large moustache and plenty of jewellery on show, was placed in a small hut on the forward deck usually 'reserved for invalids'. As the *Coleridge* entered the Bay of Biscay it encountered rough weather and the waves that crashed across the deck saw Deeming 'almost washed out of his cabin'.

This was the voyage where he passed himself off as a diamond merchant who was on his way to South America on a business trip. Edgcumbe said he had attempted to have a conversation with Deeming soon after leaving Southampton because 'I thought that he would be able to give me some information about diamonds. After five minutes' conversation with him, I came to the conclusion that if he was a diamond merchant at all he did not know as much about diamonds as I did, and that therefore it was useless to continue the conversation.'

It was also the voyage when, with his need to be the centre of attention overcoming any desire to keep a low profile after the events in Hull, he flirted with women and organised a concert, the proceeds of which would go to the Seamen's Orphans charity. He painted intricate invitation cards and personally handed them out to fellow passengers. Then, taking the stage, he slaughtered the lyrics to that old sea shanty 'The Dead Horse', dropping his h's to the amusement of many of the passengers, including Edgcumbe.

When the *Coleridge* anchored in Montevideo Bay, all male passengers were summoned on deck. According to Edgcumbe, everyone appeared except Deeming. The police, acting on a request telegrammed a week earlier by the Hull police, searched the ship and arrested him, discovering the diamond rings and seventy-two diamonds gouged from the bracelet he had told Nellie was for her.

The jewellers he had swindled in Hull had notified the police on the Monday after Deeming had left Nellie alone in the hotel. It turned out his bank account had been closed the previous week. But to secure his extradition required reams of paperwork that would reach all the way to the desk of Lord Llandaff, the Home Secretary.

It was not until early August that a Hull detective, Thomas Grasby, arrived in Montevideo to arrest him and return him to England. It was Deeming's bad luck that the UK had just signed an extradition treaty with Uruguay. Before then the country had been a reliable destination for those wanting to leave their troubled past behind them. South America, just like South Africa, was a place that offered a new beginning. Its internal borders were loosely patrolled and new identities easy to obtain. Had Deeming absconded just a few months earlier he would have been free to travel through the continent and plot his next move.

He was reportedly a difficult prisoner during his four months inside his Montevideo cell. In early April he wrote to the British consul in Uruguay saying his treatment was 'not fit for a dog' and was doing considerable 'hinjury' to his 'helth'. He had only come to Uruguay in pursuit of a man who owed him 9000 pounds, he said. He asked for his luggage to be returned to him because he required clean linen as he was 'dirty and miserable . . . I never see anyone to speak to, not even a spiritual adviser. I have not my prayer book nor my Bible and my Sunday has passed almost without knowing.'

At the same time the consul received an anonymous letter 'written in a disguised hand' threatening his life unless Harry Lawson was released from his Montevideo prison by a certain date.

Not long after, Deeming wrote to the consul saying he had heard a threatening letter had been sent to him. He wanted to make it known he had nothing to do with it.

X.

On 17 October 1890 – six weeks after being returned to England in handcuffs – Deeming was found guilty of defrauding the jewellers and, under the name of Harry Lawson, was sentenced to nine months imprisonment in Hull Prison.

To the inmates and those who worked inside its red brick walls the prison was more often referred to as 'Webster's Hotel', a reference to its long-serving governor, Harry Webster. Nearing retirement, Webster regarded himself as a man ahead of his time, a just and humane prison chief who tried to treat the men under his care firmly but fairly. While he had meted out punishment to thousands of criminals – some of them the most hardened and duplicitous in England – he would never forget the prisoner he knew as Harry Lawson.

After retiring Webster moved to Australia and settled in Melbourne. He took with him dozens of mementoes of his career. Visitors to his East Kew house could have been forgiven for thinking they had stumbled into a museum dedicated to crime and punishment. On display were 'ingenious contrivances' – tools, keys and weapons made by prisoners hoping to escape or avenge themselves on a rival. Webster, too, was not without his own talent. He had kept a cat-o'-nine-tails of his own making that had once lashed the backs of more than a few inmates.

He was an old man when he invited a reporter from *The Argus* inside his home years later. He still clearly remembered Harry Lawson not just as a fraudster and bigamist, but a man with a 'restless, crookedly developed mentality'. Webster recalled how he suspected the man had money and friends outside the prison, and he had not wanted to give him the opportunity of bribing one of the poorly paid guards to help him escape.

Webster began moving Lawson to a new cell within the prison every week, often on a different floor or separate wing. Lawson had protested and, when finally granted a meeting with the governor, had asked him, 'What is the reason for my being bandied about from pillar to post?' Webster wouldn't say and a frustrated Lawson began nursing a grudge against him.

But Webster had his reasons. Not long after Lawson's incarceration Webster had been approached by a former businessman who had been appointed a magistrate in Bedford. The magistrate claimed the description of Harry Lawson matched that of a man who had swindled him and others in South Africa. He gave Webster 'a graphic account of plotting and robbery on the South African diamond fields which, of itself, could fill a book with the kind of facts that makes fiction seem tame'. The magistrate had hired detectives to track the suspect and when Webster allowed him to see Lawson in his cell, he confirmed him as the culprit who had run a series of bogus schemes that cost investors thousands of pounds.

Lawson declared he had never seen the magistrate before. At that point the visitor turned angrily on Lawson and told him 'that he had robbed him out of thousands of pounds and that when he got him to Johannesburg it would be many a year before he got away as he would prosecute him'.

The next morning Lawson's memory of the man improved. He asked Webster if he would allow him to write to the Bedford magistrate 'as he had remembered that this gentleman owed him several thousand pounds . . . and if the money was not remitted within a few days he should issue a writ'.

The sheer front and chutzpah of prisoner No. 1528 was breathtaking. He soon lodged an official complaint claiming his treatment inside Hull Prison was ruining his health ('Not true,' wrote the prison's medical officer in a memo to Governor Webster. 'He is in good health and has gained 1lb in weight since his exception into this prison.')

Before long Lawson was petitioning bureaucrats in the Home Department saying 'on the grounds of innocents' he deserved to be freed. He also issued a writ against Hull's chief constable 'to recover certain specific articles of jewellery now in the possession of the police, and for damages for detaining same'.

The police were unperturbed by his claims. They had already received a telegram from a police detective in Kimberley saying some of Deeming's jewellery and a Freemasons outfit had been stolen from a Mr W. da Silva in South Africa the previous year and asked the local inspector 'to be good enough to forward them'.

Soon after dismissing Lawson's complaints about being constantly shifted from cell to cell, Webster heard that Harry Lawson had 'developed alarming fits and foamed convincingly at the mouth and, before long, he was enjoying the comforts and comparative delicacies associated with bed and meals in the hospital ward'. It was a repeat of what had occurred during his time in Darlinghurst Gaol.

The doctors and guards remained baffled by the seizures, which were frequent and, to them, appeared genuine, involving 'shivering fits . . . lapses into inertia, ghastly rolling of the eyes and frothing about the lips'.

'Soap chewing is all that is wrong with Lawson,' Webster told the prison doctor. It was an old shamming method he had seen plenty of times before.

Webster decided to personally investigate the case.

'Get up, Lawson,' he barked as he entered the hospital wing. He told an orderly to closely examine the bedding while Webster turned over the mattress and ran his fingers along the bedframe. He felt something hidden beneath a ledge and used his fingers to dislodge it.

Several tiny balls of soap fell to the floor. Webster ordered Lawson out of the hospital wing and back to a normal cell.

In April 1892 the *Liverpool Echo* published a statement by a former Hull prisoner, Fred Wilson, who said he had served time with Harry Lawson in Hull after being gaoled for six months for larceny. He had met Lawson a day after the man had swapped his suit for prison clothing. Lawson had quickly announced: 'I have got nine months, but when I get out of this here I will let this world know something that they know little about.'

Lawson's fits were a source of amusement to Wilson and other prisoners.

'One day after we came off parade he went up into his cell, reeled right over and went into a shaking fit.'

Fred Wilson was ordered to stay with Lawson for a short time and keep an eye on him. 'We had not been in long before he again fell down in a shaking fit. He had two or three of these fits that day, but they were only put on . . . it was to our benefit to make the doctor believe they were fits because we were eating Lawson's victuals and living well.'

Later, when Wilson was about to be released, Lawson asked him to smuggle a letter to his wife that read: 'Dear Marie, when I get out of this I shall be free to be your husband once more, if you are willing to take me back, which you cannot help but do, or else I will round on you.'

The letter went on to say no-one had any idea how much he was worth, that he had 'thousands and thousands' of pounds hidden away and if he died in prison no-one would find it, not even Marie. According to Wilson he had written several similar letters, including one imploring Marie to 'take care of those diamonds'.

He had also written to Nellie telling her he was innocent and that he hoped his new bride would stand by him. According to local newspaper reports in Hull, Nellie had been approached by Marie, who told her she was still legally married to the man she knew to be Frederick Deeming. By then Nellie Matheson had had enough and refused to see him.

Inside the prison's walls, Harry Lawson's mood darkened further and he began blaming Governor Webster for many of his troubles.

'When I get out of this I will make the people stand on their heads,' Fred Wilson recalled Lawson telling him one day, 'and if Webster don't look out, and that chief warder, I will put a bullet through them or else knife them.'

'My friend, don't you do anything of the kind. If you do, it means rope,' replied Wilson.

'Never mind, my boy. I have done worse than that and I am not frightened by the rope.'

But what concerned Governor Harry Webster most about his prisoner was not his regular shamming, or his background as a fraudster.

He thought the man capable of murder. One day Marie arrived unannounced at the prison asking to visit her husband. She was carrying a baby in her arms, her fourth child, presumably conceived with Frederick during those brief weeks after his return from South Africa.

According to a sworn statement made by Webster, Marie told the governor she was a cousin of Harry Lawson. But she was as hopeless at lying as her husband was gifted, and quickly confessed she was his wife and was living near Liverpool. Webster allowed them to meet and stood by with growing alarm as the pair spoke. Webster 'was disturbed not so much by what was said as by the venomous glance which the man bent upon her in the first instant of their meeting'.

Lawson was furious and believed that by visiting him in prison Marie had 'given herself away' and that he would be arrested on bigamy charges as soon as his sentence had finished. Webster also read one of the letters he had written to Marie. Its contents confirmed the man was undoubtedly a bigamist, but Webster was more concerned at the threatening tone Lawson employed against his wife. After reading the letter, he said, he turned to one of the warders and observed: 'That man will do murder when he gets out.'

There was no chance of bigamy charges being laid, even though it became widely known among gaol officials and other prisoners that Harry Lawson now had two wives and was rumoured to have more. Under a clause in the treaty between Uruguay and the United Kingdom, any British citizen arrested in Uruguay and returned to England for trial could only be charged with the offence that had led to his or her extradition. Any prior offences were off-limits. It was a technical point and became the subject of a flurry of memos for months between Hull police, the Home Department and the Foreign Office.

In October 1891, three months after Harry Lawson had been released from Hull Prison, a clearly impatient Nellie Matheson wrote to the authorities saying, 'I shall be very glad if you will take any steps necessary on my behalf in the matter relating to the bigamy committed by Harry Lawson, alias Fred Deeming.'

Nellie cited information she had been given that Deeming had been married ten years previously and that his wife remained alive. 'I am not able to go to any great expense in the matter,' she wrote, 'but should like to know if the Government does not prosecute such cases.'

A decision had already been made. Even if the clause in the extradition treaty could be overcome, Deeming would in all likelihood have disappeared again. Pursuing him would be too complicated and costly.

Nellie, unknowingly, had also made a mistake. She said his first wife was still alive. By the time she wrote that letter the bodies of Marie Deeming and her four children were mouldering beneath a concrete slab in a villa in Rainhill.

And Frederick Deeming was preparing to sail to Australia with a new bride on his arm and more thoughts of murder on his mind.

PART III.

'I'll never get married any more'

The Singing Canary and the Anxious Wife – The Lugubrious Fiend Identified as a Madman – A Nasty Fracas Instigated by a Drunken Brute – His Conversations with the Canary – The Case of the Missing Necklace – Deeming's Seizures of Madness – The Final Days of the Girl with the Long Dark Hair

I.

He cradled the tiny bird in his hand so gently, so tenderly. He puckered his lips beneath his thick moustache and made a soft kissing sound. The bird should have been afraid. Its beak should have been wide open, gulping air like a panting dog. Its feathers should have been tightly wound around its body, head swivelling, eyes darting from side to side, the way canaries behave when stressed.

They were timid things at the best of times; anxious and wary, constantly unsettled, like horses after catching a threatening scent on a shifting breeze. Not even the monks and courtiers who bred them to flatter all those Spanish and English kings and fill their courts with birdsong had found a way to rid the species of its shyness. But this one? It showed no fear. It always felt safe with him.

It let out a chirp and began stepping confidently on delicate matchstick legs along the sleeve of his shirt.

The man's wife, Emily, watched on, admiring her new husband and his way with the canary. Such patience. Such attention to detail. All those hours training the bird, stripping it of its fears, rewarding it with a seed or two for every brave step. It was an impressive attribute other passengers on the ship had also noticed, for they often found the man they knew as Albert Williams on the deck, taking in the fresh air, doting on his bride, the canary nestled comfortably in his wavy sandy hair, its empty brass cage glinting gold in the bright sun.

Quite the character was Mr Williams. He was a smallish chap with muscular shoulders and a magnificent ginger moustache that hung over a pair of thin grim lips. Williams was proud of that moustache. It gave him a military bearing, which was exactly the sort of image he hoped to project. It suggested a stoic man of rigid discipline and patience, of hours in front of mirrors diligently trimming errant bristles and straightening fraying edges, a man who believed a big moustache made a bigger man.

He was not alone. Facial hair had long been a nineteenth century obsession, an emblem of masculinity, a civilised version of the way exotic male birds used their bright plumage to lure prospective mates.

Moustaches and beards ignored class distinctions and crossed social barriers. 'The moustaches are glorious, glorious,' Charles Dickens had written to a friend during his first trip to North America. 'I have . . . trimmed them a little at the ends to improve their shape. They are charming, charming. Without them, life would be a blank.'

If Mr Williams was self-conscious about his height, not even the *Kaiser Wilhelm II*, the giant 7000-ton steel behemoth carrying him toward Australia through the heaving seas of the Atlantic in late 1891, could dwarf his personality. He had been making a name for himself since the ship had embarked from Southampton in early November. When one tired of admiring the man's moustache, one's eyes were immediately drawn to a large diamond ring on the third finger of his right hand. Or to the black bowler hat he often wore when his canary was not perched on his head. And who could miss the diamond stud in his collar? Or that fashionable silver umbrella he liked to carry, even on days when the skies were clear?

He was a man determined to be at the centre of everything. Williams had confided to Max Hirschfeldt, a German-born draper and a fellow second-class passenger, that he was an experienced engineer with a military background and had a small fortune – six or seven thousand pounds – that he planned to invest in the colony of Victoria once the ship reached Melbourne.

He had told Sydney Oakes, a corn merchant on his way home to Australia after a stint in Europe, that he was now drawing a healthy pension of 150 pounds a year after nineteen years as an inspecting engineer with the Royal Navy. Others thought they had heard him say he was an ex Major-General. The details were a little vague and seemed to change depending on who was listening. If anyone had bothered prying a little deeper they might have noted all the inconsistencies. But one didn't stoop to such common behaviour in the late nineteenth century. He was a military man, it seemed. A garrulous one at that.

The fellow was certainly not shy in coming forward. Always up for a chat in that soft Lancashire accent, always quick to let you know what a seasoned traveller he was and how those strong shoulders and arms had steered him safely through many a scrap. Was there a place he had not visited? Williams had told Hirschfeldt he had hunted buffalo across vast prairies in the United States. He had been in Mexico, too, working in 'negro camps' that Hirschfeldt, who had also visited Mexico, had no idea even existed. There had been lucrative stints in the diamond fields of South Africa, not to mention an expedition following the course of the great Congo River. Was it any wonder that by the time he reached the dusty plains of India he had required teams of servants to carry him for days beneath that nation's burning sun?

Truth be told the man's constant prattling and boasting had become a tad wearisome. He monopolised conversations and was uninterested in the offerings of others. Those subjected to his lengthy monologues began to think it was impossible for someone to have crammed so many adventures into such a short space of time. He appeared, at best guess, to be a year or two shy of forty. Every anecdote felt exaggerated. Every tale always seemed to end with Williams triumphing after heroically placing himself in harm's way. But if Hirschfeldt and others were harbouring growing doubts about

Williams' loyalty to the truth, there was no disputing the man was good with his hands and did, indeed, have some engineering talents.

One day he had shown several passengers how he had taken a pair of knitting needles and, with just a little wire and ingenuity, turned them into a formidable set of pliers. Before that he had drawn some intricate designs of machinery no-one quite understood, but which he claimed was a new invention that would soon revolutionise the colony's railways.

Williams could often be found on the deck leaning back in a wicker chair he had brought on board for the journey. Constantly by his side was Emily and everyone agreed she played the role of dutiful spouse with great aplomb. 'Devotedly attached,' was how one fellow passenger would remember her. 'Docile and innocent,' another would recall. She paid loving attention to his stories, laughed and smiled at all his jokes and seemed extra careful not to divulge too much information about herself.

A passenger had asked her where she intended to live in Melbourne with her husband once the ship reached its destination.

She thought they might move to the inner suburb of Carlton, she replied. And then she had smiled. 'But then I am a mere child in these matters . . . my husband knows all about Australia and he will see that we do not go astray.'

But if she hoped to remain in the shadow of her husband, Emily could not help but leave a lasting impression on those she met. She was barely five foot and petite with beautiful dark auburn hair that fell so far below her waist she could sit on it. She often formed it into thick plaits that ran down her back like the tails of dressage horses. Hirschfeldt was quite taken with her appearance and whenever he grew bored with her husband's boasting he would sneak a glance. Being a draper with a good eye for quality cloth, he would admire the brown dress that hugged her body, or the light grey tweed skirt she also favoured, often with a dark belt around the waist.

Hirschfeldt had also marvelled at the size and plumpness of her earlobes. She did not favour earrings but had a silver-mounted tiger claw she often wore as an ornament on her dress. She had a diamond boat-shaped ring almost as large as the one worn by her husband. But if Hirschfeldt was enamoured with Emily, or at least appreciated the distraction she provided from the endless prattling of her husband, there was a small but significant physical flaw he had failed to notice.

Emily, always polite, always the loving new wife, had always taken the utmost care with her appearance. But she was not as serene as she appeared. Something was bothering her. She had started biting her fingernails.

II.

When the *Kaiser Wilhelm II* stopped at a new port to take on passengers and supplies, Emily Williams made sure she had a letter ready to post to her mother back home in Rainhill. It was her first journey abroad and there was so much to describe. The ship was magnificent and their cabin all she could wish for. On 19 November 1891 they stopped briefly at Aden in Yemen to collect mail and new passengers and 'a number of natives came to the ship'. Albert, that seasoned traveller familiar with Aden, had bartered with the locals and bought two pairs of buck horns – souvenirs that would certainly make wonderful talking points mounted on a wall.

The last of the letters from Emily to her mother was dated Friday 26 November and was posted when the ship reached Ceylon. Its four dense pages, the words written in red ink in her 'exceedingly attractive style', proudly boasted that many passengers were now referring to her husband Albert as 'The Doctor'.

Several nasty illnesses had broken out, as they often did on these global voyages when hundreds were crammed into tight, poorly ventilated spaces. The ship's physician had been caring for those in first and second class. But Emily told her mother he had been ignoring the plight of many in the cheap steerage section below the quarter deck. When one of them came down with a bad dose of dysentery,

Albert had whipped up a concoction that quickly eased the sufferer's symptoms.

After that he had turned his attention to a woman who 'was ill with a slight brain-fever, caused with the heat'. There was only one way to fix that. Albert rubbed the woman's neck with mustard oil and her fever, according to Emily, quickly disappeared. Ailments like that tended to erupt when a ship has just crossed the equator and so much soft white English skin was exposed to the fierce glare of the sun and the moist tropical air. Word soon spread that a fellow with a large ginger moustache in second class knew how to ease and even cure the nasty blotches and itchy bumps they called prickly heat. Albert soothed the rashes and red welts on the skins of a mother and her young baby. After that he had restored to health an exhausted young lady who herself had been awake for five long nights caring for her sick brother.

At least, that was according to Emily, the loyal and devoted wife. Other passengers had started sarcastically referring to him as 'Dr Williams' because of his 'tendency to prescribe impossible remedies for all sorts of incredible ailments'. And always, money lay at the heart of it all.

One of the passengers familiar with the couple was Dr Robert Scott, a former Presbyterian minister who was returning home to Melbourne after earning his medical degree in London.

'He seriously asserted that he had distributed a good deal of medicine, and that his benevolence had resulted in a distinct pecuniary loss to him,' Dr Scott would say later. 'A good natured passenger endeavoured to raise a subscription to recoup him. As he was unable, however, to give any particulars of his expenditure the money was not handed over to him, but returned to its subscribers.'

But if Emily was aware of the growing scorn and derision about her husband, she would not even hint at it in her letters home. Albert Oliver Williams, according to Emily's letters, was a constant source of wonder to his twenty-six-year-old wife, a man with endless patience and boundless energy and enthusiasm. He saved food scraps from their meals in the second class dining room to give to the poor wretches on the decks below. If he wasn't healing the sick or regaling fellow passengers with tales of his adventures, he was in their cabin making intricate models of inventions he had dreamed up that would one day revolutionise the world and bring him even further riches.

In one letter to her mother Emily explained how a fellow traveller had been sent a plum pudding as a Christmas present a couple of years earlier after moving to New Zealand. The pudding had made its way all those thousands of miles from London to the small colony on the other side of the world for only eighteen pence.

Albert must have been leaning over Emily's shoulder when she wrote this because she added a quick line: 'Albert says I am only throwing hints to you.'

There was more she could write, of course. So much more. But she had already crammed a great deal into those four pages and there was a Christmas card painted by Albert – so artistic, such a dab hand with the brush – that she also had to leave space for in the envelope.

She sent her love and told her mother she had to sign off because her husband's voice was filling their cabin. 'Albert is just now singing "*I'll never get married any more*,"' she wrote.

So much love. So much admiration.

So many lies.

If only Emily Mather had the courage to overcome her embarrassment and tell her mother the truth; that it had all been a horrible mistake. The quick courtship after Albert Williams's sudden appearance in Rainhill just a few months earlier, the rushed marriage that soon followed, the laughter and dancing on that newly cemented kitchen floor in his rented villa, the swift arrival – and mysterious disappearance – of a woman and her four children he had said was his sister. Not to mention the urgent desire of her new husband to escape Rainhill and cross to the other side of the world. What had she been thinking? She had fallen for it all – his charm, his playfulness, his tenderness as a lover, his claims of wealth and status.

Turned out none of it was true. There was no fortune. There was no career studded with achievements, no powerful positions of influence. That tenderness he had shown during their whirlwind courtship had quickly given way to a sharp tongue and a fearful temper and something far, far darker; there was something twisted and broken inside him, a brooding malevolence so black and evil the very thought of it scared her.

But she had to give him credit for one thing.

Albert Williams was a clever man. He had fooled Emily while wooing her, convinced half of Rainhill he was a man of substance and even managed – eventually – to overcome the doubts and suspicions of her mother. And that was saying something because Dove Mather, a widow running a small stationery store, was nowhere near as naïve and trusting as her daughter.

The man who had arrived in their village in July 1891 with his high-falutin' airs and big spending ways and a chest adorned with military medals hadn't quite seemed right to Mrs Mather. She had no idea, of course, that he had just been released from Hull Prison, or that he was already married with four children.

Perhaps it was a mother's instinct, or she was simply being over-protective because his arrival coincided with a vulnerable time for the family. Dove's husband had died a few months earlier and Emily was still getting over a broken engagement to a man from Sheffield. Dove had warned Emily not to move quickly. This Williams fellow was at least a dozen years older than her. He was flashy and forever boasting. He had just retired from the military, he had informed some of the locals, and was a nephew of Sir Wilfred Lawson, the 2nd Baronet of Brayton and one of the greatest speakers in the House of Commons. Sir Wilfred had even paid for his education, Williams claimed.

Dove Mather first met Williams when he appeared in her stationery store after renting a room at the local hotel. He told her he was looking for a property to rent in the area. It just so happened that Dove Mather had the key to Dinham Villa, a vacant home owned by a woman who lived three miles away in Huyton. Williams asked Mrs Mather to organise for the owner to meet him there at 10am on 21 July.

Williams was punctual and after inspecting the home told his prospective landlady: 'I like the house, but I am not taking it for myself. I am taking it for a Mr Brooks, who is retiring from the regiment and he wants to come to a quiet place. This house would just suit him, and I like it very much.'

When told the annual rent was thirty-five pounds, Williams replied: 'I will take it for six months, and will pay you three months in advance. But you must make me a promise that you don't let or sell it up to the six months' end. Then we may buy it.'

Williams had one more condition. He led the owner into the kitchen and pointed to the floor. 'You see, this floor is very unlevel and Mr Brooks will have nothing to do with the house if he saw it like this.'

She shrugged. The floor looked level to her and previous tenants had never raised it as a problem. It seemed such a minor issue. The landlady stood her ground.

'The house is in thorough order,' she said. 'I shall not go to any expense.'

'Well,' said Williams, 'we go in for cementing abroad, and I will not put you to any expense. I will do it myself.'

Two evenings later Williams arrived at her home to sign the lease and at his side, willing to witness the documentation, was the clearly smitten daughter of Dove Mather.

If Dove had been concerned about Williams' motives and character, her son Joseph had taken an instant dislike to him. Joseph, keeping a protective eye out for his younger sister now their father was no longer around, warned that Albert Williams seemed more interested in getting his hands on their mother's money. How long had the man been in town? A week? Two? Not only had he immediately started wooing his sister but Williams, after learning the Mathers owned some property around town, had suggested they should consider selling some of it.

Joseph was adamant; the man was a swindler trying to take advantage of the Mathers. There were rumours in town that he was married to someone else. A woman with several young children had stayed for several days at the villa and Williams, claiming it was his sister, had moved in to the Commercial Hotel during their visit. They had arrived by train but no-one had ever seen them leave. Joseph warned his mother and Emily to keep away from a man he believed was clearly an imposter.

But Emily was in love. When Albert proposed to her she had stood up to her brother, her mother, and even the local reverend who had also expressed misgivings. The man was genuine, she insisted. He was already talking about a luxurious honeymoon before embarking on a trip overseas.

Yes, Albert had proved to be quite the talent when it came to lying. Emily, desperate to find a man to help her escape the small world of Rainhill, had fallen for him, quickly and heavily. When some of his claims didn't quite seem to add up in those first weeks of their romance, she had been more than happy to justify them one way or another. But as the steamship *Kaiser Wilhelm II* carved its way across the ocean, more than two months had passed since their wedding and keeping up that pretence was now far harder. She had no idea, of course, just what a complex web of deception he had constructed. Or that Albert Oliver Williams was not even his real name.

He was certainly not the man she had thought she was marrying that day back in September when she had so willingly said 'I do' in St Anne's church. All she knew was that despite all those claims of being an adventurer, an explorer, a soldier and an engineer, Albert only had one genuine ability.

She only had to watch him on the deck of the ship to appreciate his talent for deception. Not even that fragile little canary – an animal always alert to potential danger – had managed to glimpse the monster that lurked within.

III.

A few weeks before Albert Williams and his new wife boarded the *Kaiser Wilhelm II*, Sidney Dickinson had been lying dazed and bleeding in the lobby of a Melbourne hotel.

Blood spilled from a gash in one of his lips. He could not see clearly because his spectacles had been knocked from their regular perch high on his nose. If he squinted enough he might have been able to make out the vague outline of a man's boot as it swung toward his head. But it was difficult to get one's bearings when one was lying stunned on the floor of the Sandringham Coffee Palace. He could hear high-pitched screams, which suggested his wife Marion was somewhere nearby, even if he could not see the scratch running down one side of her face, or that another woman was dragging her across the foyer by the hair.

Things had taken a decidedly unpleasant turn. That much was certain.

Fortunately Marion, as usual, had had the good sense to throw his revolver to him just as the fracas turned nasty. It was unloaded but when Sidney finally managed to get to his feet he was able to wave the weapon about and look like a man in some sort of control of the situation. He might have resembled a drunken gunslinger staggering down an empty street looking for an opponent willing to test his quick draw. But a gun of any sort tended to have a quietening effect on any gathering of badly tempered brawlers.

The Dickinsons had been lodging at the Palace – one of many temperance hotels around Australia that had sprung up as part of a movement to give weary travellers a place to relax without the presence of noxious and intoxicating liquor. And weary the Dickinsons were. It felt like they had been on the road for years, which essentially had been the case ever since they had arrived in Australia in 1888 lugging several suitcases, the valuable stereopticon and those 400 pounds of heavy projection equipment that supported it.

A year before their arrival in Australia the Dickinsons had toured California and Sidney's lectures, backed by the hundreds of slides Marion projected for him, had filled halls and won critical praise. In San Francisco he had been introduced to Queen Kapi'olani of Hawaii, which led to an invitation to lecture at the Honolulu Opera House.

The couple had then gone to Paris to buy a collection of coloured lantern slides. London had followed – it was probably on that visit that he had dropped in on Wilkie Collins for his verdict on Marion's psychic abilities. The Dickinsons had then hastily returned to the US before packing their bags for the Australian colonies, which Sidney believed was 'a capital place for money-making, and almost any price is paid for the right man'.

Their Australian reception had exceeded their expectations. They had been welcomed to Sydney by the American consul, who introduced them at Government House and insisted on having Sidney read the Declaration of Independence during a Fourth of July harbourside picnic celebration. His public lectures in Sydney and Melbourne were reviewed favourably and then a three-month holiday to New Zealand had resulted in the government of that colony combining with a steamship company to offer Sidney a lucrative contract to promote New Zealand as a tourist destination.

The southern hemisphere, it transpired, had certainly turned into a capital place to make money. The NZ deal had required Sidney and Marion to travel by train to all of Australia's colonial capitals and twenty of its smaller towns. First, however, they were given a hefty advance to return to Paris to have their images of New Zealand colourised.

They had surely been exhausted when they checked into the Sandringham Coffee Palace while they looked for a more permanent residence. They had decided Melbourne would be their new base, at least until they returned to the US to be reunited with Sidney's young daughter. Sidney had taken on a role with a New York-based insurance company and was continuing to act as a correspondent for several American publications, including *The New York Times*. He had also established himself at the centre of Melbourne's emerging artistic scene. He was now the art editor of a new monthly magazine, *Australasian Critic*, and was writing articles with headlines like 'What Should Australian Artists Paint?'. In July he had studied the work of a group of committed outdoor artists that included Frederick McCubbin, Arthur Streeton and Tom Roberts. Referring to the suburb in which they painted, he had dubbed them 'The Heidelberg School' – a title that would stick, marking a major turning point in the colony's art history.

Marion, of course, never needed any encouragement to throw herself into hard work. When she was not helping run the Austral Salon, a club for local female intellectuals, or embedding herself elsewhere in the upper echelons of the city's ruling elite, she was giving poetry readings, examining people's palms, and holding well-attended séances that attracted some of Melbourne's most prominent spiritualists.

But if the Dickinsons had embraced Melbourne, their lodgings at the Coffee Palace left them far from impressed. Sidney, recovering from a bout of typhoid, found the manageress of the hotel, Catherine Pyle, inattentive and sloppy. The service was so bad he had been forced one morning to travel a suburb away to find something satisfactory to eat. He was two weeks in arrears on his rent and refused to pay. To make matters worse Mrs Pyle's stepson, William, was an unpleasant drunk determined to make everyone's stay at the Palace a miserable experience.

The Dickinsons were certainly not abstainers. Sidney was partial to a drop of whisky and no dinner party they hosted was ever complete without quality wine. But the constant presence of that drunken stepson and the consistently shabby service had forced Sidney to complain to one of the hotel's directors. After Sidney detailed his issues with the hotel, its director had accompanied Sidney to discuss matters with Mrs Pyle. But William, who had clearly been on the drink again, suddenly appeared and took a swing at Sidney. The esteemed art critic was sent sprawling. Then, with Mrs Pyle cheering on her stepson – 'Give it to him, Willy!' she was heard shouting – William threw several more punches at Sidney and began kicking him.

Marion, bless her, had managed to grab Sidney's revolver from their room just as the situation became heated. When she returned she slipped the weapon to her husband before Mrs Pyle stormed over and dragged her across the foyer by the hair. By then, William had moved on from clobbering Sidney and was in the midst of assaulting the hotel director. But the sight of the near-blind American getting to his feet and waving his gun about quickly sobered him. Police officers soon arrived and, when the matter ended up in court almost two weeks later, charges laid against the Dickinsons of assault and threatening to shoot were dismissed. Mrs Pyle lost her job and her stepson, described in court as 'a ferocious beast, a brute in human form and an infuriated lunatic' was fined more than thirty pounds and given a suspended six-month gaol sentence.

The whole affair had been distasteful, to say the least. The courtroom had been filled with reporters whose breathless accounts of the melee filled several column inches in their newspapers the following day. The Dickinsons decided it was time to find more permanent lodgings. By the time the *Kaiser Wilhelm II* had left Southampton on its way toward Melbourne, Sidney and Marion were searching for a home where they could settle for the next twelve months.

That search would eventually lead them to a breezy hilltop home in one of Melbourne's most desirable suburbs. It sat on a corner lot and was surrounded by vacant blocks and old gum trees that were home to a riot of noisy kookaburras or, as Sidney liked to call them, 'laughing jackasses'. There were flower beds and an orchard and plenty of dry space beneath the house for their two dogs, Schneider and Tokio. Not only that, but the empty paddock next door was crying out to be filled with chickens, ducks and geese, guaranteeing the Dickinsons would never be short of eggs and poultry.

It almost seemed too good to be true. It was luxuriously furnished and boasted plenty of quality table linen, silverware and cutlery. But even better was the price. The rent was 'absurdly low' and the elderly owner quickly agreed to lease it to Sidney for half his original asking price. His wife had only recently died and he planned to take his two unmarried daughters – 'themselves of mature years' – with him to Europe for a year-long vacation.

The old widower seemed to be in a rush to leave the house. Sidney placed no great importance on that detail at the time. The man was worn out after caring for his wife, who had just passed away after a lengthy illness. Who would not be anxious to leave those bad memories behind?

Sidney had also paid little attention to a comment made by one of the man's daughters one evening when he dropped by to sign the lease. She was a nervous woman whose pale features made Sidney wonder if she was anaemic. When the paperwork was completed she had exclaimed: 'Well, it will be a relief not to see mother about all the time!' Her sister quickly shot her a sharp glance and the subject was immediately dropped.

'Her observation touched my mind too lightly to leave any impression upon it,' Sidney would recall. But he would certainly remember it because in the months that followed, the Dickinsons would take possession of that house and quickly conclude they were not its only occupants.

IV.

Kate Jensen had heard something that troubled her within days of the start of the voyage to Australia. She had been given the cabin directly opposite the room occupied by a newly married couple and for weeks had been woken at night by a man's distinctive voice.

Albert Williams was deep in discussion. With his canary.

The conversations – animated but clearly one-sided – went on for some time. Jensen would be adamant William was not talking to his wife. These were 'extraordinary conversations with his canary as if it were a human being'.

The bizarre behaviour had continued when the *Kaiser Wilhelm II* docked in Suez to pick up new passengers. Williams returned to the ship clutching a saw. He had flashed it in front of Kate and several other travellers and, with a big grin, announced: 'This is a very useful instrument. I have just half sawn a man's hand off.'

It had not taken long for Jensen, returning home to the colony of Queensland, to conclude Williams was 'a madman'. She began whispering her concerns to others. One day, with Emily standing dutifully alongside him, Williams had brandished a knife and proudly declared: 'I have killed many Zulus with this.'

He professed to be a religious man, pious and charitable. One morning he had even conducted a sermon on the main deck with all the formality and polish of a man with clerical training. But what sort of God-fearing man would strut about the ship, as Williams once had, openly boasting 'of stealing pearls from a blackfellow'?

Still, like everyone else on board, there was nothing she could fault when it came to the tenderness he displayed toward Emily. 'They seemed much attached to each other,' Jensen would observe a few months later, 'and she spoke to me of him in the most affectionate terms. At the same time she referred to his excitable and restless nature and told me he was most anxious to reach Melbourne.'

Another passenger, Samuel Bradley of Sydney, found Emily to be a 'pretty little woman, of a dark complexion, modest and of a retiring disposition, full of sweet gentleness, which made her a favourite with all'. She seemed 'devotedly attached' to her husband, which somewhat mystified Bradley because Albert Williams was her opposite. He was a braggart who had insisted on showing Bradley his scars – the bullet wounds on his head, the slash of a sword on his shoulder and even the scars on a calf muscle. Worse, though, was the constant pretence he kept up that he was a man of high standing. Williams 'murdered his aspirates, and spoke in a stilted way, as if trying to ape a style better than his normal one. His voice was pitched high and when excited it almost reached a squeak.'

As the ship neared its Australian destination, Williams' behaviour became more erratic. Several passengers, including Max Hirschfeldt, had started interrogating him in greater detail about his exploits around the world. The more questions, the more holes they exposed. They were soon convinced the man was not only a braggart but a liar and word had spread through the ship that 'The Doctor' was actually a contemptible villain with an 'overbearing and violent disposition'. What they could not understand was the attachment the man had formed with Emily. With that long dark hair tumbling down her back, her good manners, her obvious intelligence and sweet nature, her word was 'as much respected as her husband's [is] disbelieved and condemned'.

But there was one passenger she did confide in. Several months after the *Kaiser Wilhelm II* arrived in Australia, a letter would arrive at the home of Emily's mother in Rainhill. It would be written by a woman who had also been on that voyage and revealed a very different Emily, a young bride so scared she had confessed her husband was 'a villain and had treated her most brutally' and that she had already decided to leave him and return home.

The problems, it seemed, began early in their honeymoon in London when his personality quickly changed. Gone was the whimsical, constantly joking, deeply affectionate Albert Williams and in his place was a nasty, ill-tempered and often irrational brute, sneering and constantly belittling her.

One day in their room at Seyd's Hotel in Finsbury Square, Albert had fallen into another dark mood when he heard that Emily's suspicious brother had been to a solicitor to make certain his mother's business and home were kept from Albert's grasp.

Albert hastily wrote a letter 'in a somewhat rude and schoolboy hand' to Joseph.

'I can't address you as brother,' he began, 'for I should be ashamed to own you as such.

'We have heard from home of the way you have been treating your mother by going to a solicitor and saying you have her bound hand and foot. You call yourself a son; why, you are a disgrace to the name. And as for your word I find it is not to be depended upon. I beg to call your attention to the state of mother's health. And should this trouble cause her Death, which would not surprise me, remember her death for ever will it lay at *your* door.

'You are a Father, and ought to know the trouble of bringing Children up. In what way are you repaying your mother for the way she has cared for you and the love she has shown you? I can only leave you in the hands of One with more power than myself, and I am sure that He will one day repay you for your sins and ungratefulness.

'Your mother will not live long (thanks to you), and you will soon have what you call your share, and much good may it do you. I am – A. O. Williams.'

V.

By the time the ship reached the Australian coast Emily had seen her husband go from being the life of the voyage to an outcast. People who had earlier chatted pleasantly with them on deck or joined them for a game of quoits now began ignoring them.

Albert looked exhausted. He was constantly tetchy, overreacting to the smallest of slights. Something was simmering within. In the dining room he berated the stewards and awarded them ratings according to their level of ineptitude. He had his food sent back to the cooks because it was slop not fit for a dog. From a discreet distance Hirschfeldt and others watched him stalking the ship's passages and decks, walking furiously this way and that, 'until his passion was exhausted'.

The ship was soon consumed by an allegation from Albert Williams that a thief was on board. Someone, he announced, had stolen Emily's necklace. With its precious stones and gold chain, he claimed it was worth an enormous 100 pounds. He made such a fuss the ship's master, Captain Ludwig Stormer, was summoned. An agitated Williams told Stormer his ship should be searched from the hold to the masthead and if the necklace was not found the ship's German owners, Norddeutscher Lloyd, should compensate him for its loss.

Stormer launched an investigation and after interviewing several passengers – including forcing a confession from Albert that he was not quite the man of wealth he had pretended to be – concluded the whole thing was a scam cooked up to raise some much-needed cash.

That suspicion – held by so many others – gained more currency not long after when a man who had joined the ship in Ceylon alleged Williams had robbed him of three valuable pearls.

With his fantastical stories no longer believed, the man resembled a puppet whose strings had been suddenly severed. The props and illusions that had been the foundation of his world were gone and there was nothing left to stop him falling apart. Each day Hirschfeldt saw an increasingly irrational and desperate man and he was not surprised when Williams was accused of trying to keep a collection of coins and notes taken up for one of the poorest passengers on the ship.

Then, just hours after the ship left Adelaide for Melbourne, an anonymous note was found pinned to the door of one of the public lounges. It named Kate Jensen – the woman in the cabin opposite the Williams's room – as the culprit behind the theft of the necklace. The hastily scrawled note claimed two witnesses who watched her take it were prepared to come forward once a reward was offered.

Jensen, embarrassed and greatly annoyed, took the note straight to Captain Stormer, denying any knowledge of the theft. Stormer examined the handwriting and quickly decided it had been written by Albert Williams. He shrugged. There wasn't much more he could do except, like everyone else on board, patiently wait for two more days until the ship arrived in Melbourne.

In the early hours of 15 December 1891, the *Kaiser Wilhelm II* navigated the notorious rip guarding the entrance to Port Phillip Bay. By the time the sun rose it was anchored in deep water as a flotilla of small craft made their way to her side. Once the ship had been cleared by health and immigration officials, everyone stood to attention as the ship's brass band launched into a rendition of 'God Save The Queen'. Then the disembarking passengers gathered their luggage and boarded the tender *Albatross*, which would take them ashore to Port Melbourne.

Dr Robert Scott was sitting not far from Albert and Emily Williams on the *Albatross* and was shocked by the change in the man. 'Williams had slunk away into a corner, and during the whole of the trip never spoke so much as a word,' Scott told *The Age* later. 'He appeared anxious and apprehensive and his absolute silence contrasted strangely with the verbosity which had characterised him during the voyage.' He had also been in such a hurry to land he had forgotten a large part of his personal cabin luggage 'which had to be sent after him at a later hour' – a lapse Scott thought peculiar given the man's 'systematic method and attention to detail'.

Scott lost sight of the couple when the tender landed at Port Melbourne. But afterwards he saw them at the train station where Williams 'was engaged in a congenial row with the representatives of Messrs Tate, Customs House agents, to whom he stated that he was 'Major-General Williams' and that it was the duty of the steamship company to clear passengers' luggage and carry it up to Melbourne free of charge'.

Kate Jensen had also watched on with a growing sense of unease. Even given the man's drawn and surly appearance in the last week of the voyage, he looked 'unusually pale and haggard'. She put it down to the manner in which he had been 'shunned by the other passengers on account of the accusations he had made against them'.

But later she would change her mind. By then she would have heard so much more about the man. So many distasteful things. She would look back on that morning in Melbourne in a completely different light.

'I now think a fit of madness was coming on him and that he was trying to control it,' she would say.

VI.

If Emily was anxious about her floundering marriage and preoccupied with thoughts of escaping it, the sight that greeted her when she walked into the entrance of the Federal Hotel and Coffee Palace, the grandest and most opulent of Melbourne's many temperance hotels, would surely have been a welcome distraction.

Situated in Collins Street, one of the city's most picturesque boulevards, the Palace was a monument to the colony's decade-long property boom, a flamboyant exclamation mark punctuating years of optimism and excess. Built four years earlier out of five million bricks, it was a hotel perfectly in keeping with the standards expected by a man like Albert Williams. The four-storey lobby was cavernous, its centrepiece a magnificent wide staircase, its stucco exterior studded with sculptured figures. A domed turret on the roof reached 165 feet into the sky. There were 370 guest bedrooms, all of them elegantly furnished.

At the front desk Albert Williams asked for a 'double bedded room' and one of the hotel's bookkeepers, Ethel Clair, promptly handed him the keys to the room.

A double-bedded room. That was how they described a room with two separate beds in the nineteenth century. Did that mean he was already sleeping apart from Emily? If the stories he would tell his doctors a few months later were true, the spectre of his syphilis infection had become a constant in his life, along with the ghostly presence of his mother.

According to the claims he made to his doctors, he had paid a South African prostitute five pounds for sex because he had been a long way from home and that overpowering need to be with a woman had taken hold once again. It had not taken long for the first rashes to appear and quickly turn into ulcerating gashes. He had the lacerations on his legs to prove it. The only good fortune was that he had been able to hide the disfigurements as battle wounds because the disease had never reached his face and eaten away at his nose or mouth, as it sometimes did.

But he would say a day rarely passed when he did not think about the woman who had infected him and that once, when the infection was coursing through him and Mother was constantly shaking him awake, he had unsuccessfully gone looking for the woman in the hope of exacting retribution. Adopting a new identity seemed to help.

'Mother always tells him if he has a lady friend to kill her, or a wife, to kill her,' one of the doctors who examined him would write in his notes. 'Has never seen anyone in this way but her; hears no other voices. Changed his name to try and escape from this. On the next day he always felt easier; that he thought to get out of his life by parting with the past. Did not see why he should be responsible under new names. As an instance, he said that when in London with the syphilis he changed his name, and the syphilis disappeared.'

That deep scar at the back of his neck – the hole he often boasted to the curious was a bullet wound? It was most likely a lesion, the doctors would conclude, the remnant of a seton applied during his stint in the Calcutta hospital years earlier. A common treatment for epilepsy in the nineteenth century, doctors took a large needle and inserted a skein of threads – quite often silk, cotton or rough fibrous twine – beneath a flap of skin at the back of the head. By manipulating the skein each day – pulling the threads back and forth along the length of the wound – they created a chronic running sore that allowed the 'bad humours' inside the body to seep out.

But if the ghost of his mother had indeed begun waking him at night after his arrival in Melbourne, he showed no signs of tiredness the day after checking into the Federal Coffee Palace.

John Stamford, a butcher in High Street Windsor, a suburb three miles to the south-east of Melbourne, heard the door of his shop swing open and saw 'a mild mannered man of gentlemanly demeanour' standing in front of him.

Stamford noticed the man had a large moustache surrounded by whiskery stubble. He was short but had solid shoulders that suggested 'considerable strength'. The man introduced himself by saying his surname was 'Drewn' and that he was an engineer's toolmaker from Sydney.

Drewn said he understood that Stamford had a house available to rent around the corner at 57 Andrew Street. He had tried to see Stamford's agent, but he had been unavailable.

The house had been empty for several weeks and Stamford was keen to install a tenant before Christmas. He didn't ask too many questions. Mr Drewn was polite, extremely well-dressed and, judging by his expensive jewellery and offer to pay a week's rent of eighteen shillings in advance, would clearly be a reliable tenant. He quickly signed a receipt and handed Drewn the keys.

Albert Williams and Emily were busy over the next couple of days preparing to move into their house. They were often seen in the lobby of the Federal Coffee Palace. On 17 December, a passenger who had travelled with them to Melbourne on the *Kaiser Wilhelm II*, a retired Master mariner, Captain Robert Firth, bumped into them on the street. 'He said he was going to Portland Bay to start an engineer's shop,' Firth would recall later.

Firth did not notice anything unusual about the couple. But others had. A worker at the Coffee Palace would recall how Albert Williams had been 'studiously insulting and unkind to the lady, for whom a great deal of sympathy was expressed in the hotel'. Others were also taken aback by the contempt he displayed toward Emily, including John Harford, a local luggage carrier hired by Williams to collect some of his luggage.

Williams told Harford his name was 'Drewn'. As Harford loaded the man's bags into his dray, he overheard the man complain to his wife 'most brutally' about how much she was costing him. The voyage alone had cost him seventy pounds, Harford overheard him say. The room at the Federal Coffee Palace was expensive. And now he had to wear the additional cost of renting a house.

Later that day Mr Drewn entered an ironmonger's shop in St Kilda, not far from Windsor. He told the ironmonger's wife, Mary Wood, that he required cement, sand, soil, a broom and a small trowel. He placed an order for the materials and asked for them to be delivered to an address at the new home he had rented.

That evening he returned to Stamford's butcher shop carrying a sample parcel of cement. 'I am going to mend the nail holes in the wall and also the piece of plaster that is off in the bathroom,' he announced. Stamford was surprised because he thought the house was in perfect order. But he gave Drewn permission. He seemed to be a handy man who knew what he was talking about.

The following morning an agitated Drewn returned to the ironmonger's shop. He demanded to know why the cement and tools he had requested the previous day had not been delivered. 'He was very angry,' Mary would recall, 'and said I ought to have sent them because the men were waiting for him.'

Mary's husband, John, overheard the heated discussion and wandered over to explain he was too busy to make a delivery. The man was insistent.

'I am going to do some asphalting in the back yard,' he told Wood. 'I have a bricklayer waiting for the cement and sand.' At the urging of his wife John Wood loaded the items into a cart, attached his horse and set off for Windsor with the man next to him. When they arrived there was no bricklayer to be seen.

Wood peered into the backyard. It was well-kept and did not seem to require any concreting.

'It's a curious thing to want the cement for the yard,' he mused. 'It will be no use for the yard.'

'I never said I wanted it for the yard,' Williams said. 'I want it to re-set the copper boiler.'

Wood looked at the base of the copper – a washing tub with an enamelled exterior commonly found in many houses by the end of the nineteenth century.

'The man must have been a fool to have told you to build a copper in with cement,' said Wood. 'It will be of no use. Lime would be much better for that purpose.'

'The bricklayer told me that cement was the proper thing.'

'It is not the proper thing to set a copper with, and it does not want re-setting.'

At moments like this the practised liar, confronted by a barrage of pedantic inquiries from someone more knowledgeable, had only one option. He had to change the subject.

'Are you a gas fitter or do you know gas fitting?' he asked Wood. When Wood told him he was, he guided him inside. 'If you come into this front room I will show you where I want a new chandelier.'

Drewn then told Wood his sister was coming from Sydney. Once she had chosen her preferred light fitting, he would send for Wood to install it.

Frederick Deeming was in a hurry. He had various cover stories and aliases to juggle. He hired another carrier, John Featherstone, to take him to the city, collect his luggage and return it to Windsor. Featherstone said it would cost ten shillings. When the man scoffed at the price Featherstone lowered it immediately to six shillings.

'You are talking sense now,' the man told him. He then turned to Emily and dismissively told her to find her own way to the house in Windsor and meet him there.

Featherstone loaded two heavy boxes and various pieces of luggage into his cart. But he was worried about the brass cage and its canary and asked if the bird would be nervous at the rear of the cart.

'Oh no,' Williams told him. 'It has travelled further than you.'

Featherstone was impressed with the man's knowledge of Melbourne. He had transported many 'new chums' around town and seen the bewilderment in their eyes as they tried to make sense of a strange city. But this man seemed at home. He knew most of the suburbs and understood all the shipping movements on the Yarra River. The man told Featherstone he was an engineer's toolmaker who was importing machinery from England and planned to set up a business in the inner suburb of Carlton.

As they arrived at 57 Andrew Street, Emily was walking down the street toward them. She unlocked the front door and Featherstone began carrying the luggage inside. But when he deposited one of the bags in one of the front rooms, its owner flew into a passionate rage or, as Featherstone would tell a courtroom several months later, 'he got his hair off'. He ordered Emily to go to the back of the house and told Featherstone to leave the bags in the hallway.

Over the next few days a series of people would encounter the same man, always nervous and curt, prone to over-reacting to the smallest of trifles.

Five days before Christmas Ernest and Martha Bueller were at work at the Hamburg Laundry they owned in Charles Street, a couple of blocks from Andrew Street, when he wandered in and asked if someone could come around and collect clothing to be washed.

Ernest would later say in court that he quickly went to the house. 'A lady came to the door of the house and when I had explained my business to her she asked my price. I answered her . . . she said "Oh, that's too much. I'm sorry, your charge is too high" and when I turned to go she said kindly, "Good day".

'There was something about her, too, which made me think she was miserable,' Ernest would add. 'She was under the height of the man and much less strongly built than he, and she was dressed in black . . . and as she looked at me her brow was furrowed and her eyes looked sad. She appeared like one whose life was altogether unhappy.'

VII.

To the residents of Andrew Street, the new couple at number 57 appeared to be intensely private. The husband was sometimes seen on the front porch, a caged canary always at his side and a lit cigar in his hand. His wife was briefly glimpsed at the front gate before she scurried back inside. But they never introduced themselves and seemed determined to keep to themselves.

One night they were seen dressed up, apparently headed into the city for a night out. Perhaps they were planning to see one of the several Christmas pantomimes that were filling Melbourne's halls and theatres. The Theatre Royal was showing *Legend of Dick Whittington and his Cat* while *Jack the Giant Killer* was on at the Alexandra. The Opera House was also readying itself for a night of entertainment from Alfred Tennyson Dickens, the wayward son of the great novelist Charles Dickens. Having squandered his inheritance, Alfred had turned to giving lectures about his father, with readings from the old man's most popular works.

By then Emily must have felt trapped. A few days earlier she had approached a property owner called Mr McHale who lived in the nearby suburb of Richmond. She told him one of the staff at the Federal Coffee Palace who was aware she wanted to leave her husband had suggested he might have an unoccupied furnished house he could rent her. According to what McHale later told *The Age* newspaper, Mrs Williams 'rejoined that she had just arrived with her husband from England in the *Kaiser Wilhelm II*, and having had some differences with him she had determined to leave him, take a house for a month or two and then return home'.

The Age report stated: 'She had not much money, she added, but she had sufficient to allow of her doing this . . . the apparent truth of what Mrs Williams said, coupled with her manner, which was gentle, and excited sympathy, induced Mr McHale to promise that if she would call again in three or four days he would arrange that she should enter upon the tenancy of a suitable house which he had in mind.'

Mrs Williams never returned. But McHale had seen her in Swanston Street in the city a few days later. She told him while she had been prevented from making a return visit she fully intended taking the house he had mentioned.

But as they spoke 'a man walked across the street and approached Mrs Williams. His brows were lowering, and from the general expression of his features, he appeared to be in a passion . . . he halted and beckoned the lady away. She hurriedly excused herself to Mr McHale and joined the man who walked away with her.' McHale never saw her again.

Two days before Christmas the man calling himself Mr Drewn walked into the office of Charles Connop, the agent responsible for the home he was renting. Connop asked him if he planned on staying in the house for a lengthy period.

'No,' said Drewn. 'I expect a sister from Sydney and until she arrives I will not take it for a term.' He paid another week's rent in advance, complained about termites he had seen, and said he would keep Connop informed about his intentions.

At about 7pm on Christmas Eve, Louisa Atkinson, a widowed washerwoman, was walking down Andrew Street on her way to visit a friend when she heard a loud noise coming out of number 57.

'I heard a man and woman quarrelling in the house. I stopped and listened for a few minutes. I heard something thrown . . . I heard a crash and a woman ran out of the back door and walked up and down the side entrance. She seemed excited.

'I said to her when she came to the front "If I were you, I would leave this place for a while."

'But the woman smiled and said "It will be alright soon", and she went back into the house by the back door.'

It was the last time anyone saw Emily Williams alive.

Only fifteen inches separated 57 Andrew Street from the weatherboard house next door. Months would pass before neighbours were asked if they recalled anything about the couple with the canary who had just moved into the neighbourhood.

Like most people they would find it hard to remember exact times and dates. But one of them, Alfred Spedding, was fairly certain he had been woken at 4am on or about 25 December by thumping noises coming from next door. At first he thought it might have been a carpenter because he heard knocking. Then he changed his mind. It sounded like bricks being shifted. Perhaps it was a plumber at work.

But on Christmas morning in 1891 the only man at work in the suburb of Windsor was Frederick Deeming. And by then the only living companion with him in the house was a well-trained and unusually trusting canary.

PART IV.

'Life without you would not be worth living'

An Unbelievable Stench Exposes the Crime – Uncovering Emily in her Concrete Tomb – The Detectives Begin their Pursuit – The Snake Sheds its Skin – The Scoundrel's Web of Lies – His Courtship of Miss Rounsefell – The Canary Sings Again – A Distraught Mother Receives Terrible News

I.

Sidney Dickinson had never smelled anything so awful. He had encountered plenty of offensive odours in his travels around the world. But he had never – *never* – experienced anything quite like the stench that rose from the fetid streets of Melbourne in the early 1890s.

How did one even begin to describe it? The stink hanging over Melbourne reminded him how the great English bard Samuel Coleridge had described the German city of Cologne a century earlier:

> . . . *a town of monks and bones*
> *And pavements fang'd with murderous stones*
> *And rags, and hags, and hideous wenches;*
> *I counted two and seventy stenches.*

The problem in Cologne, as Coleridge had pointed out, was the Rhine River, which for centuries had been nothing more than a receptacle for human waste, rotting carcasses and putrefying food. The problem in Melbourne, as Sidney pointed out to the readers of *The New York Times*, was the Yarra River, on whose banks a motley collection of sod huts a little over fifty years earlier had given rise to one of the largest metropolises in the southern hemisphere.

The Yarra was 'yellower than the Tiber', complained Sidney. It was 'more varied and aggressive in stench than Coleridge's Rhine'. In fact, Sidney believed the Yarra's 'foul engorgement' and 'burden of tannery refuse' was worse than the Cloaca Maxima – the open sewer that for centuries had flowed sluggishly through Rome carrying the putrid waste from public baths and latrines.

As Sidney composed his article about Melbourne's polluted streets, construction work was finally beginning on the city's first underground sewerage system. But it would take more than a decade before more than 400,000 residents stopped emptying their chamber pots into the gutters outside their homes.

Anyone who visited Melbourne, reported Sidney, 'and sees its filthy streets, its heaps of decayed vegetables and other refuse and its reeking gutters . . . and inhales the stench that arises from all these abominations . . . might well question how the city avoids devastating epidemics and a constant experience of zymotic diseases'.

Fortunately Sidney had an answer. Melbourne had avoided waves of gruesome epidemics because of the violent winds that buffeted the city from all directions. 'Unpleasant as they often are and irritating to the temper, [these winds] are Melbourne's salvation from a health point of view,' he explained to his fellow Americans. 'The dry north winds desiccate, burn and disperse most noxious germs which, thriving only on moisture, find no nourishment in these hot Borean blasts.' Sidney had not forgotten his first summer in the city. For an uncharacteristic six straight weeks those hot northerly gales had sliced through Melbourne 'and seemed to dry the blood in the veins, the very marrow in the bones'.

But it was those brutal southerly gales, like the one that would rock his rented house in the days before the execution of Frederick Deeming, that astonished him. They often arrived without warning, turning summer into winter within a few savage minutes.

He would experience their sudden fury during that summer of 1891/92. One afternoon at precisely 2pm (Sidney was always a stickler for detail) he returned home 'fairly panting from the heat of a north wind'. The thermometer in the room had reached 96 degrees.

'In hope of finding more air on the balcony I stepped out . . . and was met by a cold wind from the south which fairly blew me backward. With difficulty I closed the door and returned to my room. Every moveable article in it had been blown down and to save the apartment itself from the seeming danger of being blown inside out I was compelled to close the window.'

He glanced at the clock. It was 2.02pm.

'In less than thirty seconds the violent wind from the north had subsided and the gale from the south taken its place. Three hours later my thermometer stood at 65, and in the evening a fire in the grate was found very agreeable.'

So these winds were also the city's saviours. But on the night of 3 March 1892 there was only a soft southerly breeze drifting through Sidney Dickinson's adopted town. If the air remained ripe, it was also filled with the rich, leathery odour of cigars and the floral scents of women dressed for an evening at the opera.

La Cigale was in its third week at the Princess Theatre. Not far away at the Theatre Royal an excited audience was waiting for the curtain to rise for the opening act of *Little Jack Sheppard* and reveal the great Miss Billie Barlow, the enchantress of burlesque who, according to that day's newspapers, 'has no dull moments', whose zest and abandon 'never flag', whose 'good voice, good looks, a good figure and good temper . . . act as a tonic for these troubled times'.

These troubled times.

For months the papers had been filled with reports of banking collapses, financial scandals and expensive land deals gone wrong. There were warnings of a deepening recession. Even the theatre business had known better times. Several promoters were said to be on the brink of bankruptcy. 'Bad times must be felt, of course, in the theatrical as in every other business,' *The Argus* would report the next day. 'But even though the pinch may be severe at the moment, the population of Australia, it may be relied upon, will always find bread, and while they have bread, they will inevitably, like the Romans, demand circuses too.'

The pinch may be severe.

You would never have known it. Summer had just finished and the city was still basking in its warmth. Thousands had turned out at the Flemington racecourse earlier that day to watch some of the finest horseflesh in the southern hemisphere doing battle for more than 13,000 pounds in prize money. Many in the crowd had dined in a beautiful double-storey 'Swiss Chalet' specially erected for the day. Alexander Gardiner, the renowned wholesale dairyman, had journeyed on his cart from Brown's Hill in West Melbourne with a fresh supply of milk and cream.

If Sidney Dickinson's nostrils sometimes twitched for a very good reason, there was still plenty to love about Melbourne. He had gazed in admiration at its Parliament House and its towering cathedrals and elegant churches. This was a town, he thought, with the same qualities that were turning his home nation into the newest world power. 'Melbourne has more enterprise, more of the American quality of "hustle",' he would tell readers in an issue of *Scientific American*. It might have been a city with a 'less-finished air' than its sworn rival Sydney, but it boasted a 'more energetic and less conservative population . . . Sydney is the leader in intellectual, Melbourne in material advancement'.

The city had been the beneficiary of a wool boom, a gold boom, and then a land boom propelled by wondrous predictions of massive increase in population. But by 1892 there was more bust than boom about the place. Still, like any good hustler, the city continued to strut and swagger as it always had.

Which was why, on Thursday evening, 3 March 1892, there remained that unmistakeable bouquet of expensive perfumes mingling with the scent of fine leather, quality brandy and spicy tobacco. Melbourne was still putting on a show and stubbornly refusing to surrender its optimism and arrogance.

But only four miles away from the city's centre another smell had begun to emerge in the night air. It was far worse than the one that usually suffocated the town and which Sidney Dickinson had come to detest so much. It was an odour so awful it would force those who encountered it to retch and burn their clothes to remove any lingering trace.

It was the unmistakeable stench of death and it would hang over Melbourne for a long time to come.

II.

Constable Godfrey Webster had been a sick man. For a week he had battled a cold so severe he had been forced to stay home and leave the Windsor police station undermanned. Fortunately for the police he had been well enough to return to duty that Thursday afternoon on 3 March. Unfortunately for Constable Webster it was the worst day possible to resume work.

Webster was on duty at the station at about 8pm when he received a summons from his boss, Sergeant Patrick O'Loughlin. His presence was required as soon as possible at 57 Andrew Street.

When Webster arrived he entered a long and wide hallway. In the second bedroom to his left he found O'Loughlin with his hands stained with soil and cement dust. The floor around the fireplace was a jumble of shattered concrete. Tools, including an axe and a shovel, lay nearby. But it was not this scene in the early evening gloom that startled Constable Webster. It was the stench. His nose had been badly blocked because of his cold and he had not fully regained his sense of smell. But this odour was unbearable. Webster remained in the room for a few moments until he felt something hot rising in his throat. He fled outside.

Sergeant O'Loughlin had already been digging in the room for an hour after being notified by the owner of the house, the butcher John Stamford, of a revolting stink in its second bedroom.

Stamford had been showing a woman through the property that afternoon when he first noticed it. The mysterious Mr Drewn, whose lease on the house had expired a month earlier, had long vanished and the recession had made it difficult for Stamford to find a new tenant. As he guided the woman through the side door he smelled something rotten. She, too, had crinkled her nose and complained about the odour. Stamford had assured her it would only be a small issue. But when she left he immediately went back inside to investigate.

'I went into the second room from the front and saw the hearth-stone rising from the flooring and noticed a very bad smell,' Stamford would later tell police. He immediately sent for his agent and when Charles Connop arrived the two men raised the hearthstone 'and saw foul matter oozing through the cement'.

Sergeant O'Loughlin and another officer arrived soon after and set to work with an axe to break up the concrete beneath. O'Loughlin had managed to create a hole about twelve inches deep when he struck a skull and glimpsed what he thought was human hair.

So he had sent for Godfrey Webster to assist. Once the young constable had finished filling his lungs with fresh air outside, the officers spent the next two hours removing all the concrete. Beneath it they uncovered a human body.

It was hard going. 'The stench was horrible and unbearable and I had to leave the room several times for a breath of fresh air,' Webster would say.

They worked carefully trying not to disturb the remains. Below the cement was a layer of large concrete blocks known as hobs. As they removed more of these it was clear the body was that of a woman. She was wearing a singlet and chemise nightdress. She was curled up, her knees drawn up to her throat. Her right wrist was tied with a crimson sash and its dye had stained much of her skin, indicating she had been trussed up with the sash in order to squeeze her into the small grave. Her right hand was draped across one of her breasts. The left hand rested on her throat, next to her knees.

By 10pm O'Loughlin and Webster had chipped away enough of the surrounding hobs to lift the body carefully out of its grave and place it in a box to be taken to the morgue. It was hard for the officers to judge how long she had been buried. Her concrete grave had probably slowed the decomposition process. But she had clearly suffered a violent death. Her singlet and nightdress were stained with blood and there was a cut on her left temple. O'Loughlin chose not to examine the rear of her head too closely; some of the hair had come away from the scalp when they lifted the body from its shallow grave.

Besides, he still had a lot of work to do. He had sent a message to Melbourne Police Headquarters in the city requesting the presence of detectives and would have to wait until midnight before one of them arrived to assess the scene.

But Constable Godfrey Webster would not be there to join them. 'I had to go home,' he said. 'I was quite ill from the sickening smell.' He would burn his uniform and underclothes in the next few days because, no matter how vigorously they were washed with soap, 'they were completely saturated with the stink'.

As Webster tried to get to sleep that night, the box containing the woman's body arrived at the morgue on a horse-drawn cart. Taken inside, the dead woman was placed on a table still curled in the foetal position in which she had been found. The examiner conducting the post-mortem brushed away some of the cement stuck to the rear of her head and saw three distinct wounds, deep lacerations that in places had fractured the skull and punched small shards of bone into the membrane surrounding the brain. He thought it would have required at least six blows with a heavy object to create such damage.

When he turned the body over he found four further wounds. These were deep incisions, some of them beginning next to an ear and then drawn across the throat all the way to the opposite cheek. One of them had cut deeply through the windpipe and gullet. He decided the head injuries would have been inflicted first, although the cuts to the throat 'were sufficient to cause death within a minute'.

'*Deeming had a weakness for barmaids, and was often at hotels at night when he had led his wife to believe that he was at work.*' Frederick Deeming not long after arriving in Australia in the early 1880s.

'*Most likely Marie was simply desperate to find a husband and was prepared to overlook Frederick's eccentric behaviour.*' Formal studio portrait of Deeming and his first wife, Marie, in the 1880s.

'She was barely five foot and petite with beautiful dark auburn hair that fell so far below her waist she could sit on it.' Emily Mather before her marriage to Deeming in 1891. (Victoria Police Museum)

'What had she been thinking? She had fallen for it all — his charm, his playfulness, his tenderness as a lover, his claims of wealth and status.' Using the alias of 'Albert Williams', the already-married Deeming weds Emily Mather in the English village of Rainhill. (*The Standard*, London, 24 September 1891)

'The small upstairs bedroom in the Rainhill villa resembled a morgue in a war zone . . . hundreds were gathered outside and swore they could smell the stench of death.' Dinham Villa, where Deeming murdered his first wife and four children.

'He was a man of cultural and intellectual pursuits who enjoyed bushwalking with a loaded revolver and shotgun by his side.' Sidney Dickinson, chronicler of Deeming's crimes for *The New York Times*, photographed in 1874.
(Boston Public Library/Prints)

'*Blood spilled . . . If he squinted enough he might have been able to make out the vague outline of a man's boot as it swung toward his head.*' The Sandringham Coffee Palace where Dickinson was assaulted by 'a ferocious beast'. (State Library of Victoria)

'*Several nasty illnesses had broken out, as they often did on these global voyages when hundreds were crammed into tight, poorly ventilated spaces.*' The 6000-ton *Kaiser Wilhelm II* that Deeming and Emily sailed on to Australia. (Snapshots of the Past/Flickr)

'*A monument to the colony's decade-long property boom, a flamboyant exclamation mark punctuating years of optimism and excess.*' Melbourne's Federal Hotel and Coffee Palace, where Deeming and Emily first stayed in Australia.
(State Library of Victoria)

'*The stench was horrible and unbearable . . . the body had been removed and the room in which it had been discovered was a mess of broken concrete.*' The scene in the Windsor bedroom where Deeming buried Emily's body.
(State Library of Victoria)

'*He oversaw a department boasting the biggest collection of competing egos in the colony's police force.*' Superintendent Douglas Kennedy (centre) with detective Henry Cawsey (left) and detective Bill Considine (right). (Victoria Police Museum)

'*The Cross is a windy, dirty, dusty hole from which anyone is very glad to depart.*' The house at Fraser's Mine in Southern Cross where Deeming, using the alias 'Baron Swanston', was arrested in March 1892. (State Library of Western Australia)

'*Williams was no shrinking violet. Left fatherless soon after his birth, he had started working at the age of eight.*' Constable Evan Williams, who arrested Deeming for murder and accompanied him to Melbourne for the trial.
(State Library of Western Australia)

'*He is short of stature with a low receding forehead, indicating intellect of a low order, while his ears spread out like Japanese screens before a drawing room door.*' Deeming after removing his moustache following his arrest in Western Australia.
(Victoria Police Museum)

'He drank brandy, smoked cigars incessantly and played draughts and cards with anyone.' A possibly altered photograph of 'Baron Swanston' and Constable Williams during the voyage to Melbourne. Deeming had by then removed his moustache.

'He is a man incapable of speaking the truth. In order to make himself out a hero he would coin lies or blacken a man's character.' Richard Septimus Haynes, the Perth lawyer who fought to prevent Deeming's extradition to Victoria.
(W. B. Kimberley, *History of West Australia*)

'*Thus were explained . . . the enormous jaws, high cheek bones, excessive idleness, love of orgies and the irresistible craving for evil.*' Professor Cesare Lombroso, who labelled Deeming a 'Napoleonic criminal'. (Science Museum Group)

'*A man passionate in his opposition to capital punishment and known as the apostle of the insanity defence.*' Deeming's Melbourne solicitor, Marshall Lyle (bottom, centre), who described his client as 'this abnormal offspring of a mother's womb'.

'He had a rich baritone voice. His eyes were said to have mesmeric qualities . . . at sixteen he believed he had hypnotic powers.' Alfred Deakin, Deeming's trial barrister and future Prime Minister of Australia, with his wife, Pattie. (National Archives of Australia)

'The discovery of this body has merely proved the starting point of a long list of terrible crimes unequalled in the history of all the most terrible deeds ever known . . .' The scene at the coronial inquest that found Deeming responsible for Emily Mather's death. (Illustrated Australian News/State Library of Victoria)

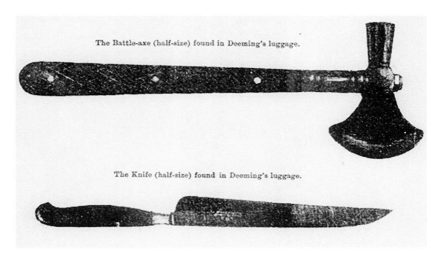

The Battle-axe (half-size) found in Deeming's luggage.

The Knife (half-size) found in Deeming's luggage.

'*The blade of a battle axe found in his luggage perfectly matched the crescent-shaped cut found at the rear of Emily's skull.*' Two of the weapons Deeming was believed to have used to murder Emily during the 1891 Christmas period.

'*She was young. He liked them like that. She had long dark hair [and] was thick-lipped with a striking bust and a narrow waist.*' Kate Rounsefell giving evidence against Deeming during his murder trial in Melbourne.

(State Library of Victoria)

'*I would gladly have given a full statement of it rather than submit myself in this court for four days to the gaze of the most ugliest race of people I have seen in my life.*' Deeming prepares to address the court before being found guilty of murder.
(State Library of Victoria)

'*The most infamous murderer of the Victorian era and a wayward son claiming to be haunted by his dead and disapproving mother.*' London's *Illustrated Police News* passes judgement on Deeming on behalf of his murdered wives and children following his trial.

DEEMING AT THE GALLOWS

THE WIFE MURDERER HANGED AT MELBOURNE THIS MORNING.

HE RETAINED HIS COOLNESS TO THE LAST—PERSISTENT DENIAL OF THE BAINFUL CRIMES—A GREAT CROWD OUTSIDE THE PRISON.

BRAZILIAN WAR SHIP LOST

THE SOLIMOES WRECKED ON THE URUGUAYAN COAST.

ONLY FIVE OF THE CREW OF 125 PERSONS SAVED—CAPT. CASTROT AMONG THE LOST—THE VESSEL WAS ON HER WAY TO MATTO GROSSO.

GARZA HIDING AT KEY WEST

THE MEXICAN HEAD HAS BEEN POSING AS CUBAN REVOLUTIONIST.

A MYSTIC FAMILY SOLFERA

SEVERAL BATTLES WITH NATIVES IN WEST AFRICA.

PUNISHED BY THE BRITISH

'*The greatest criminal of the century passed forever from the eyes of the world.*' Sidney Dickinson's front-page report in *The New York Times* reporting the execution of Deeming in Melbourne on Monday 23 May 1892.

'He passed himself off as . . . "Lord Dunn", posing for a photograph with a top hat, velvet scarf and holding an unlit cigar.' Studio portrait of Deeming at the end of the 1880s.

(State Library of Victoria)

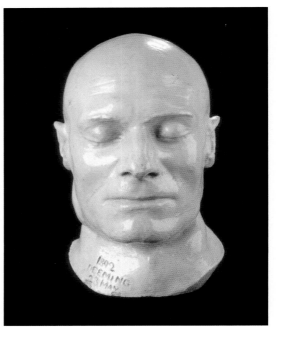

'The features are very striking – the hawk-like nose, high cheek bones, square jaw, broad chin. His love of display led to his . . . ignominious death on the scaffold.' A copy of the death mask made hours after Deeming's execution.

(State Library of Victoria)

'*Human nature could hardly endure to look upon these bodies, so disfigured and mangled were they by human hands, and also by the teeth of time.*' The scene inside Dinham Villa's kitchen after the bodies of Marie Deeming and her children were discovered.

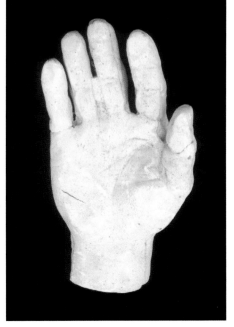

'*That right hand of Deeming, it seemed, had been dealing death around the globe.*' The plaster cast of Deeming's hand made by Sidney Dickinson and his wife, Marion, shortly before Deeming's execution.

(State Library of Victoria)

'*He had been a right strutter with his fancy clothes and diamond rings . . . and a magnificent ginger moustache that hung over a pair of thin grim lips.*' Deeming posing with his gold chain and fob watch.

'*If ever a living man was predestined gallows meat it is the keen, calculating scoundrel who is proved already to have been guilty of the Windsor and Rainhill atrocities.*' An artist's impression of the scene following Deeming's execution.
(*The Bulletin*/State Library of Victoria)

'*She was always a member of the Church of England, and if it can be done I should like her body to be placed in that portion of the cemetery . . .*' The monument marking Emily Mather's grave following her reburial in the Melbourne cemetery.
(Victoria Police Museum)

The examiner looked inside the mouth. The woman had a set of false teeth on her upper jaw. He guessed she was between the age of twenty-five and thirty-five. He stood back and considered the corpse's brown hair. He noted it was tied into three or four plaits and 'was very abundant'.

She was a slight woman, he decided, perhaps half an inch over five foot. As he looked over her body there was something else he noticed. He held up one of her hands and peered closely at it.

The fingernails were very short, their ends jagged. It appeared the murdered woman had been biting them before she died.

III.

He was a man from the old school who did not engage in small talk. After almost forty years as a policeman Superintendent Douglas Kennedy was only a year away from retirement. On the day they handed him the blue velvet case containing his monogrammed gold watch and heavy chain, Kennedy would consider himself well satisfied if his only lasting legacy was a reputation for bluntness and honesty.

Kennedy had seen many fellow officers forced out of the ranks, their names blackened by corruption. Perhaps that was why he rarely wasted a word. It reduced the chances of a man's statements being misheard or misinterpreted, a good thing given he oversaw a department boasting the biggest collection of competing egos in the colony's police force.

Kennedy, an Irishman originally drawn to Australia by the goldrush, was in charge of the Criminal Investigation Bureau and his squad of plain-clothes detectives were every bit as demanding as a cast of self-absorbed actors at any one of the popular theatrical shows around town.

The officers under Kennedy's command were driven by ambition and a desire to be noticed. A high public profile was considered a measure of success. Detectives competed against one another, positioning themselves to win Kennedy's approval and be appointed to cases likely to attract press attention. Sometimes that competitiveness spilled over into arguments and fisticuffs.

Kennedy's CIB had been created a decade earlier out of the embers of a blaze of corruption that had engulfed the force. A Royal Commission into the bumbling way the police had handled the case against the bushranger Ned Kelly and his gang had found the detective branch riddled with incompetence and bribery, labelling it 'a nursery of crime' and a 'standing menace to the community'.

It was not as though the force had fallen from any great height. The bar had been set low when, in 1836, the ruling colony of New South Wales sent Melbourne its first three police officers. The trio had already been sacked from the same role in Sydney for drunkenness. Within six months all would be fired again – one because of his constant drinking, another for accepting a bribe and the third because he simply refused to turn up for work.

A decade after that Royal Commission, Kennedy oversaw a new detective branch whose officers, he acknowledged in his economical way of speaking, enjoyed a 'healthy rivalry'. One of those ambitious detectives – and one of Kennedy's favourites – was Henry Cawsey. When news arrived on that night of 3 March that a body had been found in a home not far from the city, Kennedy summoned Cawsey to his office.

The gruff Kennedy had sideburns that flowed down the sides of his face before cascading over his jawline like a waterfall snap frozen before it reached the ground. His eyes were dark and deeply set and he parted his greying hair severely down the middle. In a photograph taken not long after the investigation into the body in Windsor, a stern Kennedy appeared like an old and reluctant sea captain pining for nothing more than his pipe and a comfortable chair on the front porch.

Cawsey, who had been promoted in 1883 as part of the new-look detective branch, parted his hair much the same way. But in his case it gave him a dashing, debonair look. He was known as a 'smart' dresser.

He was in his late thirties and tall for the time – just nudging six foot. He had high cheekbones and blue eyes and a stylishly trimmed moustache. In the same photograph that showed Kennedy with his unsmiling countenance, Cawsey stood to his right like a debonair actor staring wistfully into the distance.

Decades later, an old and weary man himself, Cawsey would recall that meeting with Kennedy on 3 March 1892.

'A woman's body has been found under a hearthstone in an empty house in Andrew Street, Windsor,' Kennedy told him. 'Get on with it. I don't want to see you again until you bring in the man.'

By Kennedy's standards it was about as lengthy a briefing as could be expected. It was close to midnight when Cawsey arrived at the scene. The body had already been removed and the room in which it had been discovered was a mess of broken concrete. He wandered through the rest of the house. It was largely unfurnished and it seemed whoever had been living there had left in a rush. A pound of rancid butter and a loaf of mouldy bread sat on a bench.

Cawsey returned early the next morning, this time in the company of a fellow detective and his senior in rank and age, Sergeant Bill Considine.

Considine was another of Kennedy's favourites, a fellow Irishman whose father had served in India as one of the British Army's highest-ranking generals. The son had tried to emulate his father's career but soon decided his future lay in the colonies, becoming a mounted trooper in the rich pastoral Western District and earning a reputation for capturing cattle thieves.

Promoted to detective ranks in 1875, Considine had managed to avoid being stained by the Royal Commission's investigation. He was known for his forensic tracking of suspects. Nine men he had arrested had been hanged and many more were in prison. He may not have had Cawsey's dashing looks – Considine was shorter, balding and had grey eyes and jutting ears – but he was a favourite of the local press, *The Australasian* regarding him as 'popular with his comrades and next to the chief, Mr Kennedy, he is in greatest demand among his brother detectives whenever advice is needed'.

Cawsey and Considine moved slowly through the interior of 57 Andrew Street. They noticed fires had been lit in every room. In one fireplace was the burned scrap of a letter. Only a few words and phrases – 'your affectionate mother', 'Nelly' and 'suffering' – had survived. They found paper fragments bearing the lettering of Melbourne bagging agents Frederick Tate and Co. Limited. There was a lead pencil drawing of a fisherman 'with crude water-colour touching on sky line and water' and the burned remains of newspapers from London and Liverpool. In the grate of the front room, half covered in ashes, was a small bottle. Cawsey and Considine sniffed it and thought they could smell alcohol. Cawsey sifted through more ashes and uncovered what appeared to be old baggage labels. One of them read 'King's X, London'.

In the main corridor sat an empty bottle of cognac. In the kitchen stood an iron water trough. The detectives noticed its wooden border was covered in a fine layer of the same sand used to cement the floor in the second bedroom. When they rubbed the sand away they found a blood stain running all the way along its edge. Nearby was a smooth block of holystone they assumed had been used in an unsuccessful attempt to remove the stain.

But it was in a small room at the rear of the house next to the bathroom that the detectives spent most of their time. There they discovered another large dark stain – this one about two feet in length – on the linoleum floor. Cawsey and Considine believed it might have been in this room – so small it would be referred to as 'the apartment' – where the murder occurred.

This theory was boosted by the discovery of three hairs stuck to the stain. The two men then ran their magnifying glasses over the rest of the room. Near the door they discovered the soft impression of a man's hand and traces of the first, second and third fingers, 'the grain of the skin in each coming up perfectly'.

As the two detectives studied the prints, an English polymath and noted tropical explorer, Francis Galton, was putting the finishing touches to a tome he would call *Finger Prints*. It was the first large-scale statistical study of human prints and would dramatically change criminal investigations for the following century. Galton, who worked out most prints belonged to eight broad categories ranging from a 'plain arch' and a 'tented arch' through to 'lateral pocket loops' and 'plain whorls', estimated the chances of two individuals bearing identical fingerprints was one in sixty-four billion.

At about the same time, a police inspector in a remote province of Buenos Aires was investigating the brutal slaying of two children. Arriving at the scene nine days after the murders, he found a brown mark on a door, which he suspected was a bloody fingerprint. He cut away the part of the door containing the print and, after ordering the children's mother be fingerprinted, identified her as the culprit. She confessed and became the first criminal in the world to be charged and found guilty on the strength of fingerprint evidence.

But it would be another decade before regular fingerprinting of criminals was adopted by police around the world. After examining the prints, Cawsey and Considine finished their inspection and walked outside to speak with waiting reporters.

'It is the belief of Detectives Cawsey and Considine . . . that the woman, probably at the suggestion of her husband, took a bath in the house, utilising the apartment in which the blood stain was found, as a dressing room,' said one report the following morning. Her assailant had then taken advantage 'of her helpless condition . . . armed with a sharp knife or a razor, probably with the latter – for with a razor the doctors believe the throat was cut – seized the woman and, putting his left hand upon her mouth and forcing the head back as he did so, slit her throat from ear to ear'.

'The particulars of the shocking crime,' thundered *The Argus*, 'indicated that the tracing of the murderer and the establishment of the identity of the victim and the motive for the deed would be a task of exceptional difficulty, and one which would tax the best efforts of the ablest detectives in the force.'

That newspaper's main rival, *The Age*, would set the tone for the enormous coverage the case would attract: 'From the outset a suspicion of insanity is almost suggested,' said the paper, 'and a tinge of the ghastly horror of the Whitechapel murders is hinted.'

In the following two days baggage carriers and workers at the Federal Coffee Palace would shed more light on the events leading up to the woman's murder. The suspect, police would announce, was believed to be a man who spoke in a Lancashire accent, 'is 35 years of age, 5 feet 7 inches in height, of stout build, with broad square shoulders. In walking his head is slightly stooped. His complexion is fair. His hair is light, with a tendency to brown, and he wears a very large ginger moustache, but no beard.'

The wanted man was always well-dressed with a black bowler hat and an umbrella with a silver-mounted handle. But it was his jewellery that everyone remembered; the diamond-studded collar, the diamond studs in his shirt and the single large diamond on the third finger of his right hand.

Not long after Cawsey and Considine left the scene, a figure slipped inside the loosely guarded front door of the house. Alfred Spedding, the next-door neighbour who had heard what he thought was a plumber busily at work in the early hours of Christmas morning, wanted to take a closer look inside the home that was now attracting a growing crowd of onlookers.

He made his way down the hall and into the kitchen. In its fireplace he found a small card, folded and crinkled, that Cawsey and Considine had overlooked. Spedding made his way to the Windsor police station and found Constable Godfrey Webster, still recovering from the wretched odour that had overwhelmed him at the murder scene the previous evening.

Webster peered at the card and realised he had a crucial piece of evidence in his hands. It read: 'Mr Albert Williams requests respectfully the pleasure of the company of . . . at a social evening at Allan's Commercial Hotel, Rainhill, on Wednesday, August 10 1891.'

He quickly forwarded the card to Cawsey and Considine. The detectives remained concerned. So much time had elapsed. The killer had a two-month head start on them.

Where was he?

IV.

Albert Williams was almost unrecognisable. Two weeks had passed since Dr Robert Scott had last seen the man who had become the scourge of the *Kaiser Wilhelm II*'s journey to Australia. He had been pale and surly, barking orders through pursed lips and insisting baggage handlers refer to him as 'Major-General Williams'.

But that was nothing compared to the figure Scott had seen shuffling toward him in Collins Street two days after Christmas. That preening, self-absorbed fellow who had 'paraded himself ostentatiously before the other passengers' and had worn 'an unreasonable amount of jewellery' seemed dazed and dishevelled.

Scott was stunned by the deterioration in the man. Williams' wavy hair, which had always been combed perfectly in place, was unkempt. His face was unshaven, his clothes shabby and soiled. Scott thought he looked distraught. He walked up to him and shook his hand and asked after Emily.

She was in good health, Williams had told him, and was in Sydney visiting friends she had made on the trip to Australia.

'Why did you not go with her?' Scott asked.

Williams hesitated. He seemed distracted. 'Oh, I have a good deal of business in town. In fact I am arranging to leave it.'

'Leaving so soon? Where are you going?'

What was it with this city? In England a man could travel a few miles to another village and be completely unknown. Deeming had proved this several times. Yet in a big city like Melbourne it was impossible to go anywhere without being recognised. Just before Christmas Eliza Hirschfeldt, the nosey wife of Max, had seen him walking down a street in Windsor. He had quickened his pace and pretended he hadn't seen her. But there was no avoiding Dr Scott.

'I am going to Bombay,' Williams told Scott. 'I have had an offer to superintend three jute mills there. I was offered 800 pounds a year by the company in England but I declined to go at that salary; but I have since seen the company's agents in Melbourne. At first they offered me 850 pounds a year. This also I declined. They then tele-graphed home to see whether they might offer me 900 pounds . . . and as this satisfies me I am going.'

Scott wished him the best. He then watched Albert Williams continue down Collins Street. The man who had arrogantly strutted the decks of the *Kaiser Wilhelm II* seemed to stagger. Scott soon lost sight of him in the busy post-Christmas crowds.

Scott did not know it at the time but Frederick Deeming was in the process of another transformation. He was discarding the persona of Albert Williams. It was the same way a snake shed its skin every few months, leaving behind a brittle, rice-paper outline of its former self. It would take him time to settle on a new identity and the next few weeks would be spent in a bewildering blur as he experimented with several aliases – some old, some new – before completing the metamorphosis into a new persona.

The process had started a few days before Christmas while Emily was still alive when he arrived on his own at the Cathedral Hotel and booked a room under the name Duncan. According to staff he came and went a great deal, although he was not seen in the hotel for a couple of days over Christmas. He wasn't a man easily forgotten. The licensee of the hotel, Maria Thomson, would always remember him as the man with a caged canary.

On about the same day of his chance meeting with Dr Scott, Thomas Lambert, a builder's labourer, had been standing on a street corner a couple of suburbs away from Windsor when Frederick Deeming came by driving a horse and spring cart. He called out to Lambert and asked him if he wanted work.

'I said "Yes" and he told me to jump up. When I asked him where we were going he said that he didn't know the name of the street but that he knew the house.'

The man seemed confused and lost. 'We pulled up at Union Street and I mentioned the names of several streets but he could not recognise them.'

'Will you have a drink?' Deeming asked Lambert as they drove past the Bowling Green Hotel. They went inside and Lambert noticed the man's hands were shaking so badly he had to hold the glass with both hands. But the brandy seemed to settle his nerves. 'I know where I am now,' he told Lambert when they returned to the cart. He gave the reins a flick and a few minutes later they pulled up outside 57 Andrew Street.

Lambert waited with the horse while the man opened the front door. It seemed to take forever. He had only been inside for a few moments when he came rushing out in a panicked state.

'What's the matter?' asked Lambert.

'I thought the horse was bolting,' he said.

Lambert was confused. The horse had not moved.

To Lambert, the man seemed frightened and did not want to return to the house. He insisted Lambert collect the luggage stored in the bedrooms. He would stay outside and keep an eye on the horse and cart.

'I told him that they [the bags] were too heavy for me and that he would have to give me a hand,' Lambert would say later. Again, the man seemed wary about going inside, particularly into the second bedroom on the left. He told Lambert to drag the bags into the passage. It was only then that he reluctantly went inside and – 'he pushing, and I pulling' – the pair removed the luggage and loaded it on to the cart. The man paid Lambert a shilling, waved goodbye and headed toward the city.

On 28 December he checked out of the Cathedral Hotel, caught a train and arrived that night in the Gippsland town of Sale, 130 miles to the east of Melbourne. Carrying the canary in its brass cage, he booked a room at the Criterion Hotel under the name of Francis Dobson. The next morning he told Lucy Colgate, the daughter of the hotel's proprietor, that he was an engineer employed by the Melbourne Tramways. He had intended to spend some time touring the lakes of the region but had just received a telegram ordering him to return to the city. He showed her the pliers he claimed to have crafted out of knitting needles.

Lucy introduced him to her older brother, John. 'He said he was looking round to start a foundry,' John Colgate would recall. 'He told me that he had been engaged in America at 600 pounds a year, but that when he came out here they only gave him 300 pounds . . . he asked me to write to him at the Prahran engine-sheds and he would get me a billet on the trams at five pounds a week. He also showed me the pliers.'

He returned to Melbourne later that day, posting a letter to Emily's mother in Rainhill dated 29 December, which said:

'Dear Mother, At last, as my dear Emily says, I take it in my head to write you. We are still in Melbourne, but since Emily wrote you there is great changes. When she wrote I was about to take the management of a mill in Queensland, but I have now settled on the management of a tea-exporting company in China, at a salary of eight hundred and fifty a year. I have signed on for three years, at the end of which time it is our intention to return to England.

'We leave here on the fourth of January, '92, with the steamer *Catterthun*, captain J. J. B. Darke. We will write to you from each port we pass. I am pleased to tell you that we have had a very happy Christmas indeed. Emily is one of the happiest little girls I have ever seen. God bless her. She does enjoy herself. I hope, mother, that you are keeping well and that you have got over your little shop trouble.

I have nothing more to tell you at present so I must conclude with love from your loving children – Emily and Albert.'

That evening Maria Thomson once again found him standing at the front desk of the Cathedral Hotel.

'Back again, Mr Duncan?' she asked.

'Yes, and I've brought my luggage with me,' he told her. Among the bags and cases was a large portmanteau that he refused to leave in the store room on the ground level. He insisted it be taken upstairs to his room and Maria had been forced to find two men to help lift it.

Mr Williams. Mr Drewn. Mr Duncan. Mr Dobson. He had employed at least four aliases in little more than two weeks. More would soon follow.

But first he required a new wife.

V.

Courting a prospective wife or husband in the nineteenth century could often be a complicated and expensive process. One needed to attend balls and soirees. One required introductions and, if things went further, underwent formal interviews with an intended's family. To circumvent this lengthy and often costly exercise, matrimonial agencies had become popular, particularly in big cities where they brought together new arrivals and those struggling to find prospective partners.

One of Melbourne's leading matrimonial agents was James Holt, who had a reputation for simplifying such a complex and delicate matter. 'Ladies, gentlemen, every station in life contemplating matrimony,' read one of his advertisements. 'Immediately consult . . . Holt's New Matrimonial Chambers, 448 Queen Street, Melbourne, opposite the Old Cemetery. Introductions privately arranged between eligible partners.'

On 2 January 1892 Frederick Deeming, using the alias Frederick Duncan, sat in his room and wrote to Holt, outlining his ideal future wife.

'Cathedral Hotel, Jan. 2, 1892. Matrimonial. The undersigned, at the above address, wishes to meet with a young lady with the above intentions. She must be good looking, age 18 or 20, and know something of housekeeping. I, myself, am 32 years, engineer by trade.

I have 360 pounds in the bank and am about to enter into a good appointment. Am sober, steady man. Am just from England, and have 14 years' testimonials from one master. Please enclose photo of lady. – Yours &c., F. Duncan.'

There were about five blatant lies in that single paragraph. But Frederick Deeming, apparently having overcome the shocked state he was in following Emily's murder, was on a roll. In the coming week he would adopt several new aliases and embark on a dizzying series of half-baked schemes that, even by his usual standards, would confuse those attempting to piece together his movements.

He rented a shopfront in Collins Street under the name of Mr Watson and displayed a collection of items including bedding, clothing, books, the wicker chair he had used on the journey to Australia, assorted silverware, a sword, a broom, a claw hammer, a can that still contained traces of sand and cement, a bent shovel and even his beloved canary and its cage.

Then, using the name Harry Dawson, he appointed Beauchamp's, a local auction house, to handle the sale.

Two more names – Watson and Dawson. Tally of aliases since his arrival in Australia on 15 December 1891: six.

On 6 January he was walking along Bourke Street, the main street in Melbourne, when he crossed paths with yet another former passenger from the *Kaiser Wilhelm II*. It was Sydney Oakes, the corn merchant who believed Deeming to be Albert Williams, a retired engineer on a healthy pension with the Royal Navy. The pair retired to a local hotel and had a glass of ale.

'Where is your wife?' asked Oakes.

Deeming said Emily had gone to Sydney to visit old friends she had made on the ship. To Oakes, Albert Williams was his usual boastful self. 'He told me he was going to a government billet in India as an inspecting engineer at a salary of 900 pounds a year.'

The following day most of the items on offer at the auction were sold for a total of seventy-two pounds. A local art dealer, Simeon Solomon, bought the canary and its cage for three pounds.

'Look after it,' the man calling himself Dawson told Solomon. He handed the bird's new owner a bag of bird seed bearing the name of a Liverpool firm. 'It's a good bird,' he said.

Accompanying Deeming at the sale was Richard Smith, an accountant who had struck up a friendship with the talkative Englishman at a city jewellery store soon after Christmas. Deeming had told Smith he was a toolmaker, but an uncle in England had recently died and bequeathed him several valuable properties, including one in Cheapside, the street running through the heart of London's financial district. He thought the building might be worth 18,000 pounds. This same wealthy uncle had also left him a terrace of houses near Buckingham.

Deeming said he planned to claim his inheritance and was waiting on his wife – a 'very superior person of an intellectual turn of mind' – to return from Sydney where she had been visiting relatives.

The next day the pair walked along the pier at Port Melbourne and Smith pointed out *Ophir*, one of the Orient Company's newest steamers, a 500-foot twin engine ship that regularly sailed the London–Australia route.

'I wish to God my little woman was over here,' Deeming said, admiring the ship that was about to leave. 'I would like to go with her. But she won't be here till Wednesday.' The following day he told Smith his wife had fallen ill and her health was deteriorating. He might have to go to Sydney to see her. But he would come back, he assured Smith.

'He said he would like to buy some property he had seen while out driving with Mr Vivian,' Smith would later recall.

'Mr Vivian' was Edward Vivian, a salesman who worked for the Kilpatrick and Co jewellery store in Collins Street. They had met on New Year's Eve when Deeming spent seven pounds on a Baume Chronograph – a display watch with a built-in stopwatch – and asked Vivian to have it oiled and serviced. He had returned on 4 January and collected the watch. He came back the following day to buy Vivian lunch and, over the coming days 'Harry Dawson' became a regular visitor to the jewellery store, paying two guineas by cheque for a set of field glasses along with a silver matchbox and a silver napkin ring that he asked Vivian to engrave with the initials 'B.S.'.

The pair struck up a friendship and Deeming bought two rings – one for twenty-five pounds, another for thirty pounds – which he asked Vivian to resize for him. Vivian did so and gave them to him when he arrived at his home in the eastern suburb of Hawthorn for lunch after catching a train from the city.

They went for a drive in a horse and cart. As the vehicle reached the top of a hill Deeming asked the driver to stop. He jumped out and theatrically produced a barometer from his vest and rattled off the exact height above sea level at which they now found themselves. Not long after they arrived at a vacant block of land that was worth an estimated 15,000 pounds. Deeming showed interest in buying it. From another pocket he produced a document with a rough plan of the house he hoped to build and asked if Vivian could recommend a local architect to finish the design and oversee the construction while he returned quickly to England for business. As they headed home the Englishman conducted a running critique on the state of the horse and the vehicle attached to it. Next time they drove out together, he said, it would be in a trap supplied by him because he was in the throes of importing 'a variety of conveyances and horses from England'.

The following day Deeming had wandered into the store and told Vivian he had just received a letter from his wife in Sydney. She was very ill with influenza and he expected he would have to travel there to comfort her. Vivian asked him to pay for the rings.

'I have been giving so many cheques lately that I don't know what I have in the bank,' Deeming said. 'I will pay you in cash.' He pulled out a roll of notes and thumbed through them.

But suddenly he announced he had to go. 'Oh, I have to meet a young lady at the post office; I'll come back when I leave her.'

It would be the last time Vivian would see the man in his store. But a letter would soon arrive for him.

'My Dear Boy,' announced 'Harry Dawson'. 'I have just received a wire from Mrs Dawson, who is very much worse with the influenza, and I regret I must go to Sydney by the 4.55 express this afternoon. I am sorry that I have not had time to see you, but will return as soon as I can, or forward you a cheque before the end of the week.'

By then Vivian had discovered another set of rings – some gold, some encrusted with diamonds and an opal brooch set in gold – had also gone missing from his store. They were now safely in the possession of a man in search of a new bride.

VI.

She was young. He liked them like that. She had long dark hair, another attribute that caught his eye. She was what the newspapers of the time, in their careful but suggestive manner, would call 'prepossessing'. She was thick-lipped with a striking bust and a narrow waist. A little pale, perhaps. But the journey through the turbulent rip guarding the entrance of Melbourne's Port Phillip Bay had been a rough one and several passengers on board the *City of Adelaide* had complained of seasickness. Still, she had soldiered through it. One of the stewardesses had even complimented her 'upon being a good sailor'.

It was the twelfth of January 1892 and that night, as the ship made its way along the eastern coast of Australia toward Sydney, Frederick Deeming made his first move on eighteen-year-old Kate Rounsefell.

He found her standing on the near-empty deck, gazing out at the water.

'Are you ill?' he asked her. 'Can I fetch you anything?'

She was fine, she replied. He persisted. Surely there was something he could do to make her feel more comfortable? It was important that he left a good first impression. Chivalry, along with a little flattery, had rarely failed him in the past. He introduced himself as Baron Swanston. He managed to strike up a brief conversation and discovered that Kate Rounsefell was on her way to Bathurst to visit her sister. She had come from Broken Hill, where she had been caring for her sick brother. He asked her if she would like a drink. She shook her head and politely rebuffed every offer.

He flirted with her on the main deck again the following day. Months later she would remember Mr Swanston being quite 'solicitous about my health, and desirous of doing me a favour in some way or other. Later on he asked me if I played whist, and when I told him I did he went away and got a couple of gentlemen who, with us two, made up a four-handed game. We played for a while and afterwards had a few words of conversation.'

That pleased him. She had not rejected him. In fact, he was sure she was warming to him. Late the next morning as the *Adelaide* entered Sydney Heads, he handed her his new pair of binoculars 'which enabled me to see the full beauty of the harbour scenery'.

As the ship neared the pier, she walked up to him and said, 'Well, Mr Swanston, I shall say goodbye to you now, and thank you for your kindness to me on board. I may not have an opportunity later because of the rush there is bound to be for the luggage.'

'Oh no!' he had said. 'Don't say goodbye just yet, Miss Rounsefell. Let me help you with your luggage to your hotel or to the train.'

'Very well. Though I'm afraid you are troubling yourself too much.'

It was no trouble, no trouble at all. He was already besotted. It was marvellous to finally be in the company of another woman. He could feel that familiar excitement coursing through him. He told her he was an engineer and when she said she was going all the way to Bathurst on the train – a distance of more than 100 miles – he said he would travel with her because he had already planned to journey further along the same line.

'I think there should be a chance of employment in one of those New South Wales mining townships,' he told her.

And then, right there on the deck of the ship as the skyline of Sydney came into view, he allowed himself to be carried away by the moment.

'Will you marry me?' he blurted.

At first she thought he was joking. But the man was clearly serious.

'No!' she said. 'I couldn't think of it. I don't know much about you, and cannot even say I like even what I do know.'

If he was embarrassed he didn't show it. By the time the *Adelaide* berthed and they had collected their luggage, they had missed the morning train to Bathurst. They made their way to the Wentworth Hotel for lunch and after it Baron Swanston suggested they visit the picturesque coastal suburb of Coogee.

'On the way he appeared to be very familiar with the streets of the city, and I told him that for a stranger he certainly did contrive to learn his way about the place quickly.'

There was no need to lie about his familiarity with Sydney. He told her he had worked in the city about five years earlier and it had barely changed since his last visit. But as they made their way down one of the streets near Circular Quay, Baron Swanston's heart must have sunk. There, marching toward him and waving, was Captain Robert Firth, another one of his fellow passengers from the *Kaiser Wilhelm II*. How was this possible in a country as vast as Australia? The damn place was little more than a tiny village.

Firth watched Swanston reluctantly acknowledge him and noticed that a young woman who was with him and bore no similarity to Emily, had walked ahead to give the two men privacy.

'Where is Mrs Williams?' Firth asked him.

'Oh, she is up here. She is quite well.'

They chatted for a few moments before Baron Swanston managed to escape and re-join Kate further down the street.

'Who was that?' asked Kate.

'That old chap is a shipmate of mine,' he said. 'He has got lots of money. I wish I had half of it.'

When they arrived in Coogee he took her down to the rocks that overlook the ocean and as they sat there watching the breaking waves, Baron Swanston revisited the subject of marriage.

She was young and very attractive, he told her. He found himself fascinated by her beauty and personality.

'He said if I would consent to become his wife I should never regret it, but would always congratulate myself upon having entered into matrimony with him,' Rounsefell would recall several months later. 'I told him I couldn't think of marrying a stranger whom I had only known several days.'

'I have had my loves before,' he said, 'but they were nothing in intensity to the passion I have for you.'

He seemed so earnest, almost desperate.

'Well, I am going to live with my sister,' Rounsefell replied. 'Wait till I see her and ask her opinion on the subject.'

He could sense her weakening. If his past had taught him anything, it was that persistence always won out.

They made their way to a nearby aquarium. As they wandered through the summer crowds and past the three big tanks with their performing seals, he asked her if she would accept a ring as a keepsake to remind her of him. He was quite the romantic, not to mention one of the most determined men she had ever met. She agreed. The ring he produced from one of his pockets sparkled with diamonds and sapphires.

That night, according to Rounsefell, they stayed in separate rooms at the Wentworth Hotel and the next morning caught the early train to Bathurst. He was a thoughtful, doting companion. When the train stopped at Mt Victoria he got out and returned to their carriage carrying food and drink from the refreshment station. To pass the time Kate read one of the Sydney newspapers and at one point glanced at her companion with a puzzled look. The shipping notices listed the names of all the passengers on the *City of Adelaide* who had arrived the previous day. But there was no B. Swanston. She asked him why. 'Oh that's because I booked on board,' he told her before quickly changing the subject.

In Bathurst he dropped her at her sister Lizzie's place in Havannah Street and then booked a room at Hurley's Royal Hotel three blocks away. But he was back within a few hours. Kate declined to see him, citing tiredness. He sent several messages through the rest of the day and into the early evening. Early the next morning they heard him knocking on the front door. Baron Swanston must have smiled to himself as he heard the latch lifted and he was invited inside.

'I had a long chat with him, and so had my sister,' remembered Rounsefell. 'After he had gone my sister said to me: "If you are going to settle down I don't see any objection to you marrying Mr Swanston. He looks like a respectable man and should be able to give you a comfortable home."'

The following day Kate joined Swanston for a ride around the district 'and again, in more earnest tones than he had yet used, he implored me to be his wife. At last I was worn down by his persevering nature, and I consented to marry him.'

He asked her if she would like to move to Sydney with him. But she didn't like the big city. He put forward several regional towns. She didn't like them, either. It sounded as if she was looking for any excuse to delay becoming his wife.

Exasperated, he asked, 'Where shall I go then?'

'Why not try Western Australia?' she suggested. 'It is a new colony and is said to be a go-ahead place where an energetic and skilled man has a chance to rise quickly.'

This pleased him. He was, of course, fully aware of the growing colony on the vast west coast of the country. The newspapers were filled with reports about new gold discoveries and how West Australia's population was swelling by the week. He would leave the next day for Sydney and organise his passage to its capital city, Perth.

Before he left he gave her another two rings – one was set with five diamonds, another was boat-shaped with a diamond at its centre – along with an opal brooch set in gold.

'I remarked that it was curious that he should have these rings in his possession.'

Baron Swanston told Kate he had bought the rings for a young woman he had been courting in England.

According to an account given later by Rounsefell, Swanston had taken the woman into a theatre box when 'a gentleman tapped him on the shoulder and said, "I trust you do not forget that is my wife you are courting." He was so astounded at the woman's duplicity that he left her standing at the entrance and walked away with the intention of renouncing her and the sex.'

He also had something else he wanted to give his new bride to be. He had a great deal of clothes with him that he said had belonged to his now dead sister. Would Kate like them?

The idea repulsed her. 'I told him that I could not wear the clothes of a dead woman even if I could overcome my objection – which I did not think possible – to taking gifts of clothing from any man not my husband.'

He left Sydney on 21 January and arrived in Melbourne the following day. He sent her a letter immediately, telling her he had booked a berth on the S.S. *Albany* which left for Perth the following day. He sent another letter to his 'dear Kitty' from Adelaide, and again when the ship arrived at the Fremantle docks just south of Perth.

He was staying at the Shamrock Hotel when he wrote to her on 6 February and told her she should come immediately because he had found a job as an engineer at Fraser's Mine in Southern Cross, a small outpost hugging the edge of WA's dry wheatbelt.

He asked her to reply by telegram and included money to cover its cost. 'I excused myself on the score of illness,' recalled Rounsefell. 'In answer to a further telegram urging me to go I declined on account of unpreparedness.'

She was hesitating, perhaps looking for a way out. But Baron Swanston was, as usual, insistent. He wired her twenty pounds through the Commercial Bank of Sydney and telegrammed again saying: 'Come at once or the rains will set in and travelling will be impossible.'

She felt she had no choice now. Besides, she had given her word. She packed her bags and wired him to say she was on her way.

VII.

The canary began singing in the House of the Dead shortly after 10am on Tuesday morning, the eighth of March. The coronial inquest into the death of Emily Williams had just opened before a packed crowd at the Melbourne Morgue, all of them grateful for the cool winds sweeping through the town.

The city had experienced its hottest day in thirty-two years the previous day, the type of scorcher Sidney Dickinson believed could dry the blood in his veins and the marrow in his bones. A report in *The Age* could easily have come from Sidney's own pen: 'From early morn the fiery sun beat down red and pitiless from a sky of brass and the streets became cast iron, and the air a stiff suffocating curtain, and the wearing of flesh a weariness.'

It had reached 104 degrees in the shade and some had sworn they had seen the mercury reach 153 in the sun. But late in the afternoon one of Dickinson's favourite cool changes had swept in from the south and the following morning hundreds had queued trying to obtain a seat at the inquest.

Those lucky enough to win admission watched the jury sworn in and then, just as the first of the morning's evidence began, birdsong filled the air. All eyes turned to the canary. It was perched in its brass cage along with several other items of evidence.

'It is singing over its mistress's body,' someone said loudly. 'A sweet dirge!'

The comment would inspire a reporter for *The Herald* to greater heights when he filed his story for that afternoon's edition. 'Amid the grim associations of the House of the Dead,' he wrote, 'and breaking in upon the ghastly details of the evidence, there rang through the listening court the beautiful warblings of the dead woman's canary. The pretty little songster, a native of the Harz Mountains in Germany, whence come the canaries of richest song, sang blithely, but to those in Court its song had a touch of weird pathos about it.'

It was the sort of music review the man presiding over the hearing would have appreciated, or even penned himself.

Coroner James Neild was one of Melbourne's most prominent identities, a short, balding man with enormous mutton chop sideburns that tumbled below his collar like wads of matted moss.

A doctor and forensic pathologist drawn to Australia by the gold rush, Neild had also spent several decades writing controversial drama and music reviews under a series of pseudonyms for a variety of publications. If his days were often spent searching for death's causes, he ended his nights by dispensing critiques that sometimes led to the death of a stage career. He was brash, belligerent and believed a critic should be fiercely independent. Neild had once accused a prominent rival in print of taking money to write a 'puff' review praising a mediocre play. His reviews were equally as blunt. He loathed the theatricality of most opera singers. 'Absurd and objectionable,' was his summary of the efforts of the visiting Bianchi Grand Italian Opera Company. The singers, in turn, had retaliated by putting up posters around town denouncing him.

Neild was a man 'beloved by his friends, and most cordially hated by his particular enemies, of whom he has a good many'. He was a notorious womaniser whose constant string of extramarital affairs were the subject of constant gossip. He hosted regular Sunday afternoon get-togethers at his fashionable home in Spring Street for a wide range of actors, directors and a group of Bohemians who dominated the city's artistic scene. He claimed to have been the first to identify the immense talents of the woman who would become one of Australia's most celebrated cultural exports – Dame Nellie Melba.

Sometimes his double life as a medical professional and theatre critic collided. One night in 1868 a young star of the Australian stage, Mademoiselle Marie St Denis, attempted suicide by taking an overdose of laudanum, that tincture of opium heavily favoured by Wilkie Collins. Spurned by a man she loved and fearing her career was in decline, St Denis left a note for Dr Neild, whom she had known for only a short time. She wanted no inquest and no autopsy carried out on her body.

'My dear doctor,' she wrote, 'I have killed myself . . . as no-one will interfere with you, I beg (if you ever had the smallest feeling of regard for me) that you will give an undertaker's certificate saying I died from any cause you like to mention . . . please oblige me in this. Fancy my body cut up and hacked to pieces! Please prevent it.'

Neild was summoned to her apartment. He quickly emptied the contents of her stomach using a pump and then 'I pumped into the stomach about a pint of strong coffee and in a few minutes removed it by the same means . . . this process was repeated several times. We then passed into the stomach four drachms of aromatic spirit of ammonia in about a pint of water.' Neild and a fellow doctor worked on her all night. But her pulse gradually weakened and she died the next morning.

Neild, always fiercely independent, did nothing to prevent that inquest taking place and even appeared as a key witness. Now, more than twenty years later, he presided over the very same courtroom in which he had given evidence about Marie St Denis' suicide. He was also having difficulty hearing witness testimony above the soaring song of the caged canary.

Little in the way of fresh information would be gleaned over the next few hours that had not already appeared in the countless newspaper reports in the days since the discovery of Emily's body. John Stamford was the first witness called and was examined by Detective Cawsey. Stamford told the court how a man calling himself Drewn had rented the home for a short term about ten days before Christmas and had then extended the lease until the end of January through his agent, Charles Connop.

After regaining possession of the house, Stamford had detected an awful smell when he opened the door to the second bedroom while showing it to a prospective tenant. After discovering its source was coming from beneath the raised hearthstone he had summoned Connop and the two men had then lifted the stone.

'Did you notice anything then?' asked Cawsey.

'Yes . . . a smell. There was a casing of cement and in the cement a rent; and then we sent for the police and the body of the deceased was dug out.' Connop's testimony matched that of Stamford and was followed by several police officers who gave their account of the body's discovery and removal.

Max Hirschfeldt, the German draper and fellow passenger of Albert Williams and his wife on the *Kaiser Wilhelm II*, was then called. He had contacted the police shortly after the body's discovery was made public and a rough description of the suspect had been published. Cawsey and Considine had interviewed him and accompanied him to the morgue where he had identified the remains of the woman as the wife of Mr Williams.

Hirschfeldt was asked if Albert Williams had ever told him where he was eventually intending to live.

'He spoke of going to India and America, and made various remarks about where he was going. He pretended to have a great deal of money – some 6000 or 7000 pounds – which he said he intended to invest in this colony. But it was found out by the captain of the ship that this was all moonshine.'

'Did you notice on the ship that Williams had a canary?'

'Yes, that is what attracted my attention in the newspapers. The cage and bird produced are those Williams had on the ship.'

Other witnesses followed, including the retired sea captain Robert Firth, the owner of the Hamburg Laundry, Ernest Bueller and the luggage carrier John Harford. But after several hours Neild banged his gavel. He had been told by Cawsey and Considine they expected several developments in the case in the coming days, perhaps even the apprehension of the suspect.

Neild adjourned the inquiry for two weeks. And, like everyone else, he began to wait.

VIII.

The strongly built man rested his elbows on the mahogany table. The icicles hanging from his thick moustache – it was so cold that morning he would later describe them as stalactites – had slowly begun to thaw. Samuel Lowe, London correspondent for *The Argus*, was grateful to be back indoors. It was 9 March 1892. For the past two days England had been buffeted by cold winds and heavy snowstorms. Rail and telegraphic lines had been down in western parts of the country and much of Wales. In the north, the wild weather had shut down quarries and coal mines, throwing thousands out of work. In Liverpool a coastal steamer, the *Hero*, had sunk in wild seas just outside the mouth of the Mersey, its crew saved by a handful of lifeboats.

Lowe was upstairs in the office of one of the biggest dairy produce dealers in London discussing the state of the market. He spent a lot of his time examining various grades of butter and comparing the differences between Danish, Normandy and Australian products. Any titbit – a new method of packaging or the latest gossip about the current glut – was valuable news for Australia's burgeoning dairy industry.

Lowe was deep in conversation with the dealer when an electric bell clanged loudly outside the room. A moment later a young office boy entered and announced Lowe was wanted on the telephone. The new contraption was becoming an increasingly common feature in business houses across the city. But there were some who wondered whether it was just a passing fad; Alexander Graham Bell's invention was expensive to install and the quality of the calls left much to be desired.

Lowe lifted the receiver and heard waves of static – a 'confused current of interwoven noises' – crashing into his ear. Then a faint voice emerged from the chaos.

'Is that you, Lowe?'

Lowe straightened his stout frame. It was Thomas Townend, the manager of *The Argus*' London bureau.

'Look here,' he told Lowe. 'I want to see you as soon as possible. There's a big murder case on in Australia and we've just got a cable from the office in Melbourne instructing us to make inquiries at this end. Be as sharp as you can.'

Lowe might have been a large man but he prided himself on his speed. He apologised to the dealer and bounded down the stairs three steps at a time. Fifteen minutes later he was standing in front of Townend in the Fleet Street office of *The Argus*, reading the telegram.

'Inquire Scotland Yard. Williams murder,' it read. 'Send portraits. Interview mother.'

Back in Melbourne *The Argus*' enterprising police reporter, Bill Salter, had learned about the invitation card Constable Godfrey Webster had handed to detectives Cawsey and Considine which mentioned a celebration taking place at the Commercial Hotel in Rainhill the previous year.

'I'll look after it,' Lowe told Townend. He ventured back out into the snow flurries, flagged down a Hansom cab – one of thousands of horse and cart taxis that were now skating across the frozen streets of the city – and made his way to Scotland Yard. A senior officer and old contact of Lowe's showed him the daily police information sheet. Item number 44 – a new listing that morning – contained a detailed description of an Albert Williams who spoke with a Lancashire accent, had formerly stayed in Rainhill and was now wanted by Melbourne police for the murder of his wife on Christmas Eve, 1891.

When Lowe returned to the office Townend was huddled over a dusty copy of the *Liverpool Post*. 'Rainhill appears to be a lunatic asylum 10 miles out of Liverpool,' he told Lowe. 'You had better hurry up or you will miss the express. It's the biggest wild-goose chase a man was ever sent on but we have our instructions . . .'

The banks were already closed. He handed Lowe a couple of pounds from his pocket and the petty cash box yielded another ten quid. Shortly after 10pm the reporter was on the Liverpool train.

The next morning he found himself in Rainhill, twelves miles to the east of Liverpool. The storms had died overnight leaving the town blanketed in snow. Lowe quickly learned a man named Williams had arrived in Rainhill in the middle of the previous year. He had rented a house – Dinham Villa – and his sister and her four children had stayed there for a short time. After they left, Williams married a local girl.

Lowe made his way to the local church. The register contained an entry showing Albert Oliver Williams, bachelor, had married an Emily Mather, spinster, on 22 September 1891.

By that afternoon Lowe found himself in the 'neat little parlour' of Dove Mather. It was furnished with a horse-hair sofa and armchair. Cheap German prints hung on the walls. In the middle of the room, positioned perfectly in the centre of a square table, sat the brass-bound Mather family Bible.

'I represent the Melbourne *Argus* . . .' Lowe announced with a theatrical pause, 'and also Scotland Yard. I want to ask you about a Mr Williams who married your daughter last September.'

Lowe couldn't believe how readily the woman spoke. She told him how Albert Williams had arrived in her shop one day interested in renting Dinham Villa. She explained how he had quickly – ever so quickly – fallen in love with her daughter Emily and had, just as quickly, proposed marriage. The wedding had been celebrated with dancing on the newly cemented floor of the villa's kitchen. Yes, she admitted. Some of her neighbours had questioned her decision to allow Emily to marry a man no-one in the district knew anything about. But Albert Williams had been a 'free-handed, well-spoken man – and he had promised her a good home'.

The couple had seemed very happy together, Dove said. Emily had written her several letters since leaving. The last had been sent from Colombo, but Albert had also written to her from Melbourne.

Lowe then said he wanted to ask Dove Mather more about her daughter. She stared sharply at him and the welcoming tone in her voice vanished.

'I want to know first what you are driving at and I will not say another word until you tell me,' she said.

'I have something very painful to say to you,' Lowe admitted. 'I am going to tell you now about two people, a man and a woman. The man, I am positive, is Albert Oliver Williams. The woman may be your daughter . . . Williams murdered his wife in Melbourne on last Christmas Eve.'

Dove fainted.

Three years later a detailed and self-serving account of Lowe's visit that day to Rainhill would be published by *The Argus*. It was unbylined and, if it was not written by Lowe himself, the man certainly served as its primary source. Bearing a sub-headline that read 'A True Detective Story', the lengthy account highlighted the amateur sleuthing skills of Samuel Lowe, a man more accustomed to charting daily butter and milk prices, portraying him as nothing less than an Antipodean Sherlock Holmes with an unparalleled ability to sniff out the truth.

The story detailed how Lowe, shortly before finding himself in the parlour of Dove Mather's home, had sought out John Higham, the local mailman, and his eighteen-year-old assistant son. Lowe had surmised that a deliverer of letters and parcels would be one of the most likely to know Rainhill's inhabitants. Once again his investigative instincts were correct. It was the younger Higham who recalled a man named Williams renting Dinham Villa and, not long after he had been visited by his sister and her four children, had the kitchen floor cemented. According to the article in *The Argus*, when Lowe was given this information he 'gave an involuntary exclamation of surprised delight . . . When hounds are hunting live game and they pick up the scent again after a check they always give tongue.'

By the time Dove had recovered from her fainting spell, Lowe had formed a hunch that this supposed 'sister' of Williams might have been the man's legal wife. On his way to Dove Mather's home several locals had told him about gossip that had circulated around town in the lead-up to the wedding. Many had noticed how the hastily arranged ceremony had been staged in the local church early one morning. A minister had presided over the event but the parish rector had not even been aware it was taking place. Not one of Albert Williams' relatives had attended the wedding or the small reception and dinner at the local hotel later that day.

Some suspected Williams was a thief, others that he was a married man, even a serial bigamist. No-one had any proof, of course. But the idea nagged at Lowe and, as the man would all but declare a few years later, his hunches usually proved accurate.

Lowe attempted to console Dove Mather when she recovered from her fainting spell. 'Mind you, I do not believe that it is your daughter who has been murdered,' he said. 'I think it very probable that his real wife, who visited here at Dinham Villa, followed him to Melbourne and that when she made herself known to him there, and reproached him for his desertion, he took her life.'

'It was a plausible hypothesis, and it was of priceless value just then, for it enabled Mrs Mather to hope,' recalled Lowe. 'With her hopes her strength revived.'

Dove Mather unlocked her *secretaire* – an old-fashioned writing desk – and produced a pile of Emily's letters and portraits of her daughter and groom at their wedding. After 'a little persuasion' and a guarantee they would be safely guarded and return undamaged to her, she handed them to Lowe.

'Now, you must tell no-one what I have told you,' said Lowe. 'It is absolutely necessary that you preserve the strictest secrecy.'

According to *The Argus* article, 'the old lady, terrified and full of vague misgivings, pledged herself to silence . . . when Mr Lowe took his seat in the express for London he had good reason to congratulate himself upon his day's work. He had succeeded beyond his most sanguine anticipations, and he had made his position secure by closing the door against any subsequent inquirers for information.'

Just to be extra certain, Lowe, 'after rifling the treasure chamber' of the *secretaire*, had relocked the cabinet and taken the key with him.

At about the same time as Lowe's train from Liverpool made its way back to London, a plain black box containing Emily's body had been placed in a horse-drawn hearse outside the Melbourne morgue.

The Windsor murder had triggered an outpouring of public sympathy the city had rarely experienced. Hundreds of onlookers had gathered as the hearse prepared to make its way to the city cemetery for a pauper's burial. Some in the crowd were so eager for a closer look, reported *The Argus*, they 'lost all sense of decency and order' and broke through a police line and pushed their way inside the courtyard, pressing against the hearse and peering at the pauper's coffin.

They would have seen two wreaths of white dahlias and Christmas lilies resting on the top of the coffin. They had been sent by the family of Captain Robert Firth, the man who had met Emily on the *Kaiser Wilhelm II* and had then bumped into her husband walking with another woman in Sydney two months earlier. The hearse, still followed by a large crowd, then made its way to the cemetery where, after a service read by a local Church of England minister, it was lowered into the ground. When the last rites were administered, many in the crowd stepped forward and placed wreaths and flower arrangements on the unmarked grave.

On Monday 14 March *The Argus* splashed Samuel Lowe's exclusive interview with Dove Mather.

'Statement by the Murdered Woman's Mother' said the headline. 'Interviewed By Our London Representative – A Painful Scene – Suspicious Wedding Incidents – The Mother Deceived As To The Destination – A Letter Sent By Williams After The Murder.'

The story – an enormous breakthrough in the investigation – trumpeted how Dove believed her new son-in-law to have been a military man whose father, a colonel, had been killed in the Crimea. There were plenty of small details – all those little things favoured by Frederick Deeming whenever he needed to embellish one of his tales. He was an inspector of stores for the British Army. He had a 'rich uncle' in England. After the marriage he had told Dove the couple would be heading to Bombay, where he had been promoted to take charge of the army stores throughout India. Dove had no idea they were in Melbourne until a letter informed her of their arrival.

The last she had heard was that letter written on 29 December when Albert had told her what a happy Christmas they had enjoyed and how they were about to sail for China, where he would manage a Hong Kong tea business.

'Though the mother appeared to have been satisfied with him,' reported Lowe, 'some of their neighbours were suspicious that he was not what he endeavoured to induce people to believe him to be. Ground for misgiving was afforded by the fact that on one occasion he was seen in company with a strange woman who was said by gossips to be his wife. It was also noticed that none of his relatives were present at the marriage ceremony, but beyond forming subject for passing comment, this circumstance was not regarded seriously.'

It was the final line in Lowe's report and was delivered almost as an afterthought. Within days this 'strange woman' – Marie Deeming – would become a central figure in the investigation as news of the crimes of Frederick Deeming ignited the world's telegraphic lines.

But it was barely noticed because another development was competing with Samuel Lowe's exclusive interview with Dove Mather.

A man answering the description of Albert Williams had been arrested at a gold mine in a small outback town in Western Australia and charged with Emily's murder.

PART V.

'God has always been my friend'

The Capture of the Baron – The Vital Clue that Led to the Murderer's Capture – A Further Grisly Discovery that Shocks the World – 'That Damned German Swine' – Silence in a Small English Village – The Prisoner Constructs a Far-Fetched Alibi – The Case of the Missing Moustache

I.

Baron Swanston had arrived in early February in a new town in one of the oldest places on earth. The small mining settlement of Southern Cross was 235 miles east of Perth and barely four years old. It sat in the middle of the Yilgarn plateau, a mass of granite and greenstone that had risen out of the boiling sea two billion years earlier to form one of the first chunks of the continent that would become Australia.

The landscape was almost Martian; its red soil pocked with craters and strewn with boulders. It seemed to stretch forever and was so bleak it could break the heart of the strongest optimist. There were prospectors who had ridden out under its endless sky and never returned, their bones turning to chalk beneath clumps of spinifex. Dried salt pans shimmered on the horizon. Piles of large, bleached rocks lay like dice rolled by the hands of giants.

The town itself was just as desolate. Slab huts with walls of calico and hessian, creaking corrugated iron sheds and misshapen wooden buildings clung to the rust-stained dirt as grimly as the stunted weeds and ruby saltbush. Its wide streets were covered ankle deep in dust and were littered with empty meat cans, old sacks and discarded rope ends that stirred only when one of the regular willy-willys, or dust devils, danced out of the desert and into the settlement.

'The Cross is a windy, dirty, dusty hole from which anyone is very glad to depart,' a visiting prospector, John Aspinall, would write a few years later.

By the time Swanston arrived at Fraser's gold mine to begin work as an engineer – he was placed in charge of one of the batteries where quartz was smashed into powder to release gold particles – the summer had been the driest anyone could remember and the only moisture fell in the form of tears.

The crumbling soil had caused two wells near town to collapse. Bullock teams had been forced to travel eighty-five miles to cart water to help slake the thirst of the Cross's several hundred inhabitants. The local cemetery was filled with small, rubble-covered graves after an outbreak of diphtheria began claiming the lives of babies and children.

In the first week of February, as a well-dressed man with a large moustache stepped out of a coach in the main street of town, the locals had been forced to dig a larger hole. When it was finished more than 300 people gathered in the late afternoon heat to watch the coffin of David Gray lowered into it. Gray was a young miner with more hope than most; he had just sent word to his father back in Perth that his fiancee was on her way from England when four tons of earth collapsed on top of him deep inside Fraser's main mine.

A hasty investigation had found an 'unforeseen slippery joint, not perceptible, was the cause . . . and that no negligence or care-lessness is attributable to anyone'. That was usually how it worked. Fraser's had seen more than its share of deaths and injuries in the short years it had been in operation. But no-one ever seemed to be responsible. A few months earlier its former manager had described the mine's founder and owner, Hugh Fraser, as a 'nincompoop' engaged in a senseless and relentless drive to dig deeper and further with 'not a piece of timber for safety of life or limb'. Fraser had begrudgingly given his miners a two-hour exemption from work to attend Gray's funeral.

The coach carrying Swanston to Southern Cross would have dropped the man and his usual large haul of baggage in Antares

Street near Blizzard Stanbrook's Club Hotel. He would not have been shocked by the shabby surrounds because he had seen his share of humpies and shanty towns on the diamond fields of South Africa. Gold had only been discovered in the area four years earlier, by two prospectors who had gone two days without water and relied on the Southern Cross constellation to guide them. The ramshackle town formed quickly and in the years to come all traffic to the goldfields of Coolgardie and Kalgoorlie further to the east would have to pass through the Cross.

After storing his luggage, Swanston would have sauntered through the dust past Shanko Jones's hairdressing saloon. He might have paused for a second glance at Shanko's charming daughter, Mivanivy. Further along he surely would have stopped outside Saunders' jewellery shop, pausing to wipe away the beads of sweat and noting its location for a future visit. He might also have breathed in the aroma of baking pies and fresh bread coming from Mrs Turner's house where, for two bob, a man could wash away the dust and indulge in a decent feed that would remind him of home.

At night the empty streets filled with the sound of the pub piano and raucous singing. But the real soundtrack of Southern Cross could be heard in the shunting of the crushers at the mine and the constant clanging that came from Jim Fairclough's shoeing forge. Big Jim was like so many others lured to Southern Cross once word emerged in the late 1880s that the Yilgarn contained more than just rock, fossilised bone and small tribes of natives. Gold seekers needed sharp axes, picks and shovels and that meant a guaranteed line of work for a blacksmith like Fairclough. So he and his brother sailed from their home in South Australia and landed at the port town of Albany on the southern tip of WA. From there they walked 350 miles to reach the Cross, and Jim, who was all muscle and sinew and stood six foot four had quickly established a lucrative business mending the shoes of worn horses and repairing all those tools blunted by the Yilgarn's stubborn volcanic skin.

If Fairclough was physically intimidating, the locals knew him as a decent man who was polite, charitable and always true to his word. But it was an incident in his blacksmith's shop with an infamous murderer for which he would always be remembered.

They would still talk about it decades later; how Fairclough walked into the rear of his shop one afternoon, the heat from the furnace making the whole place feel several degrees hotter than Hell, to discover a pale Englishman with a large moustache using his tools and forge without permission.

Baron Swanston would surely have begun irritating many of those around him by then. If his clothes and jewellery immediately marked him as unconventional, his inevitable boasting and one-upmanship would also have worn thin. According to one newspaper article published after Fairclough's death at the 'advanced age of 77 years' in 1940, Big Jim lost his temper and a heated argument ensued.

'Fairclough, who had been threatened, collared Swanston, threw him out into the street and applied the boot, at the same time speeding his progress by calling him a rogue . . . Swanston got up, and, to the surprise of all, walked away.'

Baron Swanston had told the mine's owners he would require a cottage close to their site because he was soon to marry and was expecting his fiancee from the east coast at any time. They had knocked one together for him quickly and if it lacked many of the creature comforts Kate Rounsefell might have expected, Swanston had moved quickly to make it as welcoming as possible. He had ordered a large stove – so big the newspapers would later say it was 'large enough to roast a human being'. More tellingly, he had also requested two barrels of cement from the mine's legal manager. The contents of one of the barrels was used to concrete part of the floor of the small shack. Weeks after his arrest the other barrel remained untouched and, as *The Inquirer and Commercial News* in Perth would later remark without a hint of irony, 'was probably intended for use on some future occasion'.

He was also pining to be reunited with Kate Rounsefell. A few days after arriving in Southern Cross he wrote to her imploring her to leave immediately.

'My Dear Kitty, Don't keep me waiting, dear. If you love me half as much as I love you, you would not keep me waiting a day. As we are to be man and wife, why not let it be at once. I have written to your brother at Broken Hill informing him of our approaching marriage, and I have got everything in readiness here, so do come quickly dear. The appointment I have got gives me 6 pounds a week for the first six months, and thereafter 8 pounds and 10 shillings a week: and in addition I have a house rent free and should be able to earn 3 pounds a week extra.

'I do not intend to stay here all my life. I shall make enough money in two years so that we may take a trip to England so you may look forward to that treat. Write as soon as you get this, or wire if you can come at once. I am longing to hear from you. Send me your photo. I feel very lonely here, and that would be company for me. Do try and come over quick, dear, and you might send me any Sydney and Melbourne papers you can get.'

'My Dear Baron,' Kate had replied in one of her letters. 'Bathurst is awfully dull. I shall be glad to leave it. I wish my sister could come with me. Do you think she could get work? What is the town like? How large? Where would you meet me? I never dreamt it was so far away. What sort of place is it, and what sort of dresses ought I to get? . . . How do you spend your time? How many hours do you work? Is it dirty work? Write all the news, because I want to know everything.'

He was sitting in his partially built house at about 1pm on Friday 11 March, an unfinished letter to Kate sitting nearby, when Constable Evan Williams arrived with Big Jim Fairclough at his side for support. Williams was in his early thirties and had been stationed in the gold-fields for several years. He was accustomed to difficult assignments; the mining districts were filled with rugged men on the run with little to lose. Many saw no reason to go quietly when the local constabu-lary caught up with them. He might have had Fairclough's towering frame for support, but Williams was no shrinking violet. Left father-less soon after his birth in Wales, he had started working at the age of eight, and after saving enough for a berth on a ship to the colonies had walked 120 miles from Perth to the wheatbelt town of Dandaragan to take up his first job in Australia with a wealthy pastoralist.

Yet the telegram from Perth police headquarters that morning had been different to the usual requests to arrest thieves and violent offenders.

'Albert Williams alias Baron Swanston charged with the wilful murder of Emily Williams at Windsor Victoria on the 24th of December last,' said the telegram. 'Williams under the name of Swanston is now in charge of machinery at Frasers Gold Mine. Arrest at once and wire when effected.'

A detective in Perth had also sent a further warning. The suspect was said to be 'determined and dangerous . . . prevent access to arms and weapons, if necessary handcuffs may be used, also services of special constable if required'.

Constable Williams, according to testimony he gave later in court, put his hand on Swanston's shoulder and told him: 'I arrest you in the Queen's name for the murder of Emily Williams at Windsor, Victoria . . . you need not say anything to me unless you like, but what you do say will be put down and given in evidence at your trial.'

Swanston appeared shocked. 'I shall say nothing,' he said.

But he couldn't help himself.

'I am innocent,' he said, trying to compose himself. 'I have never been to Windsor to the best of my knowledge. I do not know where it is. When I was at Melbourne I was staying at the Cathedral Hotel. The lady there made the remark – I never went out by night. [And] my name is not Williams. My name is Baron Swanston.'

Constable Williams took him to the local lockup and returned to the house accompanied by the manager of the mine. They went through Swanston's possessions and confiscated two large cases, several travelling bags and a wicker basket containing a large amount of women's clothing.

An hour later Swanston sent word he wanted to talk to Constable Williams. He was fishing for details and asked if he could have his newspapers brought to his cell when the daily mail coach arrived. Constable Williams agreed and, after reading the reports about the Windsor murder, Swanston asked to speak to the officer again.

'I can't make out how they can fix upon me as an innocent man,' he told Williams.

'There is many an innocent man arrested on suspicion,' said Williams.

'There is many an innocent man hanged these days. Can you tell me what day Christmas Day fell on? When an innocent man gets into trouble he loses his memory.'

Williams told him it had been a Friday.

'Did anyone see the murder?'

Williams explained that all he knew about the case had been contained in that morning's telegram.

'Someone must have seen the murder or else they could not have put the date – the twenty-fourth of December,' replied Swanston. '. . . There will be a doubt as to this, for no one saw it.'

But Constable Williams detected a significant shift in the mood of his prisoner the following day. His story was already beginning to change.

'I think I know the party who has been murdered,' Swanston told Williams. 'I don't believe anyone would have the heart to murder a girl like that. She was a tender-hearted creature. A man could not help but like her.'

'There is always some motive,' replied Williams. 'Perhaps she was murdered for her money.'

'She had no money,' Swanston said. 'She had not a penny to call her own.'

II.

One of the newspapers Baron Swanston might have read after his arrest was the Perth-based *The Daily News*. It contained a report sourced out of Melbourne stating: 'The detectives believe they have discovered a strong clue concerning the whereabouts of Williams, the alleged perpetrator of the Windsor murder.'

Detectives Henry Cawsey and Bill Considine would claim later that they had wandered into the front bar of Young and Jackson's hotel in Melbourne's Flinders Street one evening several days after Emily's body had been discovered. Frustrated and under pressure from the gruff Superintendent Kennedy and the intense press coverage, they feared their investigation had hit a dead end.

They had identified their suspect as Albert Williams and tele-grammed his description around the country. Passengers from the *Kaiser Wilhelm II*, including Max Hirschfeldt, had given them plenty of information not only about the man's appearance, but his idio-syncrasies as well.

Inquiries with police in the colony of New South Wales suggested his description matched that of a Frederick Bailey Deeming, an English plumber who had served two stints in gaol in Sydney in the 1880s. But Cawsey and Considine were sceptical. Even if Williams and Deeming were the same man, they feared their suspect had probably long since left the colony and was, by early March, overseas and using another alias.

The detectives took their seats at the bar and ordered a round of cold beers. It was the week of Melbourne's record-scorching heatwave when the city's fetid air was close to unbreathable and even human shadows seemed to cringe when struck by the sun's rays.

According to Cawsey and Considine, they were forlornly sipping their drinks when they overheard a man with broken English telling the barman he had been on a steamer travelling to Perth in late January when a fellow passenger had shown him a pair of scissors or pliers made from knitting needles.

Forty years later, retired and revelling in his almost legend-like status as one of the greatest detectives the city had seen, Henry Cawsey would take up the story again with a reporter from *The Herald*.

After listening to the conversation at the bar, 'the two weary detectives were at once all ears,' said *The Herald*. 'They fired questions eagerly at the German, who was a wine and spirit merchant. He told them the stranger on the steamer had given him a card bearing the name Baron Swanston.'

Early the next morning Cawsey and Considine were waiting at the merchant's door. When he arrived he showed them the card. The handwriting was identical to that found on some of the partially burned letters discovered in the home in Windsor. Telegrams were immediately sent to WA. Police there quickly traced Swanston's movements, from his arrival and short stay in Perth through to his journey to Southern Cross. Late that evening 'the reply came back that Frederick Bailey Deeming had been arrested at the Yilgarn gold mine'.

'If Considine and I had not had that drink Deeming might never have been traced,' Cawsey would tell *The Herald*.

Considine, too, dined out on the tale. In an article in *The Argus* several years after Baron Swanston's arrest, the newspaper would recall 'the clue which directly led to the discovery of Deeming's whereabouts – perhaps the most valuable piece of information which any

Victorian detective ever picked up . . . Detective-sergeant Considine took much pleasure in relating how he and his colleague, Cawsey, while having a drink at a city bar, heard a man telling some friends of how he had met a most interesting travelling companion when on his way to Western Australia a few weeks earlier'.

It was a neat and compelling tale that would not have been out of place in a pulp fiction novel: two weary, hard-working, down-on-their-luck detectives walk into a bar, overhear a conversation containing a vital clue in their investigation and, within hours, track down their suspect and solve the case.

But it never happened like that. The man the two detectives claimed to have overheard in the bar was not a German, but a Frenchman called Ambrose Lamandé, who worked for the prestigious Paris-based cognac producer James Prunier and Co.

And the overheard conversation? It was a complete fabrication. Cawsey and Considine might have gone to the bar for a beer, but they did not emerge from it an hour later convinced they had all but solved the case.

Ambrose Lamandé had been reading newspaper accounts of the Windsor murder. The description of the suspect, Albert Williams, had troubled him. His appearance – and mannerisms – were almost identical to a strange fellow he had met on the steamer *Albany*. That fellow – boastful and prone to unpredictable mood swings – had shown him a set of pliers made out of knitting needles (they would later turn out to have been made by Joe Pickering, the husband of Emily's sister, Maria). He told Lamandé he was a wealthy engineer considering a job offer from the WA government at an annual salary of 1000 pounds.

Lamandé contacted Superintendent Kennedy and told him of his concerns. Kennedy, in turn, summoned Cawsey and Considine and ordered them to meet with Lamandé. The Frenchman, he told them, had a business card that belonged to a man calling himself Baron Swanston. He had listed his address in Perth not as the Criterion, but the Shamrock Hotel.

Without Lamandé's story, for which he would receive a reward of twenty-five pounds, the Windsor murder case might not have been solved.

Baron Swanston, said Lamandé, had been an engaging, if eccentric, companion. But several other passengers had formed a different opinion. On the night before the *Albany* sailed out of Melbourne, Swanston had shared dinner with the ship's captain, its purser and a couple, Mr and Mrs Wakeley, who were accompanying their niece, Maud Branch, to Western Australia.

Swanston was in a foul mood. He barked at the captain and purser, telling them the *Albany* was 'not fit to carry dogs'. The purser, trying to lighten the mood, jokingly suggested the ship's usual practice was to 'chain passengers up to their necks'.

According to an account given later by the Wakeleys, Swanston 'got up and stormed out of the cabin in a terrible rage. From that time out he cherished a grievance against the captain and the purser'. When the *Albany* reached Adelaide he summoned local police and, in a repeat of so many of his previous performances, claimed his black dressing case had been stolen and told them he suspected the captain and purser to be the thieves.

After departing Adelaide, Swanston told Wakeley that a portion of his goods had been discovered in one of the city's pawn shops and detectives were certain to arrest the captain and his purser when they docked in WA. By then Wakeley was growing weary of Swanston and his boasting. He claimed he had just signed a 2.5 million pound contract for his English engineering firm. The firm had offered him a sizeable promotion, but he had rejected it because his 'business affairs' in WA offered greater rewards. Wakeley, just as Hirschfeldt and others had done on the *Kaiser Wilhelm II* several months earlier, began challenging his claims. If Swanston's possessions had been recovered in Adelaide, he told him, he would obviously have to return to that city to identify them.

Not a problem, said Swanston. He would appoint a lawyer to act on his behalf in Adelaide.

'But how is your lawyer to identify goods which he has never seen?'

According to Wakeley, Swanston, unable to offer an answer, 'turned on his heels, and needless to say nothing more was heard of the subject'.

The Wakeleys had other reasons to be concerned. Swanston had openly flirted with several women on the *Albany*, one of them a married woman who was travelling to WA to be reunited with her husband. But another target of his affections was their own niece, Maud Branch.

'Take my word,' Mrs Wakeley had warned her husband at one stage. 'That Swanston is either a married man now or has been married and he is not what he represents himself to be.'

A day before the *Albany* reached Western Australia, Swanston approached Mr Wakeley proposing he marry Maud. Until now, he told him, he had been a single man with plenty of money who had been strong and reserved when it came to women. But Miss Branch, he said, was clearly the girl who would make him thoroughly happy.

Wakeley had heard enough.

'Mr Swanston, may I tell you plainly that I don't believe your stories, and that I am not in the habit of allowing men of your class to enter my family circle. If my wife or niece see you on shore they will bow to you, but that is as far as they will go.'

It was the last they heard from Baron Swanston until, a few weeks later, a letter arrived in Fremantle for Maud Branch. The sender was writing from the small mining town of Southern Cross. He had not forgotten Miss Branch. He politely inquired after her health and signed off, expressing his wish that one day he might see her again.

By then, thanks to Lamandé's information, the WA police had tracked Swanston's movements to Southern Cross and ordered Constable Williams to make the arrest.

Three days after that arrest, Swanston composed a letter to Kate Rounsefell from inside his cell in the police lockup.

'My Dear Katie, what I am now about to write you I know will be a heavy blow to you. I was all joy when I got your wire to say you were leaving Bathurst, and I just got the house finished and everything ready for your comfort, and was looking forward to nothing but hap-piness, knowing how happy I could make you, when on Friday . . . I was arrested on a charge of murder of which I know nothing whatever about.

'The murder has taken place near Melbourne and I am being taken from here today on my way to Melbourne for trial, but I don't see that I shall have any trouble in clearing myself, knowing that I am not guilty, and trusting in God to carry me through is my only comfort. I should not say my only comfort, for knowing that my dear Katie will never believe me guilty of such a fearful crime is more than comfort to me. Knowing that your love is steadfast, and that my trouble will draw me nearer to you, is more comfort to me than words can tell. Oh, Katie, were you in trouble would it not be the time you would most need my love and help. Were you at the other end of the world I would come to help and comfort you. Do write to my solicitors, whose address I have inclosed, and tell them that my trouble does not shake your love for me, and that when it is over you will be the same to me as you are now.

'I know that my position is critical, and that many a man has been hung for a crime that he has never been guilty of, but God forbid that it should be so. With the assurance of my Katie's love to the last, and with one look at your dear face again, I can die happy. I don't know that I ever wronged anyone in my life and as for harming anyone, why, Katie, I think you would know I would not harm a cat.

'God has always been my friend, and I have always trusted in God for all the wants of life, and should death, which I do not fear, be my fate in the present case, I know He will not forsake me, and with my Katie's love I shall be strong enough to face it all. Oh, Katie dear, look to God for all your wants; remember me in your prayers and ask Him for your sake to carry me through this fearful trouble; give my love to Lizzie and ask her not to think bad of me. I know she will take care of you until I get this over, then I shall never ask anyone to care for you again but myself. Of course, my situation here will be open to me again, should I think of coming back, and if death is my fate for which what I am not guilty of, all I have in this world will be left to my dear Katie. God bless you. You are all I have in this life. Life without you would not be worth living, so if my trouble alters your love for me, and you think that after such a charge being brought against me you could not marry me, why, then, death would be better than all, for without you I could never live.

'I feel too ill to write more . . .

'P.S. – Dear Katie, if you can send any part of the 20 pounds I sent you to my solicitor to help to pay for my defence, I should be very glad as I have gone to a big expense getting a home ready . . . if you can't send much please sell the five-stone ring I gave you for whatever you can get for it. I will soon get another.'

By the time he finished the letter a large and unusually orderly crowd by Southern Cross standards had gathered in the street near Blizzard Stanbrook's hotel. They looked on as the handcuffed prisoner was bundled into the waiting coach. Then, with Constable Williams by his side, they set off on the 150-mile, four-day journey to York, where a train would be waiting to take them to Perth.

The people of Southern Cross had much to celebrate. A small windswept town perched on an ancient plain sprinkled with gold dust was about to achieve fame as the place where one of the world's most notorious murderers had been captured.

But more importantly, it had begun to rain. The crowd no longer stepped through mounds of ankle-high dust. Every stride was met with a gloriously deep sucking sound as heavy boots were wedged in puddles of thick, beautiful mud. They laughed and cheered as the horse-drawn coach swayed and slid along the rutted and mushy track leading out of town. Three inches of rain had fallen and more was expected in the coming days. In one of the oldest places on earth, the land felt renewed and filled with hope.

III.

Samuel Lowe, the London-based reporter for *The Argus*, had good reason to be pleased with himself. A few days earlier he had been an anonymous journalist charting the prices of butter and milk. But his exclusive interview with Dove Mather had changed everything. That story – and another he was determined to reveal – would, he believed, become the first of a series of 'perhaps the most remarkable coups ever known in the history of Australian journalism'.

Samuel Lowe had proven himself to be the equal, if not the superior, of the best detectives Scotland Yard had to offer. Proof of that surely lay in a comment by one of the Yard's prominent superintendents. He had greeted Lowe with an outstretched hand and said: 'Let me congratulate you upon the smartest piece of detective work that has been done in England for many years.'

But Lowe was not satisfied. He was sure there was more to come. Over the next several days he shuttled between London and Liverpool 'collecting and piecing together all the ravelled ends of hearsay, all the tangled inference, all the stray fibres of circumstantial and direct evidence, until he had made a rope that was strong enough to hang a man'.

What 'kept on intruding into Mr Lowe's busy brain' was the mysterious 'sister' of Albert Williams and her four children who had visited him in Rainhill in the middle of 1891 and stayed for a short time at Dinham Villa. What had happened to them?

'She quite upset his [Lowe's] calculations,' *The Argus* would report later. 'It was odd that, in spite of all his efforts, he could find no trace of her whereabouts. She and her four children were like so many unquiet ghosts that refused to be laid until they were avenged.'

At about the same time as Baron Swanston was leaving Southern Cross in the company of Constable Evan Williams, Lowe had a flash of inspiration. He lifted his hand in the freezing London air and placed it on his forehead. It was wet. 'He was sweating,' reported *The Argus*, 'from sheer excitement.'

What if the cad Albert Williams had also murdered his first wife and four children? The entire world knew that he had buried Emily in a shallow concrete tomb. Lowe had heard from several townsfolk that Williams had also cemented the floors of his rented villa shortly after being visited by the mysterious woman and her children.

Returning to Rainhill, Lowe tracked down Ben Young, a local labourer who had helped Williams complete the cementing of the floors of Dinham Villa's kitchen and scullery (a small ante-room used to wash dishes and launder clothes).

Young showed the reporter into the villa's coach house. Three empty barrels that once contained cement sat near a wall.

'Did you use all the cement out of the three barrels?' asked Lowe.

Ben Young preferred to gather his thoughts before speaking. Lowe waited.

'Naw,' Young finally said.

Lowe was impatient. It was difficult enough deciphering Young's thick Lancashire accent, let alone having to endure the achingly slow moments that passed for conversation with the man.

'How much did you use then?' pushed Lowe. 'For Heaven's sake! Hurry up my good man. It's a matter of life and death.'

Young paused again. Then he explained he had only used the cement from two of the barrels because the third had already been used by Williams before he arrived.

'A knaw nowt aboot this 'ere other won,' said Young. 'It wur empty afoor a got that job.'

It was at that moment that Lowe experienced another of his penetrating insights: 'A great light flashed in upon the amateur detective's brain, illuminating all that was black a moment before, and silhouetting in the sharpest outlines objects which up to that moment had been wrapped in darkness.' Williams, he decided, had killed the woman and children and used the first barrel of cement to hide the bodies. He had then hired others to complete the work.

Lowe made his way to the Rainhill police station and excitedly discussed his epiphany with Constable William Chipchase, who needed little persuasion in taking the theory to the district superintendent.

By nine o'clock the following morning – Wednesday 16 March – a team of four officers led by an inspector from the nearby town of Widnes arrived at Dinham Villa. They searched all the rooms, including upstairs. Then they shut the doors and whitewashed most of the ground floor windows. It did not take long for word to spread that the police were conducting a search of the villa. Lowe, who had accompanied the police, was soon joined by a growing band of local reporters. A crowd of onlookers began forming outside. Within minutes they could hear the sound of pick axes and shovels hammering at the concrete floor of the kitchen.

It was hard going. For three hours they hacked away, concentrating their efforts on a point not far from the kitchen's fireplace. When they finally broke through a layer several inches thick they hit several large concrete hobs so hard their picks rebounded against the surface. They eventually found the edges of the hobs and, using long crowbars, were able to prise them free.

Another layer of cement lay below. At the same time they were assaulted by a stench so strong several officers were forced to rush outside for fresh air. 'There were long hours yet to go though, and an irksome task to be done, before any tangible manifestation of a criminal character could be found,' reported *The Liverpool Post*'s correspondent, who seemed to have spent much of the time during the excavation poring through a thesaurus to help describe the horror before him.

'The police became somewhat exhausted; they were overpowered with offensive odours, and a short relaxation was necessary ere they could unearth the source and origin of the malodorous effluvium,' he wrote. 'Free recourse had to be taken to stimulants, as the kitchen was now like a charnel house.'

They were still at it an hour later when Constable Chipchase, almost waist-deep in the kitchen trench, came across the first of the bodies. It was a small child lying face down. Most of the extremities had decomposed but the body remained tucked in a 'comfortable, warm-looking nightshirt'. Within moments another child's body was found next to it. The young victim appeared to have been strangled; a rope drawn around its neck had been snipped at its ends with a sharp blade.

By then it was early afternoon and the police, exhausted and overcome by the smell and the sight of the remains, took a break. They walked into the village seeking refreshments and the reporters and onlookers used their absence to enter the house and gaze at the horrific scene. 'Human nature could hardly endure to look upon these bodies, so disfigured and mangled were they by human hands, and also by the teeth of time and corruption,' reported the *Post*. 'A few spectators remained gazing in speechless horror at the awful sight . . . the bodies had been adjusted in their graves with some show of skill.'

When the police returned they decided to remove the bodies of the two children in order to continue digging but were quickly overcome by the stench. Eventually a constable with a stronger stomach jumped into the trench, gathered up the body of one of the children and carried it quickly upstairs. A moment later he returned and did the same with the second infant.

When digging resumed a third victim – an adult woman wrapped in an eiderdown bed quilt – was discovered. The body was cut free from the rubble and placed on a wooden board that served as a makeshift stretcher. Four constables then raised the board shoulder-high and began carrying it carefully toward the staircase like a group of pallbearers struggling beneath the weight of a heavy coffin. The highly decomposed corpse looked as if it might fall apart at any moment. As they tried to navigate the steps, the body bounced, swayed and almost fell. Panicked shouting followed until the *Liverpool Post* reporter stepped forward, seized the woman's head and, accompanying the officers up the stairs, held on to it tightly to prevent it falling to the floor. The group finally reached an upstairs bedroom where the woman's body was 'leisurely deposited side by side with the children'.

Samuel Lowe had also been busy. He would later boast that the digging and exhumation of the bodies had been conducted under his supervision. But that would have been impossible because he would have spent most of the day keeping an eye on his watch. There was an eleven-hour time difference between the United Kingdom and the east coast of Australia and he did not have much time to make the first edition of *The Argus*. More than twenty clerks had arrived in Rainhill to assist the swelling army of journalists to cable their stories. Lowe had sent a series of short despatches, the first announcing that police had arrived at the villa and begun taking up its floors. The second, sent several hours later at close to midnight in Melbourne, revealed that 'on taking up the floor of the kitchen, the room in which Williams had done his cementing, the bodies of a woman and of two children were discovered'.

It was sensational news and gave enough time for one of the newspaper's sub-editors to add a breathless paragraph at the top of its main news page. 'The request cabled to England by *The Argus* that special inquiries should be made at Rainhill as to the murderer Williams and his proceedings there has been fully justified by the result . . . it is evident that in capturing Williams the career of the most atrocious criminal of modern days has been at last brought to an end.'

There was more to come. *The Argus* kept its pages open as long as possible for more updates from Lowe. Not long after 3.30am Melbourne time another cable arrived. Two more children's bodies had been discovered.

The small upstairs bedroom in the Rainhill villa resembled a morgue in a war zone. The bodies were left overnight and early the next morning a doctor from Widnes, Donald McLennan, arrived to examine them.

The dead woman was clearly Marie Deeming. Dr McLennan found she had been well-nourished and healthy at the time of death, despite the disfigurement and mummification of her face that had occurred since burial. Her head was thrown back and there was a three-inch deep cut across her throat that had severed her windpipe and all the large blood vessels on both sides of the neck. She was still wearing a blue-striped dressing gown and a black corset. Her under-clothing – white frilled petticoat and drawers – were still intact and a boot and black laced stocking remained on her left foot and leg. Both legs had been drawn up and tied around her calves in a reef knot. She was still wearing a wedding ring on her left finger.

The head of the eldest child, nine-year-old Bertha, was enclosed in a pillow slip tied firmly at the neck with clothesline. Once removed, Dr McLennan quickly concluded she had been strangled. The other three children – Marie, Sydney and Leala, the baby girl – had all had their throats cut with the same severity as their mother. They had all been buried with their heads covered by pillowcases.

As Dr McLennan continued his examination, the police resumed digging in case more bodies lay beneath the concrete. The discoveries had drawn large crowds to Rainhill. Hundreds were gathered outside Dinham Villa and swore they could smell the stench of death. 'The horrors already disclosed had, as it were, whetted the appetites of those around the place,' reported the *Liverpool Post*'s main competitor, *The Mercury*, the next day. 'They were prepared for anything.'

But as the hours passed there were no new developments. The house had given up its ghosts. Yet the crowd outside continued to grow. In the late afternoon, just as the police decided to discontinue digging, a stir worked its way through the group of onlookers.

A short man with muscular shoulders and an imposing moustache had pushed his way through the onlookers and was walking solemnly toward the front door. His eyes were red and his hands trembled. He swallowed constantly. Many in the crowd were locals who had met Albert Williams the previous year.

The man now in front of them was identical to the suspected murderer.

'So closely did he resemble in outward appearance the man who has caused so deep a wave of trouble to pass over this rural village that the natives of the place actually thought that Williams himself had returned to the scene of his fearful crime,' reported the *Mercury*.

For a moment it seemed a lynch mob might be formed to exact retribution on the sadistic murderer. But the police stepped in, making it clear the man was the suspect's brother, Albert John Deeming. He had just arrived from Birkenhead to help formally identify the bodies.

The police ushered him inside and led him upstairs.

He reappeared at the front door a few minutes later. He almost fainted as he stepped outside into the fresh air. He was broken and seemed to have shrunk into himself. Albert Deeming had just seen the remains of his sister-in-law and her family and the shock had left his face ashen.

But it was not the first time Albert had seen that cold concrete grave and all those little bodies in their stained red nightshirts. Seven months earlier he had experienced a nightmare. He had dreamed he was inside this exact villa where the slaughtered bodies of Marie and his nephew and nieces had been packed tightly and expertly into a pit in the kitchen. He was sure this premonition had occurred on the same night Frederick had moved through the rooms of the villa in a murderous rage.

It turned out that Albert and Frederick Deeming didn't just look alike. They also shared an ability to see the dead.

IV.

Baron Swanston fainted twice during the four days the small coach made its way along the boggy road between Southern Cross and York. He was often agitated when he regained consciousness, falling into long bouts of silence and smoking constantly.

It was growing dark when the carriage pulled up in front of the York police station. A large crowd outside pushed and shoved to catch a better glimpse of the man whose alleged crimes were now filling newspapers around the world. They were there the next morning, too; hundreds of them at the train station to watch him begin the journey to Perth. He had slept well and appeared more confident. He paused before stepping off the platform and into the train carriage.

'Ladies and gentlemen,' he announced. 'You need not look at me; I am not guilty, but have been victimised.'

He was seen smiling through the window as the train pulled away. When it reached its next stop at Spencers Brook, the police lowered a set of flimsy blinds to cover the window. Another large group of spectators lunged forward and began ripping the blind away.

Swanston thrust his head out of the window.

'You needn't look at me,' he told them. 'I am perfectly innocent and you'll see me soon on my way back.'

It was like this for the entire journey. Western Australia had never known a celebrity criminal like Baron Swanston. It had boasted its share of villains, including the famous Moondyne Joe, a chronic horse thief and renowned prison escaper who, after serving time, had married a widow and spent time prospecting for gold at Southern Cross. Some colonists still recalled the furore in 1876 that followed the escape of six Irish Fenian prisoners from a convict garrison. They had been picked up in a whaleboat by a group of Irish independence sympathisers and taken to a merchant ship, the *Catalpa*, that had then safely transported them to America.

But Swanston was something else entirely. Bushrangers and Irish patriots could always cling to a set of principles to justify their actions and elicit public sympathy. They could claim they were victims of poverty, persecution or oppression. Swanston was something far darker, his crimes less easy to understand. Perhaps that was why more than five thousand men, women and children were crushed into the Perth station as the train neared the colony's largest city. Mounted troopers patrolled the streets, a prison carriage was drawn up outside and the Chief Police Commissioner was striding up the platform's steps to meet the villain. But it was all a ruse. The train pulled up at the Lord Street level crossing a little further up the line and the prisoner was bundled into a waiting carriage and taken to the waterside lockup.

He was sitting in his small cell when Richard Haynes, a prominent local lawyer, arrived. Haynes had received a telegram from York the previous evening. Signed 'Baron Swanston' it had requested Haynes to meet him at the Perth police station 'on important business'.

A week had passed since Swanston's arrest and Haynes thought he had 'the appearance of a man who had gone through a good deal of mental suffering and bodily exhaustion. He was dressed in a dark waistcoat and trousers, and pair of slippers. His hair was unkempt and he was unshaven.'

Haynes was drawn to Swanston's 'quick, searching, small blue eyes and a rather small head . . . [but] there was nothing in the man to lead one to suppose that he was a murderer'.

Richard Septimus Haynes was a large man known for his bluntness and caustic wit. He had moved from Sydney to Perth seven years earlier and had ambitions to stand for the colony's parliament. A passionate supporter of the eight-hour working day campaign, he was now counsel for the most infamous criminal in the Western world.

'Are you Mr Williams?' he asked Swanston.

'Yes.'

Haynes saw a man agitated 'in consequence of the reception he had met with'. He told him he would see him later in the afternoon. As he left, his client looked up at him.

'The only evidence they can have against me is circumstantial evidence,' he said.

When Haynes returned later that day his client seemed calmer. He asked him where he had come from.

'Well, I came over in the *Albany* from Melbourne, and I am the man Williams who came out in the *Kaiser Wilhelm*.'

Haynes told him that a Melbourne policeman, Detective Cawsey, was on his way to Perth. He was bringing another man with him, Max Hirschfeldt, who would be asked to identify Albert Williams.

'That damned German swine! He will be sure to know me.'

'When he comes to identify you, be as well prepared as possible and, above all things, don't say a word because he might have some doubts about your identity which might be removed upon hearing your voice.'

'Very well.'

Haynes' client then boasted about the improvements he had made to the machinery at Fraser's Mine. He urged Haynes to get in touch with its directors to make sure his salary was paid. He also had another request. Could Haynes make out his will? He rattled off a list of his debts and assets and asked whether his belongings at the mine – a cooking stove, cooking utensils and an air bed he had been using for a mattress – could be sent from Southern Cross.

Haynes said he would look into it. But more importantly, he added, was news emerging from England that police in the English village of Rainhill had arrived at a villa and begun to break up its cemented floors.

Williams grunted but said nothing.

Hundreds gathered outside the Perth Police Court the following morning. But more remarkable was the scene inside. It seemed every justice of the peace in the colony had turned up to watch the hearing. There were dozens of them, all gathered behind the Presiding Magistrate, James Cowan.

Cowan addressed the prisoner as Albert Williams and told him he had been arrested on warrant under the Fugitive Offenders Act of Victoria and that he 'on the 24th day of December last did feloniously, wilfully and on his malice aforethought, kill and murder one Emily Williams'.

It was a brief hearing. The prosecution asked for the prisoner to be remanded for a week until Cawsey and his witness had time to arrive. Cowan granted the request and Haynes asked for a list of all the articles and possessions they had seized from his client.

Although Albert Williams seemed calm and often amused by the proceedings, 'a nervous smile played about his mouth' from time to time. Reporters thought they detected 'a nervous twitching of the lips' behind his large moustache. The *Western Mail* was more curious about what lay below it: 'The appearance of the lower half of his face is rendered very remarkable by a prognathous jaw – in other words his lower jaw projects considerably and has, moreover, a peculiar upward curve.'

When the police completed their inventory of his belongings they came across a silver case with the name 'Emily' engraved on its lid. Inside it was a pair of white silk gloves. There were several photographs, including one of Albert Williams with a girl of about six years of age and a family portrait showing him with a woman and three young children. There was a pocket book listing the Rainhill train timetable, a collection of women's clothing and a prayer book with the inscription of 'Emily'.

When the hearing concluded Haynes returned with Albert Williams to his cell.

'Did they find anything at Rainhill?' Williams asked.

'Yes they did. They found the remains of a woman and three or four children.'

Williams again showed no reaction. Haynes asked him: 'Did you ever live at Rainhill?'

'No. I don't know where it is.'

'Well, they say you are Jack the Ripper.'

Williams grunted. He appeared more interested in the whereabouts of Kate Rounsefell. He was unaware she had arrived in Melbourne a week earlier. The night before she was due to sail for Western Australia to be reunited with him, she had taken an early evening walk with a friend. At a newspaper stand they had bought an afternoon newspaper and read, for the first time, that a Baron Swanston had been arrested in the WA goldfields and charged with the murder of Emily Williams. Shocked, she had approached the police and offered her assistance.

Haynes had wired Rounsefell's sister in Bathurst, learned Kate was in Melbourne 'and that her address was known to the Commissioner of Police'.

'This looks really bad for you,' Haynes said. 'She will give them all the information concerning you.'

'No fear,' said Williams. 'I would trust my life in Katie's hands.'

Haynes asked him again about his movements the previous year in England. Surely he must have stayed in Rainhill. 'If you are the Williams who came out on the *Kaiser Wilhelm*, he had come from Rainhill.'

'I suppose I had better say so.'

Haynes said the man who had lived in Rainhill had also used the name Deeming.

'Oh, that is quite correct. I will tell you all about it afterwards.'

It was one of those rare promises in his life that he would keep. In the coming days Frederick Bailey Deeming would warm to the pugnacious Haynes and reveal a remarkable story of fortune-seeking, betrayal and bigamy that would also include a far-fetched alibi placing him far from the scene of Emily's murder.

As Haynes prepared to leave the cell that Saturday afternoon, his client asked if he could bring a dictionary to him on his next visit.

'I can never spell well,' he admitted, 'and that is always what kills me.'

V.

The parish bell in Rainhill began tolling in the late afternoon of Friday 18 March. For the first time that day, the several thousand people who had flocked to the small English village fell silent.

It had been two days since the discovery of the bodies of Marie Deeming and her four children. With the arrival of every train and horse-drawn carriage, the village had taken on the carnival atmosphere of a summer public holiday. The previous week's snowstorms had been replaced by an endless blue sky and the warm air was filled with laughter and chatter. Women wandered down the main street in fancy coloured shawls and bright hats. Even the men – many of them coal miners and labourers from nearby districts – were shaved and dressed in their finest.

But the pealing of the church bell high in the tower of St Ann's church signalled an end to the festivities. A solemn procession of hundreds of onlookers began marching toward the Anglican church's small cemetery as a hearse and two carriages slowly approached.

'I wish they could bring the wretch over and let him try to walk through Rainhill now,' spat one woman.

Another woman next to her shook her head and stamped her foot in defiance. 'No!' she said. 'Let him be hanged out there [in Australia]. He might be shipwrecked coming over and escape his deserts.'

Several hours earlier many of them had squeezed into the assembly room of the Victoria Hotel when the Coroner of South-West Lancashire, Samuel Brighouse, swore in a jury and opened a formal inquiry into the deaths. The jurists had then gone to Dinham Villa to view the bodies.

On their return Albert Deeming had been the first witness called. His voice broke constantly and rarely rose above a whisper. He identified himself as a fitter in the Laird Brothers shipyard who lived at 55 Canning Street, Birkenhead.

He was certain, he said, that the body of the dead woman he had seen the previous day in Dinham Villa was his sister-in-law, Marie.

Asked what he would call his brother, Albert paused.

'A seaman,' he finally answered.

He was shown a photograph of Marie. He nodded and began to cry. He told the inquiry he and Frederick were married to sisters. Marie Deeming and her children had stayed with Albert and his family for about two years. Frederick had occasionally joined them but was often absent, claiming to be overseas.

Albert had last seen Marie and the children in late July the previous year. Frederick had told him he had leased a house in Rainhill and they would all be staying there for a few days before embarking for either Australia or California. Albert had taken Marie, the children and their luggage to the train station to join Frederick in Rainhill.

At that point Albert broke down. Sobbing heavily, he said he was sure Marie and the children were murdered soon after that.

Brighouse, the coroner, asked him: 'You think at that time?'

'I dreamt it. I knew it. I knew what I was going to see yesterday, seven months ago.'

The room erupted with shouts of astonishment.

The jury's foreman stood up and interrupted: 'You did not know it as a fact.'

Albert continued weeping. He said Frederick had returned to their Birkenhead home several times after Marie and the children had left for Rainhill. Asked where his family was, Frederick repeatedly said they were 'quite well' and had gone to Brighton for a short holiday before they all left as a family for overseas. At one stage Frederick told Albert they were planning to travel to Argentina.

Another brother, Walter, then took the stand and said the last time he had seen Frederick was two years earlier when he had attended his trial in Hull when he had been sentenced to nine months' prison for theft.

Several following witnesses detailed their dealings with the man they knew as Albert Williams. One of them was local labourer Joe Pickering, the husband of Emily's older sister. When Williams began cementing the floors of the kitchen at Dinham Villa, Pickering said, he had not worked into his calculations that a raised floor would prevent the doors from closing. He had wandered over to Pickering's workshop and asked him to remove the doors from their hinges and shorten them.

Pickering would later tell the *Lancashire Evening Post* that Albert Williams was a frequent visitor to his home. He would often sit on one of the workbenches, 'jauntily kicking his feet together and heartily laughing'. He told Pickering he had fought in the Basuta war – a conflict between South African colonialist forces and local Basotho tribes – and during one skirmish had been hit by a bullet in the back of his head. One day he had invited Pickering 'to put his finger in the hole to see for himself what a risk of his life he had run in the service of his country'.

Williams came and went from the rented villa, sleeping most of the time in a room at the Commercial Hotel. He had told several residents that his sister and her children had come to visit and were staying in the sparsely furnished villa for a few days. On the morning of Saturday 25 July Williams arrived at Pickering's home carrying a large blue and white jug. His sister was arriving that day, he said, and he wondered if the Pickerings might be able to supply her with milk for the duration of her visit. A niece of the Pickerings delivered the milk later that day. Over the next two days several locals remembered seeing a woman and several children in the front yard of the house. A local gardener had given two of the children – a young girl and a boy – a basket of strawberries one afternoon. But their mother – short and dark haired – had kept to herself.

Two days later Albert Williams' demeanour had changed. Neighbours reported hearing children crying over that weekend, while one claimed she thought she had heard two adults engaged in a heated argument. When the jug of milk was delivered on the Monday morning Williams refused to fully open the front door. It appeared he was wearing a nightdress but he would not allow himself to be seen. He grabbed the jug with a bare arm and asked for further milk to be left on the front porch for the rest of the week. The woman and her children were never seen after that, and no-one had seen them leave Rainhill. Not long after, Williams had asked Ben Young and others to help cement the floors.

It was uncharacteristic behaviour for Albert Williams. Several locals would say he had spent much of his time in Rainhill adopting a high profile and forging friendships with many of the locals. He had immediately shown an eye for the local women, flirting with a bargirl and a young unattached woman at the local flower show. He had also hosted a gathering at the local hotel, news of which managed to make its way into the pages of a local newspaper, the *Prescot Reporter*.

'On Wednesday evening Mr Albert O. Williams, an Inspector of the Indian Army Service, who is on a short visit to England, and who has taken up his residence in Rainhill while in this country, entertained at the Railway and Commercial Hotel, Rainhill, a number of residents of the village, whose friendship he has made during his sojourn among them.'

Williams footed the bill for a sumptuous meal which included oxtail soup, boiled salmon, roast beef, roast duckling, Snowdon pudding, jellies and creams. There were toasts made to his health and thanks expressed for his generosity and good humour.

'Mr Williams, in reply, thanked his guests for the hearty and kind way in which they had received his name,' said the report in the *Prescot Reporter*. 'He had been in many climes and countries and had mixed with many nationalities, but he must say he had never in his life met a more sociable number of friends than he had done in Rainhill.'

That hotel where he often stayed had been one of several venues visited by the large crowds in the days since the bodies had been found. Hundreds had watched the gravedigger going about his work that morning. Others had stood outside the closed stationery store of Dove Mather before making their way to view Dinham Villa, a house whose owner was now saying would be demolished. Within a fortnight Madame Tussaud and Sons Limited would make a lucrative offer to buy the house, with the intention of reconstructing the rooms damaged during the police excavations.

But late on that Friday afternoon the crowds fell into a respectful silence. The funeral cortege arrived at St Ann's and the five coffins were taken inside the church followed by the tottering Albert Deeming and a group of other relatives and friends of Marie.

The largest coffin bore the inscription:

MARIE DEEMING, AGED 39 YEARS.
'Nothing in my hands I bring,
Simply to Thy cross I cling.'

On the children's coffins were the words 'This lamb shall not perish'.

Thirty minutes later they were lowered into graves in the paupers' enclosure of the church graveyard. The Reverend Thomas Johnson completed the final rites and then turned and addressed the large crowd.

'Thus we have placed in their final resting place the victims of one of the most, if not the most, atrocious tragedies of modern times,' he announced.

'Thus we have placed from human gaze the discovered bodies of the fivefold murder which recently took place in our midst. To warn those present against a similar crime would be an insult to their manhood, such crime being almost without parallel in the annals of brutality.'

Surely, he said, there were lessons to be learned from such a tragedy. Reverend Johnson was speaking from personal experience. He had married Emily to the man calling himself Albert Williams the previous September. He had also been privy to some of the gossip that had swept through Rainhill that Williams was not all he seemed to be. The reverend had privately urged Emily to be cautious. Perhaps she should think again about going ahead with the marriage? But he had quickly been 'censured by the bride-elect for expressing a doubt as to her intended husband's genuineness'. When Williams had entered the vestry for the marriage ceremony he had announced he had just received a telegram from the War Office saying it had decided to award him 300 pounds in recognition of his services to the country. To the reverend it was just another example of the man's crassness and he could 'only pity a young person whose destiny was about to be linked with that of such a man'.

The reverend wanted to make it clear to the large crowd that they should take heed of what had befallen those who had placed their trust in the murderer.

'First, the danger of taking up with strangers,' he said. 'The more plausible the unknown is and the more wealth he exhibits, the more cautious we should be. Diamonds are not as common as pebbles; the boasted possession of wealth does not indicate riches. When strangers praise our weak points, and we respond to the magic touch, we become the victims of a delusion that more or less prevents the exercise of those precautionary safeguards with which unvitiated nature is endowed.

'The painful event also suggests that we should not allow unknown persons to cultivate intimacy with our families. Prevention is always better than cure.'

His comments could easily have been interpreted as a direct criticism of Dove Mather's family. But if it was, it fell on deaf ears.

Dove, overcome by the news of her daughter's murder, had already left town and was staying with relatives in Liverpool.

There was danger, said the reverend, in 'young people taking up with and joining their lives to those whose names and characters are unknown. The momentous functions of life should not be linked to mere boast and glitter.

'What transformed the man into the monster perhaps will never be revealed . . . he must have undergone some marvellous moral trans- formation before he became the monster that the sad and painful revelations of Wednesday prove him to be.'

Reverend Johnson urged everyone to avoid bad companionship. And then he added that if his memory was not defective, there had been a festive event in Rainhill some years previously which had ended 'with people lying helplessly drunk by the wayside in scores'. He was pleased to be able to say that even though thousands of people had thronged the village in the past two days, he had seen 'no-one the worse for drink and everyone had conducted themselves in a decent and orderly manner'.

He spoke too soon. That night the crowds filled the inns of Rainhill. It was as if, after a macabre day spent viewing the crime scene and the heart-wrenching burial of the victims, everyone wanted to forget that the border separating the living from the dead was flimsy and tenuous, that evil, in all its guises, might tap them on the shoulder at any time to tell them their time had come. So they told old stories and sang old songs and drank to their good luck. As the night wore on several 'disputations' erupted and spilled into the streets, forcing police to close every pub and bar ninety minutes earlier than their usual closing time.

It was the most momentous weekend Rainhill's locals had known. By the time it ended so many tales had been told about Frederick Bailey Deeming – *he captured an African lion with his bare hands!* – it seemed the man had left his fingerprints all over the world.

VI.

Was he insane or a self-obsessed, chronic liar? Richard Haynes had never known a client quite like Frederick Deeming. In the days following the first court hearing in Perth, Haynes had watched his client lurch from being a man who spoke with absolute clarity and confidence into a nervous wreck Haynes suspected was contemplating suicide.

Haynes had asked a doctor to examine Deeming for signs of mental illness, thinking it might form part of a defence that could prevent his extradition to Melbourne. The doctor said he could find no evidence of insanity. But if Haynes remained puzzled about the man's split personalities, he was sure of one thing. 'A good many of his statements to me must have been empty bombast,' he would recall. 'In all his narratives, there was one hero, and that was himself.'

There had been several requests for Deeming to pose for a photograph. Deeming had asked Haynes whether he should agree to sit for one and the lawyer firmly advised against it. Potential witnesses asked to identify him at any trial in Melbourne would be influenced by any image they had seen in the newspapers, he told him. At one stage Deeming asked for a razor so he might shave in case he was photographed, but the officer in charge of the cells had refused to grant him one.

'From his strong desire to get a razor and his anxiety to have his will made, I had a strong suspicion that he meant suicide,' Haynes would recall. When a hairdresser was sent to his cell to shave him, Deeming indicated he wanted his moustache removed as well.

'I will take it all off,' he said as the hairdresser lathered his face.

The hairdresser, surprised and unsure what to do, 'looked in amazement' at a police officer who was supervising the visit and asked: 'Am I to take it off?'

'Not the moustache,' the officer said.

'I have not been accustomed to have a moustache on,' said Deeming.

Haynes intervened. 'The removal of the moustache will make it appear to the jury that you had some motive in altering your appearance,' he told him.

'Oh, well,' said Deeming. 'I will have it off, even if I have to break a tumbler and shave it with a piece of glass.'

Two days later detective Henry Cawsey and Max Hirschfeldt arrived in Perth. After conferring with the local police and examining Deeming's belongings seized after his arrest, a meeting was scheduled for the following afternoon so Hirschfeldt could formally identify the prisoner he had met on the *Kaiser Wilhelm II*.

Haynes arrived ten minutes early and found Deeming wearing a pair of thick gold-rimmed spectacles he had requested on the pretence of improving his writing and reading. Haynes, reminding him not to say anything in the presence of Cawsey and Hirschfeldt, asked Deeming if he was apprehensive about the meeting.

'I do feel a little nervous,' he admitted. Haynes had already instructed the guards to give him spirits whenever he needed to relax. He watched Deeming take 'a good large dose of brandy and it seemed to give him new life'.

'Aah,' said Deeming. 'I don't think I shall flinch now.'

Deeming was taken into the corridor outside the cells where Cawsey and Hirschfeldt were waiting. Haynes thought the two visitors seemed nervous. They had come a long way and Hirschfeldt's identification would be vital if a Perth judge agreed to allow Deeming to be extradited to Victoria.

Hirschfeldt didn't need long. Deeming was standing in a group of seven men that included two local plain-clothes detectives who had been pulled in to form a hastily arranged line-up. He was the only man not wearing a coat.

'That is the man,' said Hirschfeldt.

'Which one do you mean?' asked Cawsey. 'Touch him.'

Hirschfeldt touched Deeming.

'Is your name Williams?' Cawsey asked him.

'No.'

Cawsey read from a piece of paper charging Albert Williams with the murder of his wife Emily. Haynes thought he could detect a tremor in Cawsey's voice. But he could also see that Deeming was readying himself to say something.

'Say nothing,' he told his client.

When Cawsey and Hirschfeldt left, Deeming seemed pleased with himself.

'Well, now, how do you think I stood it?' he asked Haynes.

'Very well indeed,' said Haynes.

By then the lawyer had concluded Deeming was an inveterate liar. 'My impression of him is that he is a man incapable of speaking the truth,' Haynes would say. 'In order to make himself out a hero he would coin lies or blacken a man's character, and when asked to give the same account a few hours after, he would give a totally different one.'

Deeming had already begun composing a lengthy statement for Haynes about his time in Rainhill, his marriage to Emily and their journey to Australia. Littered with spelling and grammatical mistakes, the statement claimed that Emily was also a bigamist.

'Many times on the Passage I noticed that my wife was in trouble,' Deeming wrote. 'I begged her to tell me the cause of the same and I would help her out and do all I could if only she would confide in me, but she said if she told me I would never forgive her.

'I told her I would forgive her any wrong she had done if only she would only tell me, I loved her too well not to forgive her, but she told me nothing until we arrived in Adelaide. She then told me she had been married to a man by the name of Hughie Hughes about two years ago unknown to her family and that her Husband had gone to Melbourne about six months before we left England, and begged on me to land in Adelaide but I told her to have no fear whatever took place I would stand by her.'

He had used the surname Drewn to rent a house in Windsor because he feared 'Hughie Hughes' might find them. On a Sunday evening, 20 December, they had attended a service at 'St Porls Cathedral' and as they left a man approached and introduced himself as Emily's husband. He had said if she did not go with him he would have her arrested for bigamy.

'I told her she was to go with him and never to forget that I would always be a brother to her but I could never [be] more now.'

He was not just *heroic* Frederick Deeming, but a man of empathy and grace. After discovering 'Hughie Hughes' had nowhere to live, *charitable* Frederick Deeming suggested the couple take the house in Windsor while he, the *martyr* Frederick Deeming, took a room at the Cathedral Hotel. It turned out that Hughes was an unemployed scoundrel who stole the rent money Deeming gave them. He had then beaten Emily. So *kindly* Frederick Deeming had gone to Windsor to pay a month's rent in advance. He had also organised for their washing to be done.

If anyone had murdered Emily it was the mysterious 'Hughie Hughes'. He was also innocent, he said, of the Rainhill murders.

He had moved to Rainhill to get away from Marie. But after renting Dinham Villa and wooing Emily, he had made several trips to London and when he returned from one of them, 'what do you think I found? My wife and the youngsters had taken possession. You can see the fix I was in. I was about to be married. I told the wife I should never live under the same roof as she did, and I went and lived at the Commercial Hotel in Rainhill.'

How to solve the problem? He turned to a local watchmaker and handyman he had engaged to do odd jobs around the house named Ben – the same slow-talking Ben Young who had shown *The Argus* correspondent Samuel Lowe the barrels of cement at the rear of Dinham Villa.

According to Deeming, the following conversation had taken place:

'I went to Old Ben and said to him "Look here, for heaven's sake, clear my wife and family out of that."'

'Where shall I send them?' says he.

'Anywhere you like,' said I.

'I understand,' said he.

'Well, you will want some money to pay their fares,' said I.

'And a bit more when they arrive,' he said. I gave him 200 pounds and I have not seen Old Ben and my wife and family since.'

Haynes thought the stories dubious, at best. 'That would be a very poor answer to make to a charge of this kind before a jury,' he told Deeming.

'Well, I want you to . . . write to the Inspector of Police at Rainhill, and have them watched,' Deeming said.

To Haynes, Deeming's account had just destroyed any hope of arguing a case of insanity. Insane prisoners were not known to put forward such elaborate alibis.

VII.

The angry mob no longer wanted to see him. They wanted to tear him apart. Before the train shuddered to a halt dozens of them began pummelling on the windows with their fists.

Deeming sat inside the carriage, biting his moustache and hiding his face every time someone managed a brief glimpse of his pale and drawn face. He could hear the cries of the crowd. They were ready to lynch him.

'Murderer!'

'Coward!'

'You only kill women!'

A well-dressed woman thrust her face at the window and shrieked: 'Drag him out. Put him on a pole. There's only a few of us here but we can find a bullock team to tear him to pieces.'

It was Friday 25 March 1892. Cawsey and a group of police had managed to get Deeming out of Perth that morning using a series of decoy vehicles after the judge finally granted his extradition. Richard Haynes had tried his best for his client and turned the crowded court hearing into a series of dogged legal arguments. At one stage he seemed to have succeeded because, according to one report, the hearing was 'ridiculously mismanaged and blundered . . . no solicitor was present to watch the case for the prosecution and combat

Mr Haynes' ingenious arguments'. But the judge eventually ruled he was satisfied that the prisoner was, indeed, Albert Williams, the man sought for the murder of Emily Williams.

Cawsey had thought the worst was behind them as the train finally pulled out of Perth and began the almost twenty-four-hour trek to Albany, where the steamer *Ballaarat* would then take them to Melbourne. But with every station they passed the crowds had grown and their anger increased.

Deeming puffed on a cigar and grew increasingly irritated. He had asked for his spectacles but a quick search had revealed they had been left behind in Perth. He scowled at Cawsey and muttered: 'that's done for a purpose'. He complained about being handcuffed – Cawsey was using a new style of American-made cuffs – and said: 'I don't see the use of those things unless a man's obstreperous.'

He said he had a headache. Max Hirschfeldt offered him smelling salts but Deeming, who could not hide his loathing for the German-born draper, 'ungraciously refused'.

'It's no use,' he told Hirschfeldt. 'The pains are in the back of my head. The Kaffirs smashed my brains and I have not been right since.'

No-one had expected such a large and aggressive crowd at the York station. Deeming, growing increasingly despondent, asked several officers just before the train's arrival to 'stand in front of me. Don't let them see me.'

Sitting near Deeming in the carriage was Davison Symmons, a reporter with *The Argus* who had travelled to Western Australia with Cawsey and Hirschfeldt, and was now accompanying them back to Melbourne.

Symmons, a short Englishman who dabbled in poetry and was regarded as one of the best descriptive writers in the country, had heard the crowds in Perth crying out 'Killer!' and 'Jack the Ripper!'. But much of the abuse had seemed sarcastic rather than violent.

'It was not until York was reached that their attitude changed,' he wrote in his despatch that night. 'The whole of the population for miles around seemed to have gathered on the platform and long before the train drew up to the platform yells and execrations could be heard. The blinds of the carriages were drawn up but these were of the flimsiest construction.

'Before the train stopped the footboards of the carriage on both sides were stormed, and dozens of hands were busy at every window trying to pull down the blind . . . every moment one of the blinds would go down with a crash, and there would be a momentary free fight before it could be closed again.'

When the train finally eased out of York, the 'yells and hootings' only increased.

'Goodbye, old man,' shouted one bystander. 'You're going to get your neck stretched.'

At the next station security was tighter. But the public's distaste for Deeming remained. 'Give him some cement, the murderer,' yelled one bystander.

Deeming looked afraid. 'He lay down at full length on the seat and dropped off into an uneasy sleep,' reported Symmons.

About two hours later he woke and asked for water. 'There was none in the carriage,' wrote Symmons, 'but he was given a little brandy, which he had no sooner swallowed than he fell down in a faint.'

For the next fifteen minutes the passengers in the cabin tried to rouse Deeming.

'Then he was apparently seized with a fit. The four men in the compartment threw themselves upon him, but although his arms were useless his struggles were so desperate that it was hardly possible to hold him. The fit was succeeded by a collapse, and then the seizure was renewed constantly with such violence that the next hour and a half of the journey was nothing but a continual struggle.'

At two in the morning the train reached Katanning and the prisoner fell into a sleep which lasted until later that morning. When he woke, those alongside him were astonished. Deeming looked refreshed 'without the slightest sign of exhaustion'.

He looked at his wrists, which were swollen after his frenzied straining against the handcuffs during the night. 'Hulloo, what's this?' he asked. 'I must have been doing something last night.'

'Nobody answered,' Symmons noted, 'and no-one is able to tell whether the fits were really genuine or not.'

Later that morning the train reached Albany. Rumours of a public lynching failed to materialise and Deeming was taken straight to the local prison where, after being searched and placed in his cell, he showed signs of experiencing another fit. After staging another remarkable recovery, he spent the afternoon in the prison yard under the watch of two constables, playing draughts and practising the shot put. 'In both of these he was defeated, and he excused himself by saying that having a mental strain had unfitted him,' reported Symmons. 'He asked repeatedly for his spectacles and for brandy.'

Cawsey checked on the uncuffed Deeming in his cell at ten o'clock that night and left thinking all was in order. At 5.30 the next morning he returned to prepare him for the sea journey to Melbourne.

Standing in front of him with a triumphant grin on his face was a clean-shaven Deeming. The distinctive ginger moustache was gone. Cawsey was infuriated. When he asked how he had managed to remove it, Deeming laughed and said he had been in need of a shave. An investigation would later reveal he had used a broken shard from a small glass phial he had found in the prison yard. That night he had pretended to go to sleep with the bed covers drawn over his head to block the light from a nearby room occupied by two guards. Over the next few hours he had painstakingly used the glass to remove his whiskers, although it seemed seventy-five per cent of them 'appear to have been plucked out by the roots'. A small pile of hairs were found in a corner of a cell, buried beneath cigar ash.

It was a phenomenal effort and Symmons was left gobsmacked by the man's ingenuity and desperation. 'The whole affair deepens the impression that the fits in the railway carriage were only part of a clever scheme to get his handcuffs taken off,' concluded Symmons. 'They were removed in the gaol, and thus the plot succeeded.

'The effect has been to alter his appearance in the most extraordinary manner. He looks twenty years younger and the whole contour of his features is altered. The change is noticeable especially in the outline of his mouth, chin, and nose. I myself would utterly fail to recognise him.'

That morning the *R.M.S. Ballaarat* raised its anchor and set sail for Melbourne. On board were about 200 marines making their way to Victoria. Cawsey swore in four of them to help watch the prisoner. He also made sure, after the events of the previous night, that Deeming was back in handcuffs.

Over the next few days Deeming showed all the signs of a man being accustomed to life at sea. He drank brandy, smoked cigars incessantly and played draughts and cards with anyone willing to participate. Symmons was one of those who chanced his hand with the prisoner and found the man 'devoted himself to cards with such fidelity, that were he expected to pay his losses the little money found in his possession would have been spent many times over'.

Symmons concluded Deeming was 'a man of very mediocre intelligence, and that pure self-confidence and assertion have accounted for his past successes. For instance, all through his career he has acted on the assumption that mere change of name would conceal his identity, and in endeavouring to hide his tracks he made blunders which no man of ordinary intellect could have perpetrated. He knows how to tell falsehoods, but not how to give them an air of specious reality.'

Deeming even overcame his contempt for Max Hirschfeldt.

'Many innocent men have been hanged,' he told Hirschfeldt. 'I don't want the people of Victoria to put up a statue to my memory after I am dead. If I must die I'll die like a man, but I'll make some revelations first that will astonish the world.'

He talked sparingly about the Windsor murder case, but maintained he would be able to produce a witness who would swear they had seen Emily alive five days after the alleged murder took place. He also asked constantly about Kate Rounsefell.

'Poor little girl,' he said at one stage between cigar puffs. 'She will break her heart over me. I must see her when I get to Melbourne.'

On Friday morning, 1 April, a flotilla of seacraft greeted *Ballaarat* as it made its way through Port Phillip Bay. Hundreds of onlookers were already waiting at St Kilda and by mid-morning their patience was rewarded when a small launch edged close to the pier. A pale Deeming, eyes darting nervously, chewed on the stub of a cigar as he stepped on to the launch. He had made a show of bravado by turning and waving goodbye to the marines gathered on the deck. No-one waved back.

Cawsey, recovering from a bout of seasickness, was joined by Considine on the pier. They led their prisoner toward a waiting carriage as dozens of plain-clothes and uniformed officers kept the baying crowd under control.

'A hundred menacing cries were hurled at the wretched man,' reported *The Age*. 'Knots of men pressed forward vowing vengeance and the whole mass of people seemed about to rush forward. Deeming seemed utterly cowed by this fierce outburst of public hate and he almost collapsed in the grasp of the officers, who had to half lead, half drag him down the jetty.'

Some in the crowd began to fling objects – one piece of wood struck Deeming in the face – before he was shoved into the carriage. The driver immediately thrashed the reins and the horses took off at a full gallop, pedestrians and other horse-drawn vehicles in pursuit.

Deeming was taken straight to the City Watchhouse before being bustled into a courtroom. Everyone stood to attention – 'if the Sovereign had entered the act could not have been more spontaneous' – as Cawsey presented his prisoner to the magistrate and asked for a ten-day remand.

Deeming sported a small pair of borrowed spectacles and stood with a stoop as he was placed in the dock. The reporters strained for a closer look. 'The eyes catch the attention directly,' said *The Age*. 'They are a distinct blemish on the face. The heavy jaw and the large ears combine to complete a repugnant face, made even more repugnant by the terror that is written on it.'

The judge quickly granted Cawsey's request and Deeming, having declined to answer when asked if he had anything to say, was taken from the room. As he left the journalists continued to stare.

'How could such a man be successful with the softer sex?' asked *The Age* reporter. 'The whole face was repellent, and the only explanation of his power over women that suggests itself is that women love a tyrant, and his face has the cast of such a creature of the most pronounced type.'

That afternoon he was sitting in his cell in the Melbourne Gaol when he heard footsteps coming down the hallway. He was in a sullen mood. Another pair of spectacles had been taken from him. When the guards refused to remove his handcuffs, he had sworn at them and threatened to go on a hunger strike. Another guard had been ordered to stand watch inside his cell. He had also been abrupt with his newly appointed solicitor who had visited him shortly after noon.

But most of all he was tired of the procession of onlookers granted permission to view him. He felt like a zoo animal. Members from both of the colony's houses of parliament as well as many lawyers and judges had passed by to stare at him.

When the latest set of footsteps stopped outside his cell Deeming lifted his head and gave his new visitor a hostile stare.

'Why do you stare at me?' he said. 'I don't know you.'

The visitor allowed a small smile to cross his face.

'But I know you, Harry Lawson,' he said.

It was Harry Webster, the former governor of Hull Prison who had found the small balls of soap Deeming had secreted in his bedframe during his 'epileptic seizures' two years earlier. Webster had retired and, having stopped briefly in Melbourne on his way to holiday in New Zealand, agreed to identify Deeming as the man he had known as Harry Lawson.

Deeming was crestfallen. He stared at the floor, jaw clenched, refusing to look up until the smiling Webster left.

PART VI.

'Oh Mama, I'm so frightened'

The Prince of Devils – Making Love in a Volcanic Fashion – 'He Must Die a Coward' – The Future Prime Minister Who Speaks to the Dead – The Trial Begins! – The Singing Canary Loses its Voice – A Question of Madness – His Life Hangs in the Balance – 'The Greatest Criminal of the Century' – Witless Verses of the Condemned Man – A Dramatic Encounter between a Lawyer and a Preacher – Was Deeming Jack the Ripper? – The Fiend is Sent to Hell – His Plea from beyond the Grave – Sidney and Marion's Dramatic Escape from the Haunted House

I.

Sidney Dickinson would never forget the first time he saw Frederick Deeming. It was shortly after ten o'clock on Tuesday morning 5 April 1892, and one of the most despised men in the world had just been led into the coroner's court for the resumption of the inquest into the death of Emily Williams.

As usual Dickinson was never lost for words. 'The prince of devils himself could not have seemed more callous and indifferent,' he observed. 'His evil, magnetic, steely eyes glistened like those of the basilisk above the disdainful lips that were drawn in a sardonic grin, and the strength and inflexibility of purpose which was shown in his projecting, ironlike jaw was repeated in his general bearings and in all the features of a face which seemed set like a flint against the tempest of accusation that lightened and thundered about his head.'

The journalists sitting with Sidney agreed.

'All eyes were fixed upon him to see what kind of human monster he really was,' wrote the reporter for Sydney's *Evening Standard*. 'He is short of stature with a low receding forehead, indicating intellect of a low order, while his ears spread out like Japanese screens before a drawing room door. His cranium tapers behind . . . and corresponds in the opposite direction with his projecting chin.'

Evil steely eyes. An ironlike jaw. A receding forehead. By 1892 the questionable conclusions of an Italian scientist linking physical characteristics to criminality had become established scientific 'fact'.

Twenty years earlier Cesare Lombroso, a former Italian army doctor with a long-standing curiosity about the inner working of the criminal mind, had conducted a post-mortem on the body of a popular Calabrian bandit and arsonist, Giuseppe Villella. After peeling back the skin of Villella's skull, Lombroso noticed a small indentation that seemed strikingly similar to one he had seen in African apes.

Lombroso would never forget that moment of revelation: 'I seemed to see all of a sudden, lighted up as a vast plain under a flaming sky, the problem of the nature of the criminal . . . an atavistic being who reproduces in his person the ferocious instincts of primitive humanity and the inferior animals.'

Lombroso had identified the 'instinctive criminal' doomed by nature to a life of crime: 'Thus were explained anatomically the enormous jaws, high cheek bones, prominent superciliary arches, solitary lines in the palms, extreme size of the orbits, handle shaped or sessile ears found in criminals, savages and apes, insensibility to pain, extremely acute sight, tattooing, excessive idleness, love of orgies and the irresistible craving for evil for its own sake, the desire not only to extinguish life in the victim, but to mutilate the corpse, tear its flesh and drink its blood.'

Theories about the criminal brain in the first half of the nineteenth century had been dominated by the work of a Viennese physician, Franz Gall, whose collection of more than 120 skulls had formed the basis of the pseudo-science of phrenology. Convinced the brain was the physical organ that represented the mind, Gall theorised that a skull's contours and bumps were the map that identified a person's intelligence and personality.

Gall's theories had fallen from favour by the time of Deeming's first court appearance in Melbourne, replaced by Lombroso's work on the tell-tale signs of a criminal. According to Lombroso, offenders usually had asymmetric faces and sloping foreheads while others – presumably pickpockets – boasted excessively long arms. Murderers were prone to large jaws and bent noses and cast cold, glassy stares through bloodshot eyes. Rapists often sported jug ears. Thieves had small, wandering eyes.

Lombroso's work quickly became popular. His claims threaded together many of the popular fancies of the era – from phrenology to palmistry – and coated them in a veneer of scientific respectability. The 'instinctive criminal' was not so much a creature of his environment, forced into crime through desperate circumstances, but born to it. Immorality was not just learned or shaped, but inherited.

An acclaimed French historian, Hippolyte Taine, wrote to Lombroso to congratulate him on his findings. 'You have shown us fierce and lubricious orang-utans with human faces,' he told Lombroso. 'It is evident that as such they cannot act otherwise. If they ravish, steal, and kill it is by virtue of their own nature and their past, but there is all the more reason for destroying them when it has been proved that they will always remain orang-utans.'

By 1892 Lombroso's fame had spread around the world and he was putting the finishing touches to a museum in Turin dedicated to a wide range of crime artefacts, including a collection of plaster death masks of executed criminals (his own head would be preserved in a jar and put on display at his request following his death in 1909). Within a couple of years he would invent an early version of the lie detector by modifying a device called the hydrosphygmograph and use it to measure the blood pressure and pulse of a suspect.

Lombroso was endlessly curious about the world around him, to the point of being manic. He was one of the first to study female sexuality and, as the inquest into Emily's murder resumed, he was putting the finishing touches to a new book he would call *Criminal Woman*, which would canvass the traditionally taboo subjects of lesbianism, masturbation and frigidity. Much of that work, which summed up years of observing criminals and prostitutes, would lead him to conclude that a link existed between left-handedness and degenerate behaviour.

He set an exhausting pace. One of Lombroso's daughters, Paola, would later describe a typical day in her father's busy life that often began with him 'composing on the typewriter, correcting proofs, running from Bocca [his publisher] to the typesetter, from the typesetter to the library and from the library to the laboratory in a frenzy of movement . . . ; and in the evening, not tired and wanting to go to the theatre, to a peregrination of two or three of the city's theatres, taking in the first act at one, paying a flying visit to another and finishing the evening in a third.'

Acclaimed as the father of modern criminology, he appeared as a stern and professorial-looking figure in the photographs taken of him later in life. His lips were pursed, his eyes hooded. An ash white goatee resembling the bobbed tail of a rabbit hung over his chin. The face was fleshy, his hair receding; he looked every inch like a man of science with little interest in anything not based on fact and reason.

Which made Lombroso's late-life conversion to spiritualism all the more surprising.

An atheist for much of his life, he had regarded the rise of the spiritualism movement with disdain. But in the early 1880s he began to wonder if the occult was more than just a passing middle-class fad after friends asked him to examine their teenage daughter who had been sleepwalking, vomiting and feeling tired. Lombroso found the girl could read, see and smell without using her eyes or nose – she could do the same with her hands or even an elbow. He concluded she could see into the future and his opposition to spiritualism and mysticism began to weaken. Lombroso's conversion to occultism was completed a few years later when he met Eusapia Palladino, an illiterate Neapolitan woman acclaimed as one of the world's greatest spirit mediums.

'She is nearly thirty years old and very ignorant,' wrote Arthur Conan Doyle, the creator of Sherlock Holmes and a committed spiritualist, after meeting Palladino. 'Her look is neither fascinating nor endowed with the power which modern criminologists call irresistible.'

But Lombroso had fallen under Palladino's spell and several researchers would later suspect Lombroso became one of Palladino's lovers. Witnesses claimed to have seen Palladino move tables and act as a magnet on objects as far as six feet away. In the years to come she would be repeatedly exposed as a fraud by several investigators. But Lombroso remained in raptures. 'I am filled with confusion and regret that I combated with so much persistence the possibility of the facts called Spiritualistic,' he would write.

But it was Lombroso's work on criminal behaviour – which would influence criminal trials and investigations well into the twentieth century before being dismissed as a ludicrous hodgepodge of superstition and inept science – that had also profoundly inspired a dapper Irishman who had just become Frederick Deeming's lawyer in Melbourne.

Marshall Lyle was in his late twenties and spoke in a 'rich and excitable' Northern Irish brogue. He had emigrated to Australia after graduating with honours in law from Dublin's esteemed Trinity University and had quickly thrown himself into the legal, social and art circles of Melbourne. A passionate lover of music and theatre, he often dressed in a black cloak that, according to one publication, 'gave him the appearance of an old-time Shakespearean actor'. As the inquest into Emily's death resumed, Lyle was in the process of moving out of his cramped office in Chancery Lane and into a more impressive room two blocks away. There, visitors would find a large photograph of the actress Gracie Whiteford hanging above the front door, and his name in gold letters sprawled across the wall.

Deeming had hoped Richard Haynes would represent him in Melbourne but Haynes' calendar was already booked out months ahead. Suspecting Deeming's only chance of escaping the noose would be pleading insanity, Haynes had recommended Lyle, a man passionate in his opposition to capital punishment and known in the Melbourne press as the 'apostle of the insanity defence'.

A year earlier Lyle had defended William Colston, a carpenter and former army sergeant accused of the brutal killing of a man and his wife in the central Victorian country town of Narbethong. The trial was postponed on several occasions as Lyle, who thought Colston 'peculiar' and had seen his face twitch and his tongue often hang from his mouth, sought the advice of doctors. One of them, Dr John Fishbourne, agreed to interview the prisoner despite a warning from Lyle that Colston was penniless and no-one appearing for the defence would be paid.

Fishbourne saw 'certain physical symptoms indicative of brain disease' at his first meeting with Colston and would write later that 'the twitching of the facial and lingual muscles and defect of speech . . . were, to say the least, very suggestive of general paralysis of the insane'.

Fishbourne and Lyle faced an uphill battle. 'To declare the man insane meant a storm of derision from the public and the press, as well as a decided opposition from all Government officials,' wrote Fishbourne in an issue of *The Australian Medical Journal* later that year.

Colston was found guilty and a few days before he was hanged, a teary Lyle visited his client and apologised for not having done enough to save him. He promised to fight on after Colston's death and reform the colony's criminal laws because he 'considered that matters were yet in a barbarian state in regard to the treatment of criminals'.

Lyle then started sobbing. All he could offer Colston, he said, was his belief 'in the existence of a spiritual world' and that his execution would be 'nothing more than a sort of transformation scene'.

But if Lyle was another yet committed spiritualist who believed in an afterlife, more mundane matters involving the material world were hampering his legal career when he began to act on behalf of Frederick Deeming.

'He was a scholar, more interested in prison reform than the practice of the law, and managed by the aid of his chief clerk to eke out an existence,' noted Lionel Lindsay, the brother of the celebrated

Australian artist Norman Lindsay and a member of a group of the Melbourne bohemian set Lyle counted as friends.

A few weeks after Colston was hanged Lyle had written to the colony's Attorney-General complaining that the government had been unwilling to meet his growing expenses.

'I beg to remind you that under present circumstances I am running my business more as a charitable institution than as a source of profit,' he said. He had 'defended Colston as no murderer had ever before been defended' and the task had left him fifty pounds out of pocket.

He had also spent seventy-five pounds defending Oscar Twist, a young man found not guilty of setting on fire a hotel in which he had been working, but who was now serving eighteen months in prison on perjury charges. All he had received for that effort 'was abuse and the offer of a fee of seven guineas'.

And now Marshall Lyle, a passionate supporter of the work of Cesare Lombroso and another committed spiritualist, was about to become the latest person left out of pocket after dealing with Frederick Deeming.

II.

As Sidney Dickinson sat transfixed by the sight of Deeming in the courtroom, the editors of Melbourne's afternoon newspaper, *The Herald*, had decided their first edition would not understate the importance of that day's hearing.

'This is the day of all days in the criminal history of this colony, and indeed, in the history of the whole of the Australasian colonies,' screamed the first edition. 'Upon it is the continuation of the inquest into the circumstances surrounding the death of the woman Emily Mather, whose body was found decomposing in cement in a house at Windsor on 3rd March last.

'The discovery of this body has merely proved the starting point of a long list of terrible crimes unequalled in the history of all the most terrible deeds ever known or heard of or read of in civilised or uncivilised communities.'

In the four days since Deeming's dramatic return to Melbourne there had been a surge in new claims about his life of crime. A newly appointed Victorian police officer, detective Francis Brant, alleged he had met Deeming in the goldfields of South Africa years earlier and suspected the man to have been involved in the grisly murder of a white man and three natives in the seedy outskirts of Johannesburg. He also claimed Deeming and an accomplice had pulled off a series of swindles on the Cape's National Bank and the Great Kruger Mining Company.

The murder claims – Brant had been working as a private detective in Johannesburg at the time – would later be discounted by South African police, who did not believe Deeming was in the city at the time of the slayings.

But Alfred Harford, an actor appearing at the Alexandra Theatre in the appropriately named play *Wilful Murder*, lent weight to Brant's allegations. Harford claimed he, too, had met Deeming in Johannesburg's Theatre Royal in the middle of 1888.

Harford told *The Age* Deeming and two colleagues had obtained an advance of 30,000 pounds from a bank on the strength of an interest in a mine in the Great Kruger goldfield and were intending to go to London to sell that interest to a British company. Harford's claim was an important one. If true, it opened up the possibility that Deeming had made a short visit to England in the autumn of 1888, giving him time to carry out the Jack the Ripper killings.

Deeming, according to Harford, seemed to have 'almost unrestricted entrée' to the Johannesburg theatre. Before he and his two partners departed for England it was decided to give them 'a royal send-off'.

'A supper was accordingly arranged to take place upon the stage of the theatre,' said Harford. 'We passed an evening characterised by much good fellowship, a sentiment which was liberally promoted by the contents of eight cases of the best champagne. Deeming himself, I remember, sang a song in the Lancashire dialect.' The deal eventually fell through, Harford said, when investors realised they were being swindled and the bank eventually took possession of the mine. 'I remember the circumstances well, as I happened to be a small shareholder in the original concern,' he said.

As Harford was making his allegations, a dressmaker in London's East End, described as a 'respectable girl', was contacting the daily newspaper, *The Globe*, to say she was concerned Deeming may have been involved in at least two of the killings in Whitechapel. She had seen a portrait of Deeming in a newspaper the previous weekend and he bore a striking similarity to a man she had known as 'Lawson' in 1888. He had been courting her in London during the autumn and one September evening they had gone walking before parting at 11pm. Two hours later the body of Elizabeth Stride was discovered with her throat slashed in Aldgate. An hour after that, and only a short distance away, the mutilated body of Catherine Eddowes was found by a police constable.

Later that day the girl met with Lawson again, who spoke 'with an intimate knowledge of the details of the tragedies'. He purchased a newspaper and read aloud a report that said the murders had probably taken place after midnight.

'Look at the time!' Lawson said to her. 'I couldn't have committed them, could I?' The comment struck her as strange. The man was 'agitated' and wanted to read as much as he could about the killings. A few days later he disappeared and she never saw him again. But she distinctly remembered how the man 'always made an ostentatious display of his rings, and spoke of his travels abroad'.

They were already calling it 'Deemania'. Witnesses were coming forward from every Australian city and countless small towns with their own accounts of a man who boasted a large moustache, always wore flashy jewellery and was always working a scam.

One of them was Arthur Dingwall, a master plumber, who told the *Evening News* in Sydney: 'We never called Deeming anything but "The Demon" in our shop, and we did so because he was such a thorough liar and thief. He was a thorough blowhard, but a coward withal.'

Dingwall said he and many of his colleagues in Sydney in the 1880s had detested the man, who often left his wife and children at home at night while wooing younger women. Deeming had a high opinion about his ability to attract women and had told Dingwall: 'It's my way. I can capture any girl. Show them the diamonds and promise them plenty of money, and you always win.'

At one stage, Dingwall said, Deeming had pursued a young girl called Amelia who lived in the western Sydney suburb of Homebush. When she learned he was married and refused to see him again, he began a love affair with a barmaid called Annie Spain, who worked at Ackland's Hotel in the eastern suburb of Woollahra. According to Dingwall, Deeming 'paid frequent visits to the hotel, and made love to the girl in a volcanic fashion . . . he showed Miss Spain numerous diamonds and pieces of jewellery, which were all to be hers, and which no doubt he had stolen'.

Deeming promised Miss Spain he was single and 'thus completely deceived, [she] reciprocated his love, and a marriage was arranged – only it was to be quiet, no fuss, no bridesmaids or anything of that kind'. But Miss Spain soon 'got word of the fact that Deeming was a scoundrel and so, when on the next occasion he arrived, he got a tumbler thrown at his head. The deception told so severely on Miss Spain, who was then in delicate health, that she fell ill, and within three months was in her grave.'

The story might easily have been dismissed as yet another of the apocryphal Deeming tales consuming so much newspaper space. But Dingwall's account was detailed, in keeping with Deeming's behaviour during his years in Sydney and supported by a small funeral notice published in *The Sydney Morning Herald* in late November 1886 that read: 'The friends of Mrs Annie Spain are respectfully invited to attend the funeral of her beloved daughter, Annie Spain, aged 21 years.'

—

Deeming was in an aggressive mood when he entered the court for the resumption of the coronial inquiry. He met the stares of those he walked past and, when he reached the dock, asked Marshall Lyle for a chair. He then leaned back and, crossing his right leg over the left, looked on uninterestedly as the coroner, James Neild, read out the previous testimony from two weeks earlier. When Neild finished, Deeming laughed and leaned forward to Lyle and told him the coroner was 'the funniest little man I've ever seen'.

But Sidney Dickinson believed this show of bravado disguised the man's fragile state. 'Despite his semblance of ease, Deeming, in periods of abstraction, is visibly haggard,' he told readers of *The New York Times*. 'He has lost flesh, and his features are becoming pointed. The gaol warders keep a close watch upon him at all times, for it is believed that he will kill himself if he gets the chance.

'That his vanity is overwhelming was shown during the inquest. During the reading of evidence against him, every word of which led him nearer the gallows, he indulged in a prolonged scrutiny of the public, who filled the galleries of the City Court room, and then, turning to those nearer him, he audibly remarked: "Those are all good looking girls in the front." He straightened up, adjusted his collar and necktie, and said: "I wish I had better clothes, I would be more presentable."'

The press was dumbfounded by the large number of women who had secured passes for the hearing. Some had earlier gained entry to a large holding yard behind the court where Deeming, along with ninety other prisoners, had been held for identification purposes. One woman had approached him and offered her hand for him to kiss. A reporter standing nearby watched as Deeming 'smilingly declined to recognise the outward token of amity. He smiled, however, but his smile was not such as one would think would attract even the most impressionable girl.'

It was a widely held nineteenth century belief that women of most classes were delicate and frail creatures, morally superior to their male counterparts but feeble and prone to hysterical outbursts. A courtroom examining gruesome crimes was considered no place for the fairer sex.

'It may be remarked,' said *The Age*, 'that the majority of the ladies present appeared to resemble those who crammed a court on one occasion when the celebrated Mr Justice Maule was trying a case. The evidence was by no means adapted for the ears of delicate women and one of the counsel in the case, recognising this, asked the judge to order all ladies out of court. "All ladies," replied the judge, "have long since left."'

There would be few surprises in the evidence that followed. Much of the testimony of those who had met 'Albert Williams' after his arrival on the *Kaiser Wilhelm II* had already been widely reported. But Deeming began to take more notice when Max Hirschfeldt took the stand.

Hirschfeldt was asked by Robert Walsh, the Queen's Counsel assisting the coroner, if he had noticed Emily Williams wearing a certain ring during the voyage to Australia.

'The one produced looks very much like the one I have seen on Mrs Williams,' Hirschfeldt said.

Deeming interjected: 'You might get 500 of the same kind of rings.'

Hirschfeldt went on to identify a wicker chair, the canary and its cage, and a dress and several ornaments Emily had worn on the *Kaiser Wilhelm II*. At one point Deeming smiled and said loudly to Lyle: 'This is as good as a show: I wonder they don't bring the hearthstone . . . this is really amusing.'

Hirschfeldt then told the court about his dealings with Deeming during the journey back to Melbourne on the *Ballaarat* after helping identify Deeming in Perth.

'I went into his room and we conversed about various matters,' Hirschfeldt said. 'We also played cards and draughts and then we conversed about the murdered woman. He asked me what she looked like, how she appeared, how I was able to identify her, and what points of identification I had, and so forth. He also said to me, "I don't suppose anybody could hurt my poor little Emily, my poor little woman."'

Walsh: 'Did you have any other conversations?'

'Yes, we spoke about the moustache business. I said to him: "You have prejudiced the public against you to a great extent by taking off your moustache, and you will hang for it." He replied "You cannot swear that that is my proper moustache" and I then said to him: "I can swear to it, and you will be hung for it as sure as God made little apples."'

The court erupted with laughter.

'What else took place between you?'

'Williams said that if he was convicted he would write a history of his life which would startle the world.'

More laughter, some of it uncomfortable, followed. Neild called for silence. This was an inquest into a horrible murder of a young woman, he said, and there would be no allowance for levity. He would admonish the courtroom several times for laughing and sniggering, at one point warning them: 'There must be no jocularity here. This is a serious and terrible occasion and any person indulging in jocularity will have to retire.'

When Neild adjourned the hearing for lunch, Deeming was taken by Cawsey to the holding cells at the rear of the court. They walked down a narrow corridor crowded with witnesses who would be called to give testimony that afternoon. One of them was Simeon Solomon, the art dealer who had purchased Deeming's canary and its cage for three pounds at his auction in January.

Without warning Deeming stepped forward and swung a punch at Solomon. His left fist struck Solomon on the jaw and sent him sprawling. Cawsey pushed Deeming forward, only to find him taking a swing at another witness, John Wood, the ironmonger who had delivered the bags of cement to the house in Windsor. Wood ducked the blow and Cawsey grabbed his prisoner and hauled him off to the cells.

The following day Solomon took the stand and briefly told the court how, after purchasing the bird and cage, Deeming had asked him to look after the bird.

The coroner turned to Marshall Lyle and said: 'Any questions to ask the witness?'

'No, sir.'

At that point Deeming interrupted. 'Ask him how his eye is.' The gallery, aware of the altercation the previous day, laughed. Deeming appeared pleased with himself.

But the witness everyone was waiting for was Kate Rounsefell. When her name was called in the middle of the morning 'there was a general buzz of excitement', reported *The Age*, 'and the "ladies" present appeared profoundly interested'. Rounsefell's voice was almost a whisper when she began giving evidence by telling the court she was now residing with Max Hirschfeldt and his wife in Melbourne.

Walsh asked her to speak up.

'Shout out, Kate!' yelled Deeming.

She ignored him but raised her voice. She recounted her first meeting with Baron Swanston. In Sydney he had proposed marriage, which she had rejected because she did not know him well enough. It had not been until a few days after reaching her sister's home in Bathurst that she agreed to become his wife. He had given her a couple of rings, which were noted in court as being the same ones stolen from a Melbourne jeweller.

Rounsefell also provided the hearing with several letters Swanston had written to her, including one from Southern Cross which had read in part: 'You are now my property, and I expect it to be handed over to me in as good a condition as I left it.'

Deeming was in a sour mood on the final day of the inquest. His face was pale and his features pinched. He had been refused a glass of steadying brandy in gaol that morning and had retaliated by calling the governor 'all sorts of names'. As he entered the City Court he passed a small group of men and when one pointed his finger at him and began laughing, Deeming snatched the man's hat from his head 'with a lightening movement of his left hand' and dashed it 'full in the face of the nearest bystander'. He was immediately pinioned by the police and was led away, smiling.

The courtroom was again crowded and 'again the deplorable presence of women is noticeable', reported *The Herald*. 'The wretched infatuation a certain class have for the most horrid events has drawn them hither.'

At least one member of this 'wretched class' seemed to be livid with Coroner Neild's conduct of the inquiry. Neild swore in the jury once more and then informed them he had just received a threatening letter that he would immediately hand to the police for investigation.

'Dr Neild – I warn you that if you do not conduct Mr Deeming's inquiry in an impartial manner it will be worse for you,' began the letter. 'The poor fellow is not getting justice, as you, the jurymen and detectives are prejudiced. You ought to adjourn the inquest for six months to allow public excitement to abate. From the opinions I have heard expressed in court from other ladies, I do not think Mr Deeming will want for funds to defend his life. I for one will anonymously subscribe for that purpose. You can take this warning as you like, but I shall certainly do you an injury by attempting your life in open court, notwithstanding your allowing witnesses only in court, or those interested in the case. I will [take] the detectives at a future time. Yours &c. LILLIE.'

There were loud gasps in the crowd. But Sidney Dickinson was more interested in the man in front of him. For three days he had watched Deeming's heckling and interjections, his eyes glistening 'like those of the basilisk as he looked boldly and with a sort of savage bravado at the faces about him'. When the canary had been produced he had cried out, 'Hullo! Here comes the menagerie! Why don't the band play?' A reporter taking notes near him was writing 'like a hen'. When more evidence was tendered – including a list of his belongings seized at Southern Cross – he exclaimed, 'Why don't they bring the spade and cement.' The voice of Richard Walsh, QC, was weak and sounded like 'a consumptive shrimp'.

Just before midday Walsh began summing up for the jury by saying the large mass of evidence would lead them to conclude that Emily Williams had been killed by the man they knew in the courtroom as Albert Williams.

Walsh said he had not mentioned all the names the prisoner had assumed over the years and even though his real name appeared to be Frederick Bailey Deeming, it was enough for the jury to refer to him simply as Williams because more than twenty witnesses had now identified him.

Then it was Marshall Lyle's turn to speak. He referred to Deeming as 'this abnormal offspring of a mother's womb' and what he most desired was to prepare the man's case for any potential murder charge and 'secure for this creature' a fair trial.

Any defence, Lyle said, 'would open up a question that every English-speaking community in the world must face sooner or later. It was a defence which some of the countries of Europe had faced, and which many learned men were giving their attention to at the present time.'

It only took the jury forty minutes to return with its finding that Albert Williams did 'feloniously, wilfully and with malice afore-thought kill and murder the said Emily Williams'.

Sidney Dickinson looked across and saw Deeming smiling.

The coroner turned to Deeming. 'The jury having returned a verdict of wilful murder against you, it is my duty to commit you on that charge to take your trial at the Criminal Sessions . . . I shall now issue my warrant.'

Deeming was now standing. In a shrill cackling voice he shouted: 'And when you have got it you can put it in your pipe and smoke it!' Some in the crowd groaned. Others hissed and booed at the prisoner. Dickinson watched as Deeming looked around the room 'with a demoniac grin as if expecting applause for an effective bit of repartee'.

'I beg you will take no notice of any remark he may make,' said Neild. 'This court is adjourned. *Sine die.*'

Dickinson kept his eyes on Deeming. 'As the constables seized him and dragged him to the door, his eyes fell upon a comely young woman standing on the edge of the crowd who regarded him with horrified amazement.

'Breaking away from the officers, he danced up to her, chucked her under the chin and with his leering face close to hers, ejaculated: "Oh, you ducky, ducky!" and disappeared amid the cries of the scandalised lookers-on.'

III.

Marshall Lyle had grappled with several difficult cases in recent years but nothing compared to the task he now faced trying to save Frederick Deeming from the gallows. A fair trial seemed impossible; every newspaper in the country, from small two-page country news-letters through to the mass circulating city mastheads, had turned the Windsor and Rainhill tragedies into a daily soap opera. Deeming's behaviour at the inquest had only fuelled public loathing for the man.

The evidence, too, was overwhelming and contradicted every alibi and excuse Deeming had offered. If, as Deeming claimed, Emily Williams was alive and living with her supposed first husband 'Hughie Hughes' at the time of the murders, why had Deeming written to Emily's mother four days after Christmas saying she was well? How could he explain why a trunk of her clothing and effects – some of which appeared to be bloodstained – had been in his possession when he was arrested at Southern Cross? The blade of a battle axe found in his luggage perfectly matched the crescent-shaped cut found at the rear of Emily's skull during the post-mortem.

The day after the inquest another large trunk addressed to a 'Mrs L. Dobs' had been identified at Bairnsdale train station. A curious stationmaster, thinking the name might be a truncated version of the 'Mr Dobson' who had visited Gippsland late the previous year, had forwarded the luggage to the police. Cawsey and Considine then discovered a key found in Deeming's belongings at Southern Cross opened the trunk. Inside was a large amount of women's clothing, as well as hats, floral wreaths and collars. Attached to some of the clothes, which had been washed and neatly folded, were receipts from the Hamburg Laundry in Windsor that Deeming had used at the time of the murder. Hiding potential evidence by sending it to a remote train station was also a ploy he had used after the Rainhill murders, when a box of clothes belonging to Marie and the children had been sent down a country line and left uncollected for six months.

Lyle had only two weeks to prepare for the trial. There would be no point hiding Deeming's guilt, despite his strident denials. Pleading insanity would be the only logical defence.

Having learned that Deeming had several brothers still alive in Birkenhead, Lyle had telegrammed London asking a legal firm to obtain statements from Frederick's family in Birkenhead about his erratic childhood behaviour. He had also contacted several doctors claiming to be experts in the fledgling field of mental illness.

One of them, Dr Stephen Mannington Caffyn, was an eccentric character the late nineteenth century specialised in producing. He stuttered when he spoke and was very thin with 'dishevelled hair which shook while he gesticulated'. He had just published two novels. The first, *Miss Milne and I*, the tale of a London doctor blackmailed by a female patient, was about to be reprinted for the fourth time. He was also busy promoting his new invention – a beef juice with a malt extract he had dubbed 'Liquor Carnis' and which he was now exporting overseas.

Lyle had obtained a pass for Caffyn to attend the coronial inquest, hoping his observations of Deeming might prove useful in the coming trial. Caffyn quickly concluded the man was unstable. After three days meeting with Deeming and studying his behaviour, he decided he wanted nothing more to do with the case. The public pressure for the man to hang was too much for Caffyn to cope with, as he told a reporter from *The Herald*.

'I am retiring from it now,' Caffyn announced, 'not because there is any want of evidence to show that Williams is a lunatic, which is self-evident to any student of criminology, but on account of my being quite unable to stand the torrent of hysteria which characterises the prosecution.

'I recognise the absolute impossibility of being heard in this community which has already prejudged the man. Educated men decline to help me in the matter because we are quite unable to stand the torrent of public abuse.'

Caffyn had read much of Cesare Lombroso's pioneering work on the criminal mind and believed Deeming had an unusually small head for his height. It reminded Caffyn of the skull Lombroso had examined of a homicidal maniac who had shot a man and his wife back in 1842.

Deeming, he said, 'belongs to a special order of criminals known among students as "instinctive criminals". That is to say, he is as much wanting in moral sense as a blind man is in the sense of seeing. It is as much a part of his nature to kill as to eat.

'The man's whole character is one of extreme stupidity. His jokes are either coarse or idiotic, and his escape so far is less due to cunning than to accident. I was leaning over his chair conversing with him whilst we were waiting for the verdict of the jury, and his little jokes, his inconsequential remarks and the indifference he assumed quite corresponded with the history of every man of his order.'

But if Caffyn felt overwhelmed by the intense public hatred for Deeming, he was hardly innocent of bias, either. 'He must die a coward,' said Caffyn. 'Although I have to some extent interested myself in this man's defence, I would willingly supply the rope to hang him if it were necessary.'

At least Lyle had won the confidence of Deeming. He had given his client a quill and foolscap paper to comment on the evidence tendered by witnesses and record his own version of events. Deeming had also promised Lyle to begin work on an autobiography that, he assured his lawyer, would be filled with sensational claims and could be sold for a high price to meet his legal bills. Some of the proceeds, he told Lyle, should also go to Kate Rounsefell, to 'compensate her for the worry and annoyance of which he [had] been the cause'.

It seemed a fair trade to the money-strapped Lyle and when newspapers began reporting that Deeming was writing his life story – information presumably leaked by Lyle – offers to publish the manuscript quickly arrived, including an enormous offer of 2000 pounds from London's City Press Agency.

But Deeming remained a difficult prisoner. When his regular supply of brandy was stopped by Melbourne Gaol's resident doctor, Andrew Shields, Deeming retaliated by drinking three pots of ink supplied for his writing endeavours. 'He emptied the first pot of ink in five minutes, and the second disappeared in three,' said one report. 'Then the warder watched him and found that the third would have disappeared in even less time had he not stopped it on the way to his mouth . . . after this the ink was watered, and given in small quantities.'

If Deeming had attracted support from a small group of female fans, public sympathy remained overwhelmingly on the side of his murdered wife. Melbourne City Council's Assistant Inspector of Public Nuisances, Edward Thunderbolt, had contacted *The Argus* not long after the identification of Emily's body and advised them he was a family friend of the Mathers in Rainhill and intended to set up a public subscription so that a monument might be erected to commemorate Emily's life.

Thunderbolt was a familiar Melbourne figure. He was a part-time inventor who had patented a new mechanism he claimed would revolutionise the way train doors closed. He also considered himself to be an expert in matters of public health, lending support to a local judge who had expressed concern about the practice of witnesses kissing the Bible when swearing an oath. Thunderbolt wholeheartedly agreed. He said he was aware of a case where a young woman had contracted cancer and died within three months after kissing a Bible which had previously touched the lips of a cancer sufferer.

Thunderbolt had been working in a small town not far from Rainhill in 1877 and visited the Mather family's stationery store each day for his newspapers and mail. 'The books it contained were few and cheap and the chief business seemed to be the sale of papers,' Thunderbolt told *The Argus*. Dove's husband, John, was still alive at the time and Emily was only young and one of several children. 'Though evidently poor they were much respected . . . they were strict Methodists and Mrs Mather especially appeared to be a religious woman in the best sense of the term.'

Thunderbolt, as many of his letters in later years would confirm, had a habit of inserting himself into most of his stories and his encounter with the Mathers was no different.

One night a Roman Catholic chapel in Rainhill had been struck by lightning and Thunderbolt, who had happened to be walking home during the storm, was the first to raise the alarm. 'He remembers that this formed the subject of much chaffing in the little stationer's shop, the girls seeming to think it very appropriate that a Thunderbolt should be a leading actor in a thunderstorm,' reported *The Argus*.

IV.

To save Frederick Deeming from the rope, Marshall Lyle turned to a barrister and fellow spiritualist who for much of his life had seemed more comfortable dealing with the dead than the living.

Alfred Deakin was a tall man who often felt small. He had been so conscious of his height as a young man he developed a stoop. It was as if he found the real world so mystifying that the best way of combating its shadows and terrors was to shrink and hide. By April 1892 he was thirty-five, married and a prominent political and legal figure in the Australian colonies. Ahead of him lay a career that would see him praised as a visionary and champion of reform, a man who would become the leading voice behind his newly formed nation's constitution and its second prime minister. But he still had to remind himself to stand straight, to push his shoulders back and lift his head and raise a jaw buried beneath a thick and lustrous black beard.

He was a man who had known success and enjoyed the admiration of others. Yet he remained haunted by self-doubt. On the evening of his thirty-fourth birthday he had sat at his desk and written in his diary: 'Youth is past and manhood unfolded to its full but I find myself still feeble, still doubting, still uncertain of my life and part.'

Deakin exercised regularly. He never swore or drank. He liked to read and write poetry. He disliked conflict which, for a man immersed in the robust politics of the Victorian colony, only heightened his anxieties. He had been a vegetarian, although he had recently started eating meat sparingly. He had read the work of mystics, studied the ancient philosophers and could quote long passages from the Bible. Like most spiritualists, he rejected much of the Old Testament.

He had a rich baritone voice and could quieten even the rowdiest of crowds. His eyes – dark brown and deep set – were said to have mesmeric qualities, capable of holding a visitor's gaze even though he was, at heart, shy and aloof.

The introverted Deakin, who had spent much of his earlier years peering into the abyss in the hope he might see God's signature and find a meaning to life, had worked with Lyle months earlier on a previous case. Deakin's political career in Victoria was faltering and he had decided to return to the bar to make money after a large chunk of his family's fortune was lost in the colony's property market collapse.

Deakin was humiliated by the loss of several hundred pounds and felt his reputation was at stake. Until the end of the previous year he had been chairman of the City of Melbourne Building Society, a seemingly safe enough sinecure which gave a man greater status in the parlours of the town's private men's clubs. But the building society's funds soon dried up. The night before he was due to address a meeting of angry shareholders Deakin had been stricken with his usual anxiety. 'Disaster has overtaken me at last O God!' he wrote in his diary. 'And upon me lies in some degree the responsibility for disaster to many others.'

The next day he was racked with nerves. He walked to the podium and saw the hurt and frustration among the shareholders. The room was like a pot on the simmer, roiling and ready to erupt. The investors glared and sneered back at him. He took a deep breath and unleashed that powerful baritone voice. A reporter for the weekly journal *Bohemia* watched on almost incredulously as Deakin swept all the panic from the room, transforming those frustrated investors 'from a den of roaring lions to a nest of suckling doves'.

That speech bought the building society a little time before its inevitable liquidation. But Deakin had been right. Disaster had overtaken him. His political career had stalled and with 300 pounds of the family savings lost in the colony's great property crash, he had returned to the law and hung out his shingle as a barrister to recover some of the losses.

Lyle made it clear to him in his brief that the Deeming case would not be a profitable one. But it was a case that had attracted worldwide interest and being associated with it might well lead to more lucrative work. It also offered Deakin an opportunity to reacquaint himself with a world he was only too familiar with – that spirit world with all its tantalising glimpses of the afterlife, and all its angels and demons.

One of his first spiritual experiences had been at a séance years earlier when a medium insisted Deakin would wed an auburn-haired girl. Deakin had spent his teenage years searching for spiritual truths. He had pored over the works of history's great philosophers, among them the eighteenth century Swedish philosopher and mystic Emanuel Swedenborg, whose nights were filled with strange dreams and visions of Christ and who had proposed that death was merely a first step in the journey of the human spirit.

It did not take long for Deakin to be drawn into the occult. At sixteen he believed he had hypnotic powers and could summon a young man from another room by issuing a series of mental commands. He could then 'imprison him' by waving his hands around the man's body. In his later years he would consider his submissiveness to spirituality 'by no means a manly state of mind'. But there was clearly, he thought, some kind of connection between the real and ethereal worlds. Such was his passion for the subject he had been invited to join a select group attending séances run by Dr James Motherwell, an Irish-born doctor and prominent Melbourne identity. The young Deakin had quickly found success as a medium, channelling the words and wishes of the dead.

At eighteen he became a leader in a Sunday school for spiritualists known as the Lyceum, whose aim was 'the spiritual, moral and intellectual elevation of its members'. Among the children in his class was fourteen-year-old auburn-haired Pattie Browne, the eldest daughter of the opinionated Hugh Junor Browne, a distiller who had converted to spiritualism when his dead father sent messages to him during a séance. Inevitably, Browne became a running joke around town – a man who not only created spirits, but spoke to them, too.

The Browne family were fixated with spiritualism and Pattie, their third child and eldest daughter, soon became the focal point in their efforts to communicate with the dead. During a family séance a pencil had been passed to Pattie, who suddenly cried out: 'Oh Mama, I'm so frightened, my hand is writing.'

The pressure placed on a prepubescent girl to reach out to the spirit world became immense. She was soon able to summon the ghost of Archie, an older and much-loved brother. 'He has written a long communication to Mama and Papa and wishes them not to grieve,' she claimed. Not long after that her abilities included summoning luminaries of the afterlife such as William Shakespeare.

Deakin, captivated by the girl's talents and mindful of the medium's prediction that he would wed an auburn-haired girl, waited four years before proposing. Despite the objections of Pattie's parents – they thought Deakin 'rather too delicate . . . for a strong-willed girl' – he married Pattie shortly after she had turned eighteen and quickly discovered the waiting had been worth it. Their wedding night, he confided in his diary, had been 'beyond control, beyond recall, lip flew to lip, love all in all'.

By the time they were midway through their ten-day honeymoon in Tasmania, Pattie discovered Alfred was not quite the quiet and introspective man her family believed him to be. He could not stop talking. Perhaps he was nervous, afraid of the awkward silences that can punctuate conversations early in a relationship before a couple becomes comfortable when there is nothing to be said. They took long walks and visited many historical sites, including the Port Arthur penal settlement. Alfred gave a running commentary about everything they saw and experienced. He recited the gothic history of the island and, when he started running out of things to say, began quoting the great poets like Wordsworth and Emerson.

'What an old mind for such a young man,' Pattie thought to herself.

That old mind would be fully tested by the Deeming case. Deakin and Lyle agreed an insanity defence was the only logical tactic. But proving it would be enormously difficult. They had to show Deeming was suffering from a disease of the mind, an illness the medical world and the legal system could not agree upon. The law was still relying on an 1843 decision in the case of a Scottish wood-turner who had shot the English prime minister's private secretary. The prosecution and defence in that case had agreed the culprit – usually referred to as Daniel M'Naghten – suffered from 'delusions of persecution' and the jury had quickly found him not guilty on the grounds of insanity.

The verdict was controversial and triggered a frenzy of criticism. Queen Victoria complained to the prime minister about it. The House of Lords, in an attempt to quell growing public outrage, reverted to an ancient but rarely used right to question a dozen senior judges in a bid to obtain a definitive answer to the vexed issue of insanity.

What emerged became law: 'To establish a defence on the grounds of insanity it must be clearly proved, that at the time of committing the act, the party accused was labouring under such a defect of reason from disease of the mind, as not to know the nature and quality of the act he was doing, or if he did know it, that he did not know that what he was doing was wrong.'

But what did 'disease of the mind' really mean? To make matters more complex, Lyle wanted Deakin to employ Lombroso's hypothesis of the 'instinctive criminal' in the hope it might enshrine Lombroso's theory in law. It would be a triumph – not just for Lyle and Deeming's legal team, but also for the Italian professor.

In the years to come Lyle would send Lombroso photographs of dozens of convicted Melbourne criminals and regale him with all the details of the Deeming case. Lombroso, in turn, would tell Lyle he believed Deeming had been a 'Napoleonic criminal' capable of slaughter on a mass scale.

Lyle would write back to Lombroso with a sense of satisfaction.

'When you said he was Napoleonic you confirmed what I said at the time. By-the-bye, have you read Herbert Spencer's indictment of the "man of destiny" to be found in his introduction to the *Study of Sociology*? He puts the great Napoleon in the position of, perhaps, the world's greatest criminal. I think it is highly desirable in the interests of morality that a big scoundrel should be shown up. Just at present we have a sort of hero-worship going on; we have Napoleon plays in our theatres, and the people who will execrate the name of a Deeming, will worship a bigger murderer, Napoleon! I have no love for militarism but I confess I have a loving for the Duke of Wellington. For as you know he smashed up Bonaparte.'

By far the greatest hurdle faced by Lyle and Deakin was their client. Since his return to Melbourne he had begun claiming his dead mother was visiting him each night in his cell at 2am. A succession of doctors had examined the prisoner, including Melbourne Gaol's resident doctor, Andrew Shields.

Shields had allowed Deeming a small amount of brandy and water most evenings, which the prisoner 'drank with avidity'.

But when Dr Shields returned the next day and said he hoped Deeming had enjoyed a good night's sleep he found Deeming surly and antagonistic.

'I should have rested well after that dose of poison you gave me,' he snarled at Shields.

'Poison? It was brandy and water.'

'I know brandy when I taste it. That was poison.'

Shields stopped Deeming's brandy rations soon after and the feeling between the two men further soured. Deeming complained bitterly to Lyle about the doctor's daily visits; Shields, he said, constantly peppered him with questions as if he was a lawyer. In turn, Shields had been briefing reporters and telling them he had seen no signs of insanity in the prisoner. Deeming, he said, was certainly a man who 'possesses a great deal of cunning . . . but it is a mistake to suppose that every man liberally endowed with craft is a lunatic'.

Lyle already regarded Shields as a hostile witness. The doctor had given testimony for the prosecution in the William Colston case, declaring Lyle's client 'clear-headed and intelligent' and a man who knew what crimes he was committing.

This time Lyle decided to lodge a formal complaint with the gaol's governor, John Shegog, over Shields' behaviour.

'Dear Sir,' wrote Lyle, 'The prisoner Baron Swanston complains of being badgered by Dr Shields, the Government medical officer, who appears to be again conducting an inquisition into the defence and otherwise acting against the spirit of the British constitution. Similar complaints were made to me by William Colston and other prisoners awaiting their trial for murder. I wish you would make some arrangements to prevent prisoners being thus annoyed.'

When Lyle met with Deeming he also made sure guards were present. Some wondered whether he was afraid that Deeming might physically harm him. Not so, said Lyle. He was doing it to ensure 'there should be no grounds upon which any person will be able to say that feigning of insanity has been undertaken by the prisoner by the advice of his counsel'.

V.

Dawn broke grey and grim on the morning of 22 April 1892. Heavy rain had fallen through the night and Melbourne's Yarra River – that fetid sewer Sidney Dickinson believed had no equal elsewhere in the world – was yellow and swollen. But if the weather was expected to deter many from attending the Supreme Court for Deeming's trial, the police were taking no chances.

Not long after 6.30am in the Russell Street police barracks, Senior Constable Johnny Kirkpatrick hitched two horses to his Black Maria, covered its windows in black paper and made the short trip around the block to the Melbourne Gaol. Waiting for him outside the gates was the prison governor, John Shegog, a police inspector, three mounted officers and a large group of constables on foot. Within minutes a handcuffed Deeming was bustled into the van. Two gaol warders and another pair of constables joined him inside. The door was locked from the outside to prevent any escape. Then, with the mounted officers riding alongside and another prison van following closely behind, Kirkpatrick steered the Black Maria down the slope of Victoria Street. The procession took a left into the flat stretch of Elizabeth Street before finally turning right and climbing the hill of Little Bourke Street toward the Supreme Court.

Deeming was in 'a sulky humour' when they led him into the holding cells below the Supreme Court, one of a series of newly built law courts Sidney Dickinson regarded as 'an enormous pile of the sombre bluestone of which a large proportion of the edifices of the city are built, which gives to the streets on wet days a particularly gloomy and funereal appearance'.

Deeming was not the only one in a bad mood. As the morning stretched on, many of those fortunate enough to get a seat felt cheated. After sixty potential jurors were sworn in, the case was temporarily stood down to give the prosecutor, Robert Walsh, QC, who had assisted the coroner during the inquest, a chance to read an affidavit from Lyle requesting a postponement of the trial.

Lyle and Deakin needed to buy as much time as they could. 'I verily believe there is existing in this colony a state of public feeling against the prisoner, which is likely to continue for some time and will at present preclude a fair and impartial trial of the prisoner,' Lyle stated in his affidavit.

He listed many reasons: the press coverage had been antagonistic and had already pre-judged the prisoner as being guilty, while the coronial inquest had seen 'exhibitions of prejudice against the prisoner, the public at times hissing and making other hostile manifestations'. Lyle was also adamant there had not been enough time to prepare. His client was imprisoned, the Easter holidays had intervened and contacting potential witnesses, including family members in Birkenhead, had proved impossible. Deakin and his assisting counsel, Robert Furlonge, had only just come across information that Deeming may have been confined in an asylum in India and had been known at one time as 'Mad Fred'.

It was after lunch when Deeming was brought into the courtroom and placed in the dock with a police officer at each side. Sidney Dickinson was staggered by the transformation in the man. Gone was the maniacal, leering grin. There was no hint of a sneer, much less a swagger. 'In this frock-coated, well-groomed and gentlemanly person in the dock there was no trace whatever of the ruffian who had been the central figure of the inquest,' Dickinson would note. 'In age he seemed to have dropped some twenty years; his manner was perfect, showing no trace either of apprehension or bravado.'

Asked by the presiding judge how he pleaded, Deeming, charged under the name of Albert Williams, replied clearly: 'Not guilty.'

Henry Edward Agincourt Hodges was the most inexperienced judge on the Victorian Supreme Court. He was thirty-seven years old and in only his third year on the bench. But he already had a reputation for being a rude and humourless man with an explosive and some-times violent temper. His sarcastic asides could wound and unnerve the most experienced lawyers in town. Hodges, said one critic years later, was 'quick to resent whatever he perceived as impertinence'. Evidence of his thin-skinned nature was on offer that morning in the newspapers. Hodges had recently gaoled a swindler connected to the colony's property market collapse and the Attorney-General, Charles Duffy, had publicly complained the sentence was too lenient. A riled Hodges had released copies of letters he had sent Duffy rep-rimanding him for making misleading statements. Duffy, he wrote, 'should be the last person to say or do anything tending to bring the administration of the criminal law into contempt'.

A decade later Hodges would be admonished in a resolution passed by his peers that would deplore 'the violent discourtesy of Hodges towards litigants, witnesses and members of the legal profession'.

When Deakin read part of Lyle's affidavit saying he had sent a cable to England asking for more information about Deeming's alleged mental illnesses as a boy, Hodges expressed concern.

'That means three months to make the inquiries, and some six months more before the witnesses are got,' Hodges said.

Deakin said his client 'had been of a roving disposition, and had lived in three colonies and, it was believed, in several other parts of the world' and that evidence confirming those movements 'has not been obtained up to the present time'.

Hodges: 'Since what time?'

Deakin: 'Since when the prisoner gave the names to his solicitor there has been no time, in the ordinary course of the post, to get replies from each.'

Hodges: 'At the present time the prisoner is of sufficiently sound mind to plead . . . and why he should not have had time to communicate with those people is beyond my comprehension.'

Deakin explained that Lyle had had 'considerable difficulty in extracting from the prisoner coherent statements'. But it was the press coverage which was also concerning. Deakin cited a case from 1839 – *Queen against Bolam* – in which a judge had granted a postponement because of prejudicial newspaper coverage.

Hodges, although he agreed some of the reports about Deeming had been 'very improper, no doubt, very improper', was having none of it. 'If such matters as that were sufficient to justify the postponement of a trial there are very few persons who could be tried for a very long period . . . it is of the highest importance that punishment should be as early as possible after the offence, or the accused, if innocent, as soon as possible discharged'.

With every point Deakin tried to make, Hodges had a rebuttal. Lyle's affidavit, with its expectation of lengthy communications with England, 'is a very ridiculous one'. If the case was postponed, Hodges said, the excitement surrounding it would only be revived 'with possibly intenser [sic] interest'. Hodges was confident potential jurors would not be influenced by what they had read. And besides, from what he had seen so far, he could not even see there was any belief 'or any reason to believe, that the prisoner was insane at the time the alleged offence was committed'.

He was prepared to push the trial back a week, to Thursday 29 April. But that was all. The defence had less than a week to prepare.

VI.

The canary was no longer singing in its brass cage when it was carried into the Supreme Court the following Thursday. For months attendants at the morgue had cared for it and its songs had filled the normally sombre rooms in the House of the Dead. But the previous day it had been badly hurt when its wings became entangled in the cage bars. Now it sat at the front of the courtroom – 'silent and depressed', according to one report – as the gallery filed in for the resumption of the trial.

Dickinson continued to be amazed by the enormous interest in the case. The street outside was filled with thick fog but the foot-paths on either side were packed with spectators braving the frequent showers and cold winds. They had 'besieged all entrances and even made a few rushes to carry them. But all the doors were set three deep with policemen selected from the heaviest and strongest of the metropolitan force.'

By ten o'clock at least 450 people were crammed inside the court. Most of the floor space was taken up by reporters and Dickinson found himself again within touching distance of the dock. But he was more struck by the crowd in the public viewing gallery sitting above. 'In its composition were many women whose names are always prom-inent in reports of social functions and soirees at Government House,' he would note. Over the next few days Sidney would observe them listening 'with astonishing equanimity to the ticklish medical testimony, and regarding the prisoner with that fascinated absorption which his conquests among their sex was calculated to inspire'.

Once again Deakin proposed a postponement. This time he had two supporting affidavits from doctors who had examined Deeming in the past week. One was Dr Robert Springthorpe, the president of the Victorian branch of the British Medical Association. The other was the aforementioned Dr John Fishbourne, whose main speciality was in 'the diseases of the mind' and who had assisted Lyle in the Colston case.

Deeming remained in a holding cell below the court when Deakin opened his remarks. He and Lyle had decided on an unusual tactic – they wanted the prisoner kept out of the room and out of earshot of the two doctors when they spoke in support of their affidavit.

It was a tradition in law that a prisoner be entitled to hear all evidence against them and Justice Hodges was quick to raise it.

'There can be no harm in his being present,' said Hodges. 'It is not known but that the prisoner might resent the application.'

Deakin: 'If he were present the accused would be made aware of exactly what the medical men are searching for, and exactly what they have and what they have not found and could, if he desired, simulate the symptoms expected. The application for postponement is not made entirely in the interests of the prisoner, but in the interests of a full and fair inquiry.'

Springthorpe, a short man who parted his hair severely on the left and who gazed intently through a pair of round spectacles, was the first to take the stand. It would be a difficult morning for both he and Fishbourne, and their cross-examination would elicit some of the most sensational – and distasteful – evidence about Deeming heard so far. He was suffering from syphilis, the doctors would claim, a sexually transmitted disease regarded as so loathsome and indicative of moral decay that some newspapers of the era could not even bring themselves to print the word.

'His account of that attack is graphic and gruesome,' the doctors would write later in a joint paper. Deeming had also told them he had infected his wife and their unborn child with the disease. 'It seems to have made a tragedy of his life,' they would conclude. 'Some of the Whitechapel murders become immediately possible by way of revenge. This delusion grafted on to syphilophobia suggests also a clue to the Rainhill and Windsor atrocities.'

But just as sensational were Deeming's claims, made public for the first time by the doctors, that his dead mother had been visiting him each night at about 2am for years, always urging him to slay his wives.

Springthorpe told the court he had interviewed Deeming for five hours during two meetings earlier that week.

Prosecutor Walsh asked: 'Can you say whether he is now insane or not?'

'I am not prepared to discuss at present his mental state or sanity.'

'What do you want more time for?'

'I want more time to find out first of all with reference to the prisoner's statements to me – to what extent these are true or false, and to what extent they are hallucinations.'

Three months after the trial, Springthorpe and Fishbourne would publish their lengthy paper in *The British Medical Journal* entitled 'An Account of the Mental Condition and Trial of the Rainhill and Windsor Murderer (Deeming alias Williams)'.

The two doctors would include many of their interview notes that would detail claims by Deeming that his father 'was a brute' who had frequently and violently beat him when he was a child, and that mental illness ran deeply through his family.

'His father ill-treated him: died in Birkenhead Asylum, did not know whether Benevolent or Lunatic Asylum. His mother was always good to him; was in a lunatic asylum before his birth, came out for his birth. Had five or six brothers; one younger than himself in an asylum. Had three sisters, one dead, one was not right in her head.'

The doctors had found '*signs of blows on the head . . . a seton mark at the back of the neck, and large deep syphilitic scars on the limb and trunk . . . in giving his answers the prisoner seemed to us like one who was obliging us with what was of no particular importance to himself, earnest even where he was evidently not stating the truth. We soon saw that all his statements could not be dismissed as lies, but the facility and dexterity of his lies made it all the more difficult to separate these from what might be exaggerations, distortions and even hallucinations.*'

The doctors recorded Deeming's age '*between 36 and 39 years; does not remember anything until 12 years old, except he was in an asylum near London. From 12 to 16 was never well. Was called "Mad Fred". He used to do all sorts of things, but never did wrong; for example he would take things away but would return them again; threw a girl in a canal for calling him Mad Fred, pulled her out again; then threw her in again because she still gave him that name, then he left her in and changed his name to "Harry". About 16 ran away to London, knocked about starving and cold all the winter, was put in an asylum under the name of Teddy Williams; he ran away, climbing over the wall; was arrested for tearing up his clothes in the street and taken to a House of Correction.*'

Deeming told them he had then gone to sea, often taking different names, even on a return voyage of the same ship, because changing his name gave him a new identity and relief from his mother's visits.

'*His mother wakes him up every morning at 2 o'clock; she always appeared before him as when last seen before death, always besides him exercising an influence on him. Many a time she has held him by the right wrist (he always points to the right side when pointing to her) and he cannot get away. Mother always tell him if he has a lady friend to kill her, or a wife to kill her. Has never seen anyone in this way but her; hears no other voices. Changed his name to try and escape from this. On the next day he always felt easier; that he thought he could get out of his life by parting with the past. Did not see why he should be responsible under new names. As an instance, he said that when in London with the syphilis he changed his name, and the syphilis disappeared.*

'Had always, since boyhood, been addicted to women. Will not admit the feeling is entirely or mainly sexual; is fond of them and of making them happy. Had syphilis very severely in South Africa in 1889; treated by Dr Matthews for six weeks; only interrupted treatment for few weeks, deep penetrating scars on legs etc., appeared early. Symptoms subsided till four months ago; very bad in London and changed his name and got well. Tried to find the woman who gave him disease; went to four places after her; would have shot her if he could have found her.'

Mother had first ordered him to kill Marie more than four years earlier when the couple were living in Sydney. But he had never paid much attention to her demands until their arrival in South Africa.

'Was on his way up to Kimberley after getting to Africa; got the syphilis. Sent for his wife; worst of syphilis over. No peace after that: left her twice because they could get no rest; woke up every night to destroy her; sent her home on that account. The first night he threw his revolver out and broke a window and that awoke her; again the next night he was incited to kill her, and three more times afterwards. Told her why he sent her away. The syphilis broke out on the way home. On the south coast of England when with Miss Matheson and also in the Kaiser Wilhelm.'

Springthorpe told the court further information from England would shed more light on Deeming's claims about his family's past, and more time was needed to conduct detailed physical examinations to see how his 'very serious general disease' might have affected his brain.

Deakin asked Springthorpe: 'Was the general disorder one which has a tendency to affect the brain?'

'Certainly. And in my opinion there is no doubt whatever that he had that disorder.'

Springthorpe explained he wanted to study one of the scars on Deeming's head that showed signs of having broken open when the disease had flared. 'It is a matter of great importance . . . in relation to the results it might produce on the brain.'

At that point Justice Hodges intervened: 'But can you get the exact position now?'

'Not in reference to the convolutions of the brain underneath. Some convolutions have to do more particularly with mental and intellectual diseases.'

'Why have you not found the exact position?'

'I have not had time.'

Prosecutor Walsh asked: 'That would be best ascertained on a post-mortem, would it not?'

Deakin quickly interrupted: 'I don't think that a remark proper to make at this time.'

Deakin, a man more familiar with unearthly spiritual voices than most in the courtroom, asked Springthorpe about the visits by Deeming's mother.

'Is this a common phenomenon in connection with insane patients?'

'No, it is not common.'

'Have you met with it before?'

'Yes, it is usual as to imaginary voices.'

Deakin: 'Although hearing the voice is common, seeing is not so common?'

'No, it is not so common.'

Springthorpe said Deeming had claimed that after telling Marie in South Africa she needed to return to England to avoid him killing her on the orders of his mother, she had told him she would prefer him to kill her and bury her in a mine than go home without him.

'He also explains as a reason for his frequent change of name that by changing his name he got rid of his former self,' said Springthorpe.

'Another apparent hallucination?' asked Deakin.

'It may be so.'

'Do you attach importance to these symptoms of disease of the body?'

'Very great, because they are likely to be associated with brain disease. They need further investigation.'

But Justice Hodges had heard enough and dismissed the post-ponement application. 'I do not think I need hear the doctors on the other side,' he said. 'No matter what adjournment is granted, they would not be able to make any satisfactory statement as to the prisoner's previous state of mind at the time at which it is all important.' All the doctors would achieve in the coming weeks was obtain telegrams from England that could still not be verified as having come from a responsible person.

'I do not see anything to prevent them giving that opinion now.'

It was a decision that infuriated the two doctors. They had just been subjected to intense cross-examination and the court seemed to have little regard for their scientific approach. They would also be criticised in the following morning's newspapers. According to *The Age*, Springthorpe had made up his mind 'too resolutely that the man was insane to make his doubtless valuable scientific knowledge of much value'. Fishbourne's evidence that followed was 'vague'. Even Sidney Dickinson found their testimony 'contradictory and confused'.

'We cannot but regard the trial as having been too hasty for a proper judgement,' the doctors would tell readers of *The British Medical Journal*. 'No scientific attempt was made by others or permitted to us to discover the motives of this remarkable murderer, or to obtain a reliable "confession"; and, further, that no attempt at all was either made or permitted to test his connection or otherwise with similar atrocious murders of interest to the whole English-speaking race.'

VII.

When the trial resumed after midday Sidney Dickinson watched as Deeming rose up 'mysteriously through the floor of the dock – which in its arrangement of a trap door strongly suggested the scaffold upon which everyone present fully believed he would stand within the month'.

Deeming had not been shaved since his return to Melbourne and a month's whisker growth now 'concealed his cruel mouth and veiled the outlines of his square, ironlike jaw. His hair and beard were carefully brushed and he was attired with scrupulous neatness, and even some degree of elegance, in a well-fitting and closely-buttoned Prince Albert coat, dark trousers and patent-leather button shoes.'

Deeming stood with his right hand thrust into the breast of his coat – a hand-in-waistcoat gesture appropriated by eighteenth and nineteenth century figures like Napoleon and the Duke of Wellington when they wanted to project stateliness and leadership. Deeming then took his seat in the dock, crossed his legs and studied his shoes with an air of indifference.

He would remain that way for most of the next four days of the trial. From time to time he might show interest in a female spectator and when Kate Rounsefell was sworn in to repeat the evidence she gave at the coronial inquest, his nonchalance quickly faded as he tried to catch her eye. Dickinson could not help but admire Deeming's 'magnificent power of control'. There were even moments of cheerfulness. At one stage Deakin removed his barrister's wig, exposing a closely cut head of thick black hair that resembled the rough cut prison barbers gave their clients.

'That's a very close crop,' Deeming said to one of the guards by his side. 'I wonder where he got it?'

Before the first witness was called Deakin rose to inject more controversy into the trial. During the lunch recess, he informed Justice Hodges, Marshall Lyle had resigned from the case and withdrawn his brief. The two doctors had also withdrawn from the case. A brief, despairing look crossed Deeming's face. The court fell silent.

It was clearly a protest move by Lyle following Hodge's decision not to postpone the trial. Lyle would later explain that, had he continued acting for Deeming while the case went ahead, he would have been unable to pursue the defence of insanity; the doctors were no longer willing to participate and there would be few opportunities to further investigate the prisoner's state of mind.

But it was more likely Lyle hoped the move would force Justice Hodges to adjourn the case. If that was so, it failed – miserably and quickly. Hodges, unusually for a man of his combative nature, said he was not going to comment on the matter: 'I thought they were medical experts who came here to give the court the benefit of their knowledge and skill and opinion. I did not understand that they were partisans open to withdraw from a case of this kind.' He quickly informed Deakin he was happy for him and Furlonge to continue representing Deeming.

Lyle would continue representing Deeming, pursuing statements and evidence from overseas witnesses. But he would no longer be present in court alongside Deakin.

Deakin gave his assisting counsel Furlonge responsibility for cross-examining most of the general witnesses – and one of the first was Max Hirschfeldt, who said Deeming had appeared during the journey to Australia on board the *Kaiser Wilhelm II*. He then told the court about the train journey from Perth when he had been one of four men in a carriage holding Deeming down as he appeared to suffer an epileptic seizure.

Furlonge: 'Did it take all four men to hold him down?'

'Yes sir.'

'Before he went off in these fits he was sleeping?'

'Yes, if it was a fit.'

'You are very nasty,' said Furlonge. 'You swore that it was a fit just now.'

'I am not a medical man.'

'Now be careful. I ask you again. Was he shortly seized with a similar attack?'

'Yes.'

On the second day Kate Rounsefell took the stand. As she was sworn in Sidney Dickinson watched Deeming lean forward against the bars of the dock and make 'every endeavour to attract her attention'. But while she remained stoic and many in the crowd considered her brave, Dickinson had formed a less favourable view of Rounsefell. She had been portrayed, he said, as having an 'absurd sense of gentility' when she was really 'a weak, pretty girl, and just as such a one as might naturally be attracted by a cheap, bediamonded adventurer'.

It was the same view shared by *The Bulletin* magazine, which had taken a satirical view of the case. Rounsefell, said *The Bulletin*, 'is in truth a very passable vision in a saucy hat and a dark blue cream fronted dress, cut to give her slight figure a good chance. Emotion is not this damsel's forte, and she never gets within a measurable distance of a flood of tears, or anything of that sort . . . one would be interested to learn whether this placid young spinster, after a hasty glance at "Baron Swanston" in his present state, recognises the influences of diamonds and moustachios in the most important events of her life.'

On the third day of the trial Melbourne's cold spell saw Deeming take his place in the dock in a long overcoat. The evidence was now overwhelming linking him to Emily's murder. It was now time for

Deakin to impress the jury his client was insane and not responsible for his actions.

Deakin had spent most of his limited time reading the available medical literature on insanity and researching previous cases where insanity had been proved. He would focus much of his questioning on a pathologist, William Mullen, who had been the medical officer for two Melbourne asylums and had also researched insanity in England and Germany.

'Would you define to me what you mean by insanity?' asked Deakin.

'Much better men have tried and failed,' replied Mullen. 'I will try. I look upon it as a general term denoting a physical disease of the brain, affecting those functions known as the intellect, the emotions or passions and the will . . . I define it from the physical and not the metaphysical side.'

'What is epilepsy?'

'It may be a physical disease of the brain.'

'And it is frequently related to insanity?'

'They are often found together.'

Mullen said he believed there could be a relationship between wounds to the head and insanity, particularly where a patient had shown 'signs of suffering from syphilis and where that disease had reached the tertiary stage'.

'What is the tertiary stage?'

'The tertiary stage is when the disease attacks the inner organs.'

'It is often the brain?'

'Yes, and it may be the liver.'

Deakin went on to question Mullen about homicidal maniacs. 'When this mania exists, is it not directed chiefly against those who are nearest and dearest to the lunatic?'

'Yes, sometimes.'

'Is insanity very hereditary? Is it frequently transmitted?'

'Yes, the weakened nervous system is transmitted.'

'Have you met with such a case as this – where a child at an early age becomes subject to eccentricities, later in life probably indulges in immoral practices, becomes the most cunning of liars, and is horribly cruel and demonically vindictive?'

Mullen said he had seen such cases of moral insanity.

'And that applies to this description?'

'I won't say in every detail, but it does in the main.'

But when the prosecution cross-examined the witness they extracted this admission from Mullen: 'From a legal point of view, assuming that the prisoner murdered the woman . . . there was no reason to doubt that on or about 24 December last the prisoner had sufficient degree of reason to know that he was killing the woman, and that such an act was both legally and morally wrong.'

Further damning evidence that Deeming was not insane came from Deeming's biggest foe inside Melbourne Gaol – the prison's medical officer, Andrew Shields – who testified he had examined the prisoner's head scars and while they might have been the result of an injury or arisen from an eruption of the skin, he did not regard them as 'serious'.

Shields had asked Deeming about the Ten Commandments: 'His reply was that they were for the convenience of the well-to-do classes,' and did not apply to the lower classes. He had also told Shields he would be justified in killing a woman who had given him syphilis to prevent her from infecting others. He had searched for the woman who had given him the disease on at least four occasions, always carrying a revolver with the intention of killing her.

Deakin: 'Will you swear he is not insane?'

'I will swear it is my opinion he is not.'

'You cannot believe anything he says?'

'No, not on his own testimony uncorroborated. For example, he told me he had no recollection of having married Emily Mather, of coming out in the vessel with her, of being engaged to the girl Rounsefell, though he said he knew her . . . the accused also told me that in 1879 or 1880 he was ill all the way out to Calcutta, and that he was sick after he arrived at that place . . . he also told me he could never remember having had a birthday, and when it does arrive he becomes quite unconscious.

'He says his mother is present with him, that she comes to him at night, that she whispers to him and that he shouted back. I asked him what she said, and he replied "I cannot tell you, something that is not right."'

Dr Shields said he had checked with the warder guarding Deeming's cell and he had not heard the prisoner shouting at his mother at all on the night the prisoner claimed he had.

'On a subsequent occasion I asked the warder if the prisoner had shouted out at night since [my] former visit, and the warder replied: "Yes, on the very night you asked him the question."'

Deakin: 'Can you swear that he does not believe what he says?'

'No, but I believe he does not . . . I cannot get any clue as to his insanity . . . I believe the prisoner's knowledge of right and wrong is sufficient to make him responsible. Many a lunatic, except if he is an idiot, knows right from wrong, just as a dog would know right from wrong if beaten. I conclude that he is sane and therefore that he is responsible.'

Dr Thomas Dick, Victoria's Inspector of Asylums, said he had examined Deeming on five occasions and believed him to be an 'instinctive criminal'.

Deakin asked Dick how he would define insanity.

'I would not like to give a definition.'

'If you, the inspector of our lunatic asylums, cannot, who can?'

'I do not think a very clear definition has yet been given.'

'Is the prisoner as responsible as the average man?'

'I do not think so . . . his standard of right and wrong is, I believe, different from that of other people.'

Dick said the problem with Deeming was that 'he tried to deceive me by feigning insanity . . . he told me on one occasion that his mother appeared to him and spoke to him. His statements relating to the apparition of his mother were not always the same, but varied.'

Justice Hodges: 'Your opinion is that he is not insane?'

'Yes.'

The final medical witness of the day, Dr James Jamieson, further weakened the defence case. A Scottish-born university lecturer in medicine, Dr Jamieson said he had also failed to find any trace of insanity. 'He did not appear very sensible,' Jamieson said. 'His views are of an exceedingly low character.'

Deakin asked if he thought Deeming was a man of high intelligence.

'He is sharp, can argue, and respond quickly to questions put to him. I take it for granted that a man is sane until proof against the contention is forthcoming. The man told me in the presence of others that his mother was sitting by him at the time, but in my opinion the prisoner did not believe his own statement.'

VIII.

Sidney Dickinson believed Alfred Deakin had made 'a plucky fight'. But who could possibly believe Deeming and his claims that Emily, herself a bigamist, remained alive and in hiding? Or that she might have even been involved with Old Ben in Rainhill in the murder of Marie Deeming and her four children?

His stories seemed to be an 'extraordinary farrago . . . and had it not been for the prisoner's reputation as a brilliant and variegated liar and a man of extraordinary shrewdness and resource, it might have aroused some assurance in the minds of Judge and spectators that the state of his mind was worth a more minute and careful examination before putting him on trial for his life'.

When the trial resumed for its climactic day on Monday morning, 2 May, Dr Robert Springthorpe reluctantly reappeared after being subpoenaed. This time he went through the notes of his meetings with Deeming in front of the jury and once more declined to give an opinion on the prisoner's mental state. But he seemed prepared to go further than his earlier testimony.

'If the prisoner were not here answering a criminal charge I would certify him as a fit patient for a house of correction, or a receiving house. I think a prima facie case has been made out, and I would certify him to the receiving house so that if sane he could be discharged, or if insane he could be sent to an asylum . . . I believe his statements are either exaggerations, distortions or hallucinations.'

Springthorpe then read from a sworn copy of a letter Deeming had written a week earlier to Dove Mather in Rainhill. It was an extraordinary self-serving document and, for many, proof the man was not insane, but a conniving murderer prepared to stop at nothing to deflect the blame from himself.

'Dear Mother,' began the letter, 'I do not know what you will think of the newspaper reports, but you may rest contented that Emily is not dead, but alive and well, as far as I know. There has been a wrong identification of the body found. I have no more idea whose body has been found than you have, but it is not Emily's.

'But if Emily's whereabouts is known she will be arrested for the Rainhill murders. Of course, you know all the particulars, and who was her associate. Emily has told you all about it. My advice to you is to make the matter known to the police at once. Emily will keep out of the way. Do so at once and have the man arrested. I am sorry that you did not tell me of Emily's first marriage. You knew she could not be my wife, even if I married her. It is, of course, easy to see your idea for having the marriage so quietly conducted, and for not even letting your own friends know how or when it was to take place. If you decide upon telling the police all you know of the affair, please wire me as soon as you get this. I have sworn not to betray Emily in any way. I know what her suffering must be now . . . hoping you will think the matter over and do whatever you think best. I remain your son, Albert (Known here as Baron Swanston).'

Not long after Springthorpe's evidence, Deakin rose and began to sum up for the defence. He began on an almost apologetic note, telling the jury he wished 'an abler and more veteran counsel had been charged with the task', but that he was confident they would remain mindful of the facts in the case and be governed by them 'and not by any imperfections in the presentation of it'.

'The heat of passion must die,' he declared, 'the clamours of the crowd be stilled, and the clouds of remark passed over . . . the fame of this colony had never been stained by a resort to violence dignified by the name of Lynch law; but it was never nearer stained in this manner than when multitudes of morbid sensation seekers hunted him down by land and sea, to gloat their eyes upon his visage and fill his ears with their maledictions.'

The entire world was against the prisoner, said Deakin, and only two doors remained open to him – 'one door was that of religion, with its infinite prospects of pity and mercy and pardon; the other door was that which opens here, where crouching at the awful knees of justice he awaits the pronouncement of his doom'.

The evidence against the accused was only circumstantial and if the jury believed he had committed 'that fearful atrocity which had wrung the heart of England as it had never been wrung before, and if they believed that he had committed this other crime at Windsor, could they believe that this creature was human?'

Surely he was a man suffering a serious mental disease and the highest officer in government ranks familiar with lunacy, Dr Dick, had already characterised Deeming as an 'instinctive criminal'.

An instinctive criminal, declared Deakin, was a moral monster from whom a great measure of responsibility had gone.

'Was it not feasible to conclude that the man [is] not only an instinctive criminal, but that disease had so deeply ingrained into his physical and moral nature as to have eaten away all responsibility for his deeds?' There was a lack of motive in Emily's murder, said Deakin. No-one had seen Deeming strike the blows that killed her. Witnesses with no experience with decomposed bodies had identified her remains. There was evidence to show the prisoner was suffering tertiary syphilis and was an epileptic. He had suffered blows to the head throughout his life and still carried the mark of a seton. All these things were known to lead to brain disease 'rendering a man irresponsible for his actions'.

Prosecutor Robert Walsh then addressed the jury. A large part of Deakin's address, he said, 'had nothing to do with the case'; unsatisfactory evidence had been given about Deeming's epileptic fits and the jury must make up its own mind if they believed the man suffered from epilepsy or was simply 'shamming'. The marks on his body purporting to be syphilitic scars were of no importance and there was no proof the man was insane.

Walsh said the facts of the case were clear. Deeming had been identified by dozens of witnesses. He had purchased cement with a premeditated plan of burying Emily's body in the same manner he seemed to have killed his first wife and four children in Rainhill.

It had been a long afternoon. But as Walsh finished his summary 'a thrill' rippled through the packed courtroom.

Deeming had risen and walked to the front of the dock. He was demanding to be heard.

IX.

His face was tense and his lips drawn. He took several deep swallows. For a moment it seemed he might fall. He gripped the spike railing that surrounded the dock, took another deep breath and began to speak.

At first his voice wavered. He was making a statement that was not on the advice of his counsel, he said. But facts had been omitted or not placed in front of the jury in the manner they should have been. While both sides had given the case their greatest attention, 'my full opinion will be that I have not had a fair trial . . . it is neither fair to me nor fair to the public . . .'

Deeming stopped. He could see someone in the gallery staring at him.

'You can see me, Sir, without staring at me so!' he barked.

His voice had now reached a high pitch. The press and the public had prejudged him, he squeaked.

'No matter which way it is looked at, I have been most unjustly dealt with. I ask the jury if they could pick one person out of any two hundred in Melbourne who would not execute me without a trial, as if I am a guilty man and as if I committed this crime.

'If I could make myself believe that I had done this I would gladly have given a full statement of it rather than submit myself in this court for four days to the gaze of the most ugliest race of people I have seen in my life.'

There were several loud gasps.

Deeming continued. There were witnesses 'who have come into court to identify me who never saw me in their lives, and whom I never saw either . . .

'The Crown had undertaken this trial at one of the most unjust times to try me – a time when the whole of the public and the whole of the press and the whole of the people in the world are entirely against me and, as I say, ready to execute me here this very minute without the option of a trial.'

For one of the few times in Frederick Deeming's life no-one was sniggering behind a cupped hand or rolling their eyes in disbelief. On he went, haranguing the press, criticising witnesses and pleading his innocence.

'Daylight faded, twilight merged into darkness, and candles, brought in for the Judge, lawyers and reporters, cast ineffectual rays of light around the room,' wrote Dickinson in his report for *The New York Times*, 'while the high-keyed, whining voice pierced the obscurity with the words of incoherent oration.

'Everybody present knew that it was the voice of a dying man, and its effect was at once horrible and pathetic.'

There were several witnesses Deeming clearly despised. But his greatest loathing was reserved for Max Hirschfeldt.

'He would do anything against me that he possibly could,' he said. 'On the way from Western Australia he told me he would stand as my friend to the last. He came and played cards and draughts with me, gave me a drop of brandy now and then, and told me that whatever I said to him would be said to him alone. But what has he done? He comes to the gaol, he tells the governor of the gaol he is my dearest friend, and that if I had any confession to make it would be to him and to no one else. Then, after professing all this, he gets into the box and swears lies against me. He came and asked me if I wanted to see him or had anything to say. I told him he was the last man in the world I would wish to see. I knew him as being a liar and a card-sharper. I cannot compare him to anything else, and the Government of Victoria should know it never employed a bigger thief than when it got Hirschfeldt to identify me.

'Even a man like Dr Shields – a learned man who ought to know his own senses and other people's to a certain extent – has not examined me fairly.'

Deeming peered into the gloom. The crowd had heard enough and was impatient. Some were shaking their heads. He had seen those faces throughout his life; the disdain, the cynicism and the condescension.

'People up in the gallery before me . . . are grinning at me, pulling eyes at me, shaking fists at me. I ask you, as reasonable men, would it not be far easier and better for me to have given you an account of it? . . . the only comfort that I have got now is the knowledge that I did not commit the murder, and that the woman is not dead. If you bring in a verdict of guilty against me it will be the greatest relief that you can give me. It will finish up what has been two months' torture to me. Death is nothing to it. Death is nothing to my feelings.

'Life is not worth living now and I do not fear death. I have not gone through the world and faced the dangers I have done and become afraid of death. I have been on the Zambesi amongst the blackfellows; in the lions' caves and brought the lions out. These are facts; they are no more to me than having my meals.'

On he went, repeating himself, contradicting himself, wallowing in the self-pity of an innocent man, friendless in a room of enemies. His life was over, even if a not guilty verdict was returned. He had nothing to look forward to. His reputation was stained. He might as well take himself down to the banks of the Yarra and throw himself into its putrid depths. Emily was alive, but it was better for him to suffer than to allow her to do the same if he revealed the truth about what had happened. Look at how the Crown had turned Kate Rounsefell against him. 'She is now one of the public of Melbourne, and shares the prejudiced feeling against me.'

He was unhappy, too, with his defence – 'They think one way; I think another.' Of course, he admitted, 'I have not always been in the habit of telling the truth myself. I did not lie wilfully; it was simply a habit. Half a dozen times out of ten I did not tell the truth, but I could not help it. I saw no mischief in it . . . sometimes I might be beside myself and mad, but I do not think I would do a thing like this. If I had done this I would be as mad as a March hare.'

It was just after 6.30pm when he finished with a plea to the jury: 'As far as committing this crime is concerned, I am as innocent as any of you sitting in that box, and whatever the end may be, the consciousness of that will be my comfort. I leave it now to you, gentlemen of the jury, to give the verdict which you think you are justified in doing.'

Justice Hodges told the jury he did not need to remind them about the gravity of the case. Deeming had said he did not value his life more than a sheet of paper, and left his life in their hands. The jury must not place the same value on his life as he placed on it, Hodges said. They had to remember that 'this is a human being whose life is at stake'. They had heard the clear evidence of Dr Shields as to the man's mental state and must now decide if he was guilty of the murder, or not guilty because of insanity.

Sidney Dickinson looked across the solemn court. The scene reminded him of the work of one of the world's greatest painters.

'The scarlet robe of the Judge was the only bit of colour in the picture, which reminded one in general of a canvas of Rembrandt, with the profound shadows that filled most of the scene, relieved by touches of light as the flare of the guttering candles played upon the half-seen faces of the assembly. The almost sepulchral gloom seemed to have its effect on the prisoner who . . . crouched in the dock with an abject and despairing look.'

The jury retired at 7.30pm and were back in little more than an hour. More than a dozen white-helmeted constables formed a ring around the dock.

In the silent courtroom the small flames of the dying candles spluttered and choked on the remains of their wicks.

Justice Hodges ordered the prisoner to stand. Deeming rose and stepped forward, his face impassive.

The jury foreman was asked if a verdict had been reached. He nodded.

'Guilty,' he announced.

Deeming did not flinch and kept his face composed.

Justice Hodges asked the foreman: 'Have you answered the questions submitted to you – that the prisoner is now not insane and that if it were proved that he had been previously in a lunatic asylum, and that his father or mother had been in a lunatic asylum also, he was still not insane at the time the act he is charged with was committed?'

'Yes.'

Deeming was asked if he had anything to say. Once again he said he was innocent and had not had a just trial. 'If I am to die for this I shall not be dead long before my innocence will be proved. Better for the law to destroy me than for me to destroy myself . . . I am quite indifferent to what the public think of me. There is only one thing that would have comforted me. If I had heard from Miss Rounsefell that she believed me innocent, it would not have troubled me if the whole of the public of Australia had believed me guilty . . . I ask your Honour to remember that I have been here for four days and I ask your Honour when you are passing sentence to make it as short as you possibly can.'

Hodges: 'It is not my intention to say one word beyond passing upon you the final sentence of the law.'

'Thank you, your Honour; that is all I want.'

Hodges: 'The sentence of the court is that you be taken to the place from whence you came, and that you be taken at such time and to such place as his Excellency the Governor shall direct, and there be hanged by the neck until you are dead, and that your body be taken and interred in the precincts of the gaol in which you were last confined; and may God have mercy on your soul.'

'Thank you, your Honour,' said Deeming.

It was 9.10pm. The candles had burned down to stubs. In the gathering darkness the constables formed a ring around the prisoner. As they began to escort him from the dock, Sidney Dickinson watched that familiar cynical smile form on Deeming's face as he cast a final slow glance at the crowd.

Then, wrote Dickinson, 'the greatest criminal of the century passed forever from the eyes of the world'.

X.

If the law had ruled that Frederick Deeming's hands were stained with blood, visitors to his cell following the trial noticed they were also smeared with ink. The business of waiting to die kept a man busy. There were letters to write – daily missives to Kate Rounsefell pleading with her to visit him. There were wills to draft – 'I give and bequeath to my dear brother, Edward Deeming . . . one 18 carat gold curb albert watch chain and three gold coins attached to the same . . .' There was also his autobiography to finish – a memoir Marshall Lyle was eager for him to complete.

On Sunday 8 May the gaol's assistant chaplain, the Reverend Mervyn Whitton, visited Deeming in his cell after delivering the morning's service. He found the prisoner scribbling a verse to his dead mother which, 'with complacent satisfaction', he was happy to read aloud to Whitton.

> *Mother look me straight in the face –*
> *I'm but the wreck of our royal race.*
> *Of friends and kindred they have bereft me,*
> *I'm Bayley Deeming – 'tis all that's left me*

But Whitton was not interested in a poetry recital. He wanted to know if Deeming was penitent.

'A jury have found you guilty of this crime,' Whitton said to Deeming. 'You must know whether their verdict is a proper one.'

'Well,' said Deeming. 'I did kill Emily Mather. I murdered her and buried her, but I do not know what possessed me to do it. If you ask me what my motive was, I can't tell you because I don't know it myself.'

It was a stunning revelation, the first time Deeming had confessed his guilt. Whitton quickly informed the gaol's head chaplain, the Reverend Henry Scott, who in turn hurried to the prison to see if Deeming would confirm the details.

Scott was a prominent identity in Melbourne – a public campaigner for the poor and downtrodden who was never short on a quote for the press. He had been visiting Deeming twice a day since his arrival in the prison and had often found him reading the Bible and repeating some of his favourite hymns.

'He treated religion always with outward respect and attention,' Scott would say. 'Had I ever any hope of doing him good spiritually or obtaining a full confession from his lips? I never lost hope, for experience has taught me that the unexpected might happen.'

Scott believed Deeming was the most complex man he had met – 'an extraordinary being, difficult to diagnose, and impossible to fathom . . . in my opinion he came into the world with a low or deficient moral organisation and its debasement was complete when he gave way to vices.'

One afternoon Scott had asked Deeming how he felt.

'Not at all well, Mr Scott,' said Deeming. 'I have today a great difficulty in keeping my hands from injuring someone.'

'That is all right,' said Scott. 'I am not afraid of you.'

'I asked the governor to put handcuffs on me, I feel so dangerous.'

When Scott arrived in Deeming's cell on that Sunday afternoon he found the prisoner only too happy to elaborate on his earlier confession to Whitton. But what to believe?

Deeming told Scott he made four attempts on Emily's life. The first had been in London shortly after their marriage when Mother had woken him at 2am commanding him to kill her. He had done his best to resist these urgings. But Mother was insistent. He had crept out of bed and seized a chair 'with the intention of dashing out his wife's brains. As he raised the chair she woke up and, seeing his intention, jumped over to the other side of the bed, just in time to escape being struck by the chair, which fell on the mattress and was splintered to atoms.'

He had somehow managed to reassure Emily this incident was part of a nightmare. The second attempt took place at the Federal Coffee Palace. Mother's commands were so strong he woke Emily and implored her to leave, but she had thrown her arms around him and told him she would rather die than leave him. The last two incidents took place in the Windsor house and culminated when he found Emily sitting on their air bed one night peeling an apple with a large knife. He had wrenched the knife from her and cut her throat.

Seized with 'an uncontrollable fear of the dead body', he had rushed out of the house and eventually found a poor fisherman on St Kilda pier, who agreed to bury Emily's body for ten pounds.

It was an account filled with the usual holes and contradictions. Every time Scott pointed them out Deeming would respond by saying he could not explain them because 'sometimes he was not himself'.

When Scott left, Deeming returned to his poetry: 'The verses are characterised by a species of horse wit which the prisoner happily imagines to be the refinement of humour,' said *The Age*.

He remained obsessed with Kate Rounsefell and several of his verses about her quickly found their way into newspapers around the world.

> *Oh! Kitty, dear, Oh! Do you hear*
> *The news that's going round*
> *The Baron is by law forbid*
> *To live on Austral ground*
> *As beautiful Kitty one morning was tripping*

Along the wet deck of the ship Adelaide
When I saw her I stumbled
And after her tumbled
And before the night fell my attentions I paid

There were also poems about the trial he had just endured, with praise for Lyle and the defence team.

My lawyer, Marshall Lyle
That son of Erin's Isle
'Tis him I wish to thank
(Though he made me but a crank)
And Mr Deakin, too,
He found me in a stew
And tried to pull me through,
With Furlonge at his heels
They were all bowled out by Shields
Who put me in a fog
With his prayers and Decalogue
The jury listened well
To the story I'd to tell
And they sent me off to Hell

Hell, it turned out, was not far away.

On Monday 9 May the Executive Council of the Victorian colony met to set a date for the execution. Before them was a colourful appeal for clemency written by Lyle in which he told them he was now 'the advocate of a being who has completely lost the small particle of sympathy which is usually shown towards criminals under sentence of death'.

The press, wrote Lyle, had proclaimed Deeming to be 'some unique moral monster of such a condition that it is hoped that none other such monstrous creations are to be found in the human family'. He was unaware of any previous trial anywhere in the world where a jury had been asked to rule on a man's sanity before his counsel had received the assessment of experts. The time of the alleged murder also remained in question – as did the question of whether the prisoner was an epileptic and suffered from syphilis.

Lyle tendered a letter from Kate Jensen, the Queensland woman who heard Deeming talking at night with his canary on the *Kaiser Wilhelm II*. He also furnished a statement from the medical officer at Darlinghurst Gaol confirming Deeming had suffered from 'undoubted epilepsy' during his incarceration in 1882, and had been 'in a very bad condition'.

But the Executive Council was not swayed and set the execution date for a fortnight's time – Monday 23 May.

While the council was meeting, Kate Rounsefell's sister, Lizzie, visited Deeming in his cell. There was no way, she told him, that Kate would come to see him. If Deeming took the news badly, he did not show it. Instead he told her a story that was a slight variation on a boast he had already made to the Reverend Scott. Deeming drew a rough sketch of two tombstones he said Lizzie and Kate would find in a cemetery in Johannesburg. Buried between them, he told her, was more than 11,000 pounds she and Kate could share.

That night the governor of the Melbourne Gaol appeared in front of Deeming's cell.

'I have some bad news for you,' John Shegog told him. He would be hanged in two weeks' time.

'Bad news?' said Deeming. 'I think it is good news – the best news you could possibly have told me.'

XI.

Frederick Deeming's life had been marked by suspicion and distrust and it would remain that way as he prepared to depart it.

There was growing tension between the Reverend Henry Scott and Marshall Lyle. Scott believed his role was to minister to Deeming's soul and move him closer to God before his execution. He was increasingly annoyed with Lyle's intrusive behaviour. How could he focus Deeming on matters spiritual when his lawyer was constantly interrupting with endless requests to sign documents, read affidavits and – because of his own financial interest in being paid for the case – urging him to complete his autobiography?

Scott had read parts of the manuscript and believed it to be a 'tissue of falsehoods . . . if ever it sees the light of day it will have to be rehashed to such an extent that all its criminality will have to be abandoned. It is a combination of immoral filth and extravagant allegations.'

Lyle, on the other hand, believed Scott spent too much time with his client trying to position himself as his chief confessor and confidant. He had already raised with Deeming the poss-ibility of replacing Scott with another minister who was friendly with himself and Alfred Deakin – the Reverend Charles Strong, a controversial preacher who had been threatened with heresy by the Presbyterian Church and had founded the breakaway Australian Church.

Lyle's mood darkened the day after the decision to schedule the execution when he picked up *The Argus* to read a lengthy account of Deeming's 'confessions' to Scott and Whitton.

What did these two supposedly humble servants of the Lord think they were doing revealing potentially harmful accounts about his client? An appeal to the Privy Council in London was due to be heard within the next ten days and any 'confession' could adversely affect that hearing.

Lyle went to the gaol and ran into Scott on his way to Deeming's cell. According to Lyle, Scott stopped him and asked if it was true he was trying to replace him as Deeming's chaplain. Lyle said he was acting on the wishes of his client.

'Then you have no right to interfere with my ministrations in the gaol,' Scott said to him. 'And you are a mean cur and a cad to do so.'

'You are continually coming between me and my client,' said Lyle.

'You are continually interfering between me and my penitent,' answered Scott.

That afternoon Scott confronted Deeming in his cell and asked him if he was contemplating replacing him with Dr Strong. Deeming, relishing the discord between the two men, said he wanted Scott to continue ministering to him and that it had been Lyle's suggestion to introduce him to Dr Strong.

'Mr Lyle said I would like you to have Dr Strong as he's a friend of mine and a friend of Mr Deakin, and then we could be all friends together,' Deeming told Scott.

Scott filed an official complaint with John Shegog over the matter. Lyle, in turn, complained to the sheriff that Scott and Whitton's leaking of Deeming's confessions in the press had severely hurt his chances of having his execution postponed and that the 'prisoner's appeal to the Privy Council in London may fall through, and I fear must do so'.

Lyle must have known the odds were overwhelming. It was undoubtedly a feeling shared by the barrister he had appointed to represent Deeming in London. When Gerald Geoghegan appeared before the Privy Council – the highest court of appeal in the British Empire – on Thursday 19 May, he sounded apologetic. Seated on the bench before him were some of England's most powerful figures, including the Lord High Chancellor of Great Britain, Hardinge Stanley Giffard. The courtroom was packed with onlookers. 'There was a large attendance . . .' reported the *London Evening Standard* the following day, 'including some ladies.'

Gerald Geoghegan probably felt like a drink. Regarded as a 'brilliant but erratic' criminal lawyer with a sharp wit, Geoghegan was an alcoholic whose wife regarded him as a 'highly nervous man' and whose chemist often sold him sedatives to soften his hangovers. Within a decade he would be found dead in his chambers from an overdose of Bromidia – an elixir of chloral hydrate and potassium bromide – in what many would regard as suicide.

He had good reason to be nervous on that morning of the Privy Council hearing because Geoghegan had very little to present. His role was simple – to ask for a postponement of the death sentence. His argument did not begin confidently.

'At the present time I am afraid I have no permanent record of any matter that I can lay before the Court, because the documents which substantiate such a proceeding on our part have not yet arrived.'

Geoghegan explained that two statutory declarations made by Edward Deeming and his wife, Mary Jane, corroborating Frederick's history of mental illness were still on their way to Australia. Likewise, documents relating to the recent trial in Melbourne were still on their way to London.

He had only received a copy of an additional affidavit from Edward Deeming that morning. He read it to the court.

'During his boyhood the said Frederick Deeming was hysterical and peculiar in his habits, and was known as "Mad Fred" on account of his extraordinary behaviour. When he was about 14 years of age he ran away from home, and I did not see him again until the year 1875, when he returned to his parents in Birkenhead. I am informed that during his absence he was confined in a lunatic asylum under the name of "Teddy Williams". When he returned home in 1875 he stated that he had been to sea, but would give us very little information as to what parts of the globe he had visited, beyond stating that he had been shipwrecked off the coast of Newfoundland and that his money and clothes had been stolen. In the year 1877 he was very ill in consequence of his mother's death, and shortly after again went on several voyages, visiting, amongst other places, Calcutta, where he had a severe attack of brain fever, which necessitated his being confined in the hospital there some time, and he was eventually sent home to England in the steamer *Orion*. He remained at home ill for three months after this, and during that time his mind appeared to be affected.

'He represented himself as being a person of distinction, and dressed in a most peculiar way. Sometimes he insisted upon going out in the daytime wearing an evening dress coat, a light pair of trousers and patent leather shoes with silver buckles, a nosegay on one side of his coat and a wedding favour on the other. At other times he would go out dressed in the deepest mourning, as if going to a funeral.

'His conversation was at this time almost unintelligible. He would ramble from one topic to another without any connexion, leaving his sentences unfinished.'

Edward went on to describe the behaviour of their father, Thomas, who had attempted to take his own life by cutting his throat on four different occasions. But Edward Deeming's declaration had little impact on the court.

The Council took only a few minutes to decide to refuse the application for a stay of execution. It cited a rule that 'has been repeatedly laid down, and has been invariably followed, that her Majesty will not review or interfere with the course of criminal proceedings unless it is shown that by a disregard of the forms of legal process, or by some violation of the principles of natural justice or otherwise, substantial and grave injustice has been done'.

After receiving news of the Privy Council's decision, Marshall Lyle wrote to the Governor of Victoria, the Earl of Hopetoun, John Hope. Lyle had reached the end of his tether. The government had just seized Deeming's autobiography and was planning to destroy it. Once again he would emerge from a noted case defeated – and unpaid.

'In my attitude towards you I may be charged with being inconsiderate,' he said to the governor, 'and you, in your position, may appear to be inert, but we both with equal force can answer that we can abide our destiny.

'A Divine compassion for all things human will yet become the predominant factor in the character of Australia. A higher conception of the sacredness of human life will inevitably force itself upon the minds of our rulers and the people. Already mutterings are heard amongst the mass, and the prison system with its cross, its whip, its stake, its gallows and its axe, will stand for judgment before the enlightened opinion of the nation . . . you will take down your scaffold in the Melbourne gaol ere many years pass by.

'The melancholy twaddle of legal jargon cannot forever withstand the lessons of supreme truth . . . the cruelty and the evil of today play their part not for nothing. We must await the return of the pendulum. The true and lasting victory will remain with those who perceive in the progress of modern science the handwork of the Divine . . . I have the honour to be your obedient servant, Marshall Lyle.'

XII.

It was the big wooden beam that caught Sidney Dickinson's attention. He squinted at it through weary eyes. It was two days after the storm that had roared its way across Melbourne's Port Phillip Bay, and memories of the wind clawing at his home and the screams of his wife as she confronted the ghost of Deeming's mother remained fresh in Sidney's mind. Now he was back in the belly of the old gaol, less than a week after making that plaster cast of Deeming's deadly right hand. He peered at the beam and the rope hanging from it. The beam had been worrying Deeming for weeks. Was it in the right position above that narrow trapdoor?

It rested on large iron sockets bolted into each side wall and spanned the entire width of the gallows. It was so thick and heavy it would have required at least six men to hoist into position. But what fascinated Dickinson were its scars. Along its length were dozens of grooves and furrows where ropes had chafed and strained with the weight of hundreds of convulsing victims. The limp body of the legendary bushranger Ned Kelly had swung from the same beam a dozen years earlier. The most recent had been Marshall Lyle's hapless client William Colston.

When Deeming had told Lyle he was concerned about its placement above the trapdoor, Lyle had shrugged off his client's concerns.

'Well, the last three clients of mine went through all right,' he had told him deadpan.

It was a few minutes before 10am on Monday 23 May 1892. Dickinson was surely tired. Marion's experience with the ghost of Deeming's mother had only been the start of a series of incidents that had begun to fray Sidney's nerves. Since then he had heard open doors slamming shut and was sure he had heard footsteps in empty rooms.

Dickinson had been reluctant to leave Marion at home alone. But *The New York Times* wanted an account of the hanging for its front page and so he had joined the crowd of reporters and dignitaries packed into the iron gallery around the scaffolding waiting to witness Deeming's demise. There were close to fifty of them while more than ten thousand were said to be milling in the cold and gloomy streets outside.

After staring at the beam – a 'fearsome tally-stick' that had 'given despatch to the souls of several hundred murderers' – Dickinson turned to an old warder next to him. The man was nearing seventy and he had accompanied Sidney and Marion when they met with Deeming the previous week.

'You have been for many years a warder here, and must have seen many men under sentence of death,' Dickinson said.

The warder told him he had been in the same role since the early days of the bushrangers and had probably seen two hundred men 'depart this life by the route of that gallows'.

'Then you should be a good judge of the character and mental state of a man who is awaiting a death of that sort,' replied Dickinson. 'What is your opinion of Deeming?'

'Mad, sir,' said the warder. 'Mad as a March hare.'

Dickinson had reached the same conclusion. He now believed Deeming to be an 'instinctive criminal' and there were good reasons to 'take him from under the shadow of the gallows to lifelong incarceration in a lunatic asylum'. While he understood the urgency of the authorities to mete out justice for the killing of Emily, it seemed a pity the execution could not be delayed while more evidence was sought about the man's mental state.

'If, as many believe, he is "Jack the Ripper", his identification with that human monster ought to be determined,' Sidney would tell readers of *The New York Times*. 'If found to be the perpetrator of the Whitechapel atrocities, that fact should give force to the contention that is made in certain quarters that he is no more morally responsible than a wild beast, which kills for the mere love of killing.'

Dickinson had been increasingly drawn to the theory of Deeming as the Ripper. Emily had been heard addressing him as 'Jack' not long after their arrival in Melbourne. Could he have asked her to use it as a pet name, a 'subtle pleasantry' that appealed to the man's grim sense of humour? It would be easy, wrote Sidney, to 'imagine how he gloated upon the secret which was suggested to him whenever the word "Jack" fell from the lips of his doomed and unsuspecting companion'.

Even stronger, however, was a fact 'which has been kept from the public, but has been made known to me by the highest authority'.

It was unlike Sidney Dickinson to act like a breathless news reporter and besides, the information he was about to impart had already been reported a month earlier by *The Herald*. But this 'highest authority' – presumably Colonial Secretary William Shields who had permitted the Dickinsons to take a plaster cast of Deeming's hand – had provided Sidney with vital new information.

It had long been believed, declared Sidney, that the Whitechapel murders had been carried out not only by someone with an uncommon knowledge of human anatomy, 'but who was also suffering from disorders contracted among the unfortunate class in which all his victims were found, and that the murderer took these means to revenge himself for his affliction'.

Everything added up – except for one thing. Medical examinations of Deeming had proved he was 'suffering from serious symptoms of evidently long standing', while the autopsy had shown that Emily's throat had been skilfully cut. The windpipe had not been lacerated but all the important arteries and blood vessels on each side of the neck had been expertly severed. No bungling murderer could have inflicted these wounds, said Dickinson. Everything pointed to them being caused by 'surgical knives wielded by a skilled and practised hand'.

But the blade of the knife the detectives believed Deeming had used had been found to be blunt. When it had been put on display during the inquest, Deeming had 'manifested a grim, chuckling amusement, as one who should say to himself "Well, you are quite off the trail there . . ."'

The 'new' information given to Sidney Dickinson solved this vexing issue. It had emerged that a week before Christmas a man 'of arrogant manners and profuse display of jewellery' had wandered into Ward Brothers cutlery store in Swanston Street in the city, accompanied by a woman 'of sad expression and quiet manners' who seemed to be afraid of him.

Several days later the man returned alone. He handed over a pair of surgical dissecting knives which required cleaning and sharpening. Each blade was about five inches long 'and in some parts bore actual cakes and clots of hardened and coagulated blood'.

When the shop attendant pointed this out, Deeming had said: 'That's not blood. The stains are caused by lemon juice. The knives have been used during a sea voyage to cut fruit.'

The attendant was sure the man was lying. But he handed them to a tradesman at the rear of the store and instructed him to clean them and put a sharp new edge to them. The tradesman examined the blades and had quickly exclaimed: 'My word! These knives have seen some work. They seem regular Jack the Rippers!'

The man returned a day later and paid for the knives. But they had never been seen again.

'There may be some connection between Deeming's possession of these instruments and the semi-scientific mutilations of the Whitechapel victims,' reported Dickinson. What followed was a typically long-winded sentence preferred by Sidney when he became excited.

'The belief is gaining ground in official quarters that the murders of which Deeming is now known to be the author (at Rainhill and Windsor) and that of Miss Rounsefell, his Bathurst fiancée, for which he was undoubtedly preparing when arrested, are the same in kind as those committed in Whitechapel – being attributable to a debased and horrible view of the sexual relationship, which had been developed by morbid imaginings and, perhaps, by a brain somewhat affected by a disease caused by excesses, until it had become a species of monomania.'

As the Jack the Ripper killings became history's most celebrated crime mystery in the century that followed, Deeming's possible involvement would be downplayed. For decades amateur and professional sleuths obsessed with the case would rule him out as a suspect, mistakenly believing he was in prison at the time. Later evidence showing he was in South Africa also seemed to preclude his involvement.

But had he briefly returned to England in the autumn of 1888, as the actor Alfred Harford had alleged? It was certainly possible given the man's propensity for travel and his willingness to undertake lengthy journeys. There was the unidentified dressmaker who had told a London newspaper she had been courted by a man named Lawson at the time of the Ripper murders, and who certainly matched Deeming's description. That man had shown an obsessive interest in the murder of Catherine Eddowes on the night of 30 September. The Reuters newsagency added weight to that claim when it carried an unsubstantiated report in April 1892 that Deeming had, years earlier, been in Halifax, Nova Scotia and shown an acquaintance a letter he had received from Eddowes, hinting the pair knew each other well.

Melbourne detectives would also receive a corroborating letter that would be retained by the Public Records Office of Victoria. Marked 10 March 1892 and written by a 'Signor D'artoz', it suggested Deeming, after marrying his first wife Marie, did not travel straight to Australia and instead sailed on the ship *Sardinian* from Liverpool and disembarked in Halifax. Littered with grammatical and spelling errors, D'artoz's letter claimed he later travelled with Deeming to Chicago and on to Bell Creek (possibly Belle Creek in Nebraska) where he worked as a gasfitter for several months and used various aliases including Crothers, Squire, Campbell and Johnston.

D'artoz claimed he and Deeming fought over money and that the body of a woman he alleged was Deeming's mistress was found in quicklime beneath a boarding house in which he was staying. The body of another woman was discovered in a water closet. D'atorz also claimed he had been in Brazil with Deeming, who had 'shot two mates and committed an criminal assault [sic] on a girl and these two brothers came on him doing such & he killed the three . . . I am glad he is getting the rope before long because he shot and wounded me in the breast then Robbing me . . .'

They were teasing fragments, circumstantial at best. But they hinted, as Deeming had to several people, that there was something darker lurking in his past besides the murder of his two wives and four children. Deeming displayed several physical and psychological symptoms of neurosyphilis, and the Ripper's clear hatred of women had led many to suspect he may have also contracted the disease.

The strongest argument against Deeming's involvement in the Whitechapel killings was the manner in which the Ripper murders had been carried out. The murderer had preyed on most of his victims in public places, mutilating the bodies and then leaving them to be discovered. Deeming had not mutilated his six victims, killing them in private homes and doing his best to hide their bodies beneath layers of concrete.

In 2012 a former Scotland Yard detective, Robin Napper, would claim in a television documentary that Deeming was the likeliest Ripper suspect, while other authors would also suggest his likely involvement.

It was why the case of Jack the Ripper had endured for so long. Nothing could be ruled out and only one thing was absolutely certain – it was a mystery that would never be satisfactorily solved.

XIII.

As Sidney Dickinson contemplated that giant beam and the likelihood of Deeming being Jack the Ripper, another man had found the excitement of the day too much to handle.

The Reverend Henry Scott had collapsed the previous night with nervous exhaustion and was at home in bed. Earlier that Sunday, Deeming had summoned him twice – once in the morning and again late in the afternoon. Scott, in the midst of a busy day of sermons at his church several miles away in Footscray, had rushed to the gaol thinking Deeming was now – finally – ready to make a full confession and repent. But when Scott arrived he discovered the doomed man merely wanted to talk and repeatedly ask if there was any way Kate Rounsefell could be convinced to pay him a final visit.

Deeming had also written Scott a letter thanking him for his efforts. 'I die a fully penitent sinner and a Christian,' he wrote, 'and I still tell you as I always have that I did not intend to kill my poor Emily, nor did I know at the time I did it, and I can only look on my execution as murder. Still, death will be a relief to me and with all your kindness and consideration for my soul, I should have died happy . . .'

There was something about Deeming that drained the energy from those who spent time with him. Scott found him to be 'the most extraordinary man I ever met in my long experience . . . I don't know whether to classify him as a splendid actor or the subject of a diseased brain, but I incline to the latter explanation.'

Scott had hurried back to his church. But as he began to give his Sunday night sermon he collapsed in the pulpit.

His assistant and another pastor had been left with the task of praying with Deeming during the final hour of his life. As they prepared the man in his cell, a rumour began to ripple through the waiting crowd. The nervous prisoner, it was said, was weeping bitterly. He had suddenly dropped on bended knee and cried out: 'Oh Lord, forgive me for having despatched my wife and family without warning.'

Deeming's prison nemesis, Dr Shields, had allowed him a large glass of brandy and a sniff from a bottle of ammonia. It seemed to steady him. At a few minutes to ten o'clock Sidney Dickinson watched Governor Shegog and the sheriff, William Anderson, push their way through the crowd and climb the steps to the gallows.

In a loud voice Anderson uttered the traditional request: 'I demand the body of Albert Williams.' Moments later a clean-shaven Deeming stepped on to the gallows with several warders by his side. His arms were pinioned behind his drab prison uniform, a white cap with a long front flap was pulled over the top half of his face, just above his eyes.

He stood, swallowing heavily, swaying slightly, as the hangman adjusted the noose around his neck and pulled the flap down to cover his face. The chaplain began reading from the Church of England's 'Order for the Burial of the Dead'.

'I am the resurrection and the life, sayeth the Lord; he that believeth in me, though he were dead, yet shall he live, and whosoever liveth and believeth in me, shall never die . . .'

The sheriff asked Deeming if he had any last words. His words were choked and barely audible above the voice of the chaplain.

'We brought nothing into this world and it is certain we can carry nothing out. The Lord gave, and the Lord hath taken away . . .'

The crowd strained to hear. Those closest to the gallows heard Deeming whisper: 'Lord receive my spirit . . .'

'Man, that is born of a woman, hath but a short time to live . . .'

The trapdoor sprang open. The hangman had allowed a drop of seven feet and four inches and it seemed his estimate was perfect. Sidney Dickinson did not even hear the expected thud. The fall instantly broke Deeming's neck. So much for Deeming's engineering eye and his concerns about the size of the trapdoor and the placement of the joist. As *The Bulletin* would wryly note later, 'Deeming had gone straight for once in his life.'

For a short time the only sound heard was the rope straining on that giant overhead beam.

XIV.

Sidney Dickinson returned home from work one afternoon several weeks after the execution to discover Frederick Deeming had paid his wife a visit.

Sidney had always been proud of Marion's courage and self-control. She was more perceptive than he when it came to dealing with the supernatural and it was only her bravery and his pride – he had paid six months' rent in advance – which had prevented them from walking out of the house and never returning.

The weird ghostly occurrences inside the home had increased since Deeming's hanging. While the spirit of Ann Deeming had not returned since the encounter in the kitchen three days before her son's execution, a day barely passed without something occurring that would chill the marrow in Sidney's bones.

Ghostly figures moved through the house, muttering and sighing, apparently unaware they shared the home with the Dickinsons. Sidney, of course, could not see them. He had to rely on Marion, 'whose clearness of sight in these matters I never shared', to describe their appearance. But he was certain he heard them. One was an elderly woman who wore a black gown. Sidney knew it was made of silk because he often heard its soft rustle as she passed him in the hall. Marion told him she could see the old woman sighing and wringing her hands and assumed she was the dead wife of the owner of the house. Another female ghost seemed constantly anxious, moving from room to room on an endless search for something she could not find.

The creepy ghost child was the worst. The way Marion described it, the little girl was often sitting in the corner of a room, holding an indistinct object she treated like a doll, and singing to it in a 'queer, faraway voice'. Sometimes she would strike a wrong note and would pause before resuming. When she hit the right note she would 'give a pleased little laugh'.

None of these spirits seemed aware of Marion and Sidney's presence and, while the couple found them 'rather cheerless company', they were loath to try and order them out of the house for fear of what might replace them.

Sidney was smoking his pipe in his study one evening when Schneider and Tokio began frantically barking downstairs. As he reached the hall a fist-sized rock shattered the glass back door. Sidney rushed to his room, grabbed his revolver and sprinted into the street. It was lit by a scattering of gas lamps. But he could see nothing and even in the stillness there was no sound of retreating footsteps. Puzzled and more than a little afraid, he went to the back of the house, dragged the cowering dogs from beneath the house and unchained them. They made a dash to the rear of their kennels, buried themselves in straw and, trembling, refused to come out.

The act of vandalism was inexplicable. The force of the rock that had shattered the glass door was too strong for a boy to have hurled it. And what man, thought Sidney, would take the risk of passing hysterically barking dogs to cross a wide and exposed yard to launch a rock at a door? Even more unsettling was the behaviour of the dogs. Since when had they ever shrunk from his touch and refused to obey his commands?

A fortnight after the rock-throwing incident Sidney came home early one afternoon to find Marion distraught. 'There was a presence of fear upon her . . . and the strange expression which I had often seen when her gaze seemed to follow the movements of shapes invisible to my grosser sense, still clouded her eyes.'

He knew from past experience not to interrupt her when she fell into a trance. So he sat and waited, growing increasingly anxious, until she cried out: 'We must leave this house! I have endured all I can! I will not remain here for another day!'

She was reluctant to tell Sidney why – 'it is too horrible; it would frighten you to death' – but he persisted. What had happened?

'Deeming has been here,' she finally said.

'Deeming!' cursed Sidney. 'That devil!'

Marion said she had been sewing by the window in the front room of the house when she heard the click of the latch on the outside gate and saw a figure step into the yard.

She thought it was just another peddler trying to sell something. But when she reached the front screen door and looked outside she froze.

'I had no idea at all that it was not a living human being,' Marion told Sidney. 'But when I got to the door and looked at the figure . . . I knew it was nothing that belonged to *this world*. It was misty and indistinct and I could not make out any details of face or costume, except that the clothes seemed mean and cheap.

'In spite of the horror of seeing him I was never so sorry for any creature in all my life . . . such awful suffering! I shall never get his sad and frightful face out of my mind.'

Sidney wanted to know more about those 'mean and cheap' clothes. Marion thought they looked like they were made from flour sacks. They were coarse and ill-fitting and had 'queer triangular black designs on them'. But it was the cap on the figure's head she found the strangest item of all.

'It was of dingy white cloth and fitted close to the head, and it had a sort of flap hanging down behind almost to the shoulders.'

Sidney gasped. Marion had identified the prison uniform Deeming had worn at his execution.

When the ghostly figure moved toward her Marion had ordered it to stop. It then held out its hand and said: 'Madame, do you want to buy some soap?' Marion said she wanted to buy no such thing.

'I thought you would,' said the figure. 'You were kinder to me when you saw me in the gaol.'

'I never saw you in my life!' said Marion.

'Oh yes, you have, and you tried to get Miss Rounsefell to come and see me.'

'Are you Deeming?'

'Yes,' said the figure in what Marion said was a sad and pathetic tone. 'I am that unfortunate man.'

Marion thought she had screamed at him and ordered him to leave. The Deeming ghost had reluctantly retreated and when it reached the street it vanished.

'But I know he'll be back,' cried Marion. 'He is suffering and I am the only one he can reach.'

Sidney had never doubted the validity of his wife's preternatural ability to see what he could not – at least not since that meeting with the English novelist Wilkie Collins in London several years earlier. But this experience with Deeming's ghost seemed too bizarre, even given the extraordinary events they had experienced.

Yet . . . the details were grotesquely accurate. Sidney had not given her details about the execution and he would be adamant years later that she had never read about it in the newspapers, either. But she had just accurately described Deeming's final appearance on the gallows – 'the uncouth trousers and jacket of sacking, stamped with the "Broad Arrow" that marked both it and its wearer to be the property of the Crown, and the ghastly death cap, with its pendant flap . . . dropped over his face just before the trap was sprung!'

And the soap? Surely it signified what the hangman would have used to make the rope smoother and more pliable, a common enough technique before an execution.

Sidney Dickinson knew his wife well. If she said Deeming was certain to return he had no reason to doubt her.

XV.

Weeks passed. The sighing and moaning of the ghosts inside the house on the hill continued and were soon joined by more unsettling events. A milk jug levitated in the kitchen. A tray of roasted tomatoes mysteriously vanished from the oven. A fork was found embedded in a window frame with a piece of paper attached containing a crude drawing in red ink of a skull and crossbones. Was it a warning?

Sidney searched for an earthly explanation. He crawled through the dusty attic looking for a device – anything mechanical – that might have been rigged to create the noises. He got down on all fours and scrutinised every inch of the floorboards. He even forensically examined the outhouse in the backyard. But there was nothing. Adding to the mystery was that the nearest homes on each side of their house were at least a hundred yards away. The neighbours and the Dickinsons had clear, uninterrupted views. There was no way any intruder wanting to prank them could sneak up without the risk of being seen.

One night Sidney sent Marion to the theatre. He left the house with her to create the illusion they were both heading into town. But then he doubled back 'by a devious route' through the rear orchard that had never quite delivered on its promise of fresh figs and grapes and entered the house via the back door. Then he sat on a chair in the hall with a clear view of every direction and waited in the darkness with his revolver in his jacket and his heavily loaded double barrel shotgun resting on his knees. But when Marion returned after midnight he had nothing to report except to say it had been a long and disagreeable evening.

Sidney continued going to the office in the city and 'every day I spent in town was darkened by forebodings of what might happen at home before my return'. As he walked down the street each evening he would search anxiously until he saw Marion on the verandah with her serene and smiling face. Within a couple of weeks he allowed himself to believe the worst was over.

But one night he came home to discover Marion weeping. He knew instinctively that the spirit of Deeming had reappeared. This time, however, the fear in Marion's face had been replaced by an expression of pity. She felt weak, she said, and thought she might faint. But she was also relieved. She asked Sidney to step into the bedroom where she could rest and tell him what had happened.

'Deeming has been here and I have been crying,' she admitted. 'Oh that poor, tortured, despairing soul! He is in Hell – and one infinitely worse than that we were taught to believe in; a Hell where conscience never sleeps and where he sees what he might have been – and now never can be.'

It had happened late that morning. She had heard the back gate creak and the dogs had started barking again. At first she thought the butcher or the grocer had arrived with deliveries. But when she peered outside she knew at once the figure in front of her was Frederick Deeming. She slammed the door, locked it and ran down the hall to the front door and bolted that shut, too.

She then saw Deeming outside one of the windows, moving toward the front of the house. When she peered through the bedroom window he was standing on the front verandah, staring at the door. Finally she mustered the courage to confront him and found herself peering through the screen door at a 'sad and pitiful' figure who told her he needed her help.

'Don't be afraid of me. I won't hurt you. I need someone to show me Christian charity.'

It seemed almost blasphemous, said Marion, that a creature who had slain two wives and his four children would dare use those words. But he was insistent. He was in 'a horrible place' the ghost explained, and if someone could show him an act of Christian charity his time of suffering would be shortened and he could 'go on'.

Marion said she asked him what he meant.

'By giving me something, and being sorry for me when you give it.'

Marion went to the bedroom and took a half crown, a shilling and some copper change from her purse. When she returned Deeming told her there was no need to open the door. She should put the money on a marble shelf behind her. She put the money down and looked back. Deeming was no longer there. The coins had also disappeared.

She rushed into the street and heard his voice. 'Don't be afraid,' he said.

'But I can't see you!'

'And you never will again. I have gone on.'

When Marion returned to the house the money was on the shelf where she had left it.

Sidney was staggered. 'Are you sure you were not dreaming?' he asked her.

'I am not in the habit of dreaming at eleven o'clock on a bright sunny morning,' she said, laughing. 'And then, the dogs – do you think they were dreaming too?'

Schneider and Tokio had always slept in separate kennels. But when Sidney found them under the house they were huddled together in the straw. They whimpered and whined as he approached, licked his hand as he patted them and howled when he left and returned to the house.

They had seen something strange, that much was certain. More would follow. While the ghost of Deeming was never seen again, poltergeist activity increased in the little-used parlour down the hall. The couple kept the door to the room closed and could often hear their possessions being thrown about. When they finally dared inspect the damage, their belongings – paintings, sculptures and other souvenirs collected from their travels around the world – were sitting in a rough pile on the floor. It was a message. The house no longer wanted them.

It came to a stunning climax when Sidney heard Marion cry out from their bedroom. He rushed in, only to find her face masked in terror and with her back to the wall. She seemed to be wrestling with an invisible force. Then, according to Sidney, Marion's body appeared to be hurled across the room. She started tearing at her throat as though someone was choking her.

Sidney picked up his hysterical wife and carried her into the street. They remained outside that night, walking the streets, not daring to return. Years later he would write: 'I shall not forget those hours of midnight and early morning – the serene and amethyst-coloured Australian sky strewn with stardust and set with twinkling constellations, and the dark earth around us.'

The Dickinsons decided to leave Australia soon after. They packed up their belongings and on a sunny morning in early March 1893, a year after the discovery of the body of Emily Williams and the exposure of Deeming's other gruesome crimes, the couple locked the front door for the final time on what Sidney called their 'house of shadows'.

As they reached the street they turned back and took one last look.

It was all so deceptive. The house looked inviting in the brilliant early autumn sunshine. The lawn glistened and the shrubs and flowers were tall and healthy after surviving another blisteringly hot Australian summer.

Sidney Dickinson knew better. You could never judge anything by its appearance. It was like those dead birds he spent hours cleaning and restoring. With his scissors and thread and a steady hand he could make anyone believe they were alive.

Reality was illusory. His life with Marion and his involvement in the dark saga of Frederick Deeming had taught him that.

Perhaps there really was a hell. Hopefully there was a heaven, too.

But between those two was the only world he really understood, a world where real monsters dwelled and only a fragile thread separated the living and the dead.

AFTERWORD

In which The Author concludes this Gothic Tale by providing an Account of the Nineteenth Century Obsession with Spiritualism and why Intelligent People including Professor Sidney Dickinson, his Wife, and the Honourable Alfred Deakin along with Millions of others succumbed to its Many Trickeries.

It began, like so many things that changed the world, with an apple.

For as long as anyone could remember the apple had symbolised the search for immortality. Christians had long assumed it to be the forbidden fruit in the Garden of Eden that Eve passed to Adam, forever plunging humanity into sin and robbing it of eternal mortal life. It was the apple's youth-preserving properties that triggered many of the legendary battles among the Viking gods in Asgard. And it had been an apple tossed by Eris, the goddess of discord, that started fighting among the Greek deities that eventually led to the Trojan war.

Later, when science began rudely nudging the old gods aside, an apple changed the way mankind viewed the universe.

Isaac Newton was an English mathematician who had already defied the odds by surviving a difficult premature birth on Christmas morning in 1642. Years later, as the Plague swept through Europe and Britain, he watched an apple fall from a tree in his mother's garden in Lincolnshire and wondered what forces caused it to plummet directly to the earth. That moment inspired his theory of gravitation that would reshape mankind's understanding of the cosmos – and its place in it.

But if science had made spectacular progress since Newton's time, it had hardly triumphed over superstition by the middle of the nineteenth century. The First Industrial Revolution, which had seen the rise of machines and mechanised factories, had petered out with a whimper. The Second Industrial Revolution, which would transform the globe with inventions like the long-lasting light bulb, the electric telegraph and the telephone, would not begin until the 1870s. In the void between those two seismic periods of innovation flourished beliefs and legends that were as old as time itself.

The spiritualist movement began as a long, harsh winter drew to a close in March 1848 in the small farming community of Hydesville, deep in the wind-battered western plains of New York State.

Two girls – fourteen-year-old Maggie Fox and her eleven-year-old sister Kate – claimed to have heard mysterious knocking sounds at roughly the same time each night inside the nondescript timber home rented by their parents. There were thumps in the ceiling. Eerie knocks sounded on the thin walls. Sudden rapping would emerge from nowhere, so violent it was said to cause tables to shake and bedframes to rattle. Maggie and Kate quickly convinced their mother, Margaret, that their home was haunted by the spirit of a murdered man, a peddler whose body had been buried beneath the house years earlier to hide the crime and whose ghost was always keen to prove its presence and provide endless details of its suffering.

One evening, with horrified neighbours watching on, the apparently terrified girls clung to each other and asked the spirit to acknowledge its presence by rapping three times. Those in the room heard three clear knocks. When asked to tell the age of one of the witnesses, an accurate thirty-three taps followed.

The girls were the youngest of six children and the only offspring of Margaret and John Fox still living at home. Maggie and Kate insisted they were not playing tricks and could, indeed, communicate with the spirit.

The story of the haunting of the Fox home quickly took root in the already fertile spiritual ground of New York state. For years its small towns had echoed with the ecstatic shouts and praises of Methodists, Presbyterians and Freewill Baptists. There were Shakers and Quakers and fervent members of the Community of the Publick Universal Friend. There were Millerites, the precursors to Seventh Day Adventists, still clinging to the teachings of former army captain William Miller, despite his failed prediction that the second coming of Christ would take place in 1843. In the 1820s in Palmyra, a small town just ten miles from the Fox home in Hydesville, Joseph Smith, a young man whose parents frequently reported heavenly visions, had founded what would become known as the Church of Jesus Christ of Latter Day Saints.

Maggie and Kate Fox were soon catapulted into another emerging phenomenon of their time – the cult of celebrity. Guided by the watchful eye and constant presence of a much older sister, Leah, the girls entertained a never-ending queue of the curious, desperate to see them commune with the dead. They were invited to display their psychic abilities in the homes of prominent identities like Horace Greeley, the influential editor of the *New York Tribune*, and the renowned seer, Andrew Jackson Davis. They were subjected to an endless series of community and scientific investigations. During one of them Maggie and Kate 'wept bitterly under their afflictions' as a committee of women from nearby Rochester disrobed them and made them stand on pillows placed on a glass to minimise any chance of 'electric vibrations'. The committee concluded the thumps and knocks they heard were of a paranormal origin.

There were harsher critics – a local Methodist church denounced them as frauds and a study by scientists from Buffalo University concluded the sisters were using the clicking of their knee joints to generate their unearthly noises. The truth – and the role of the apple – would take years to emerge as a wave of excitement and relief spread across the United States. An afterlife existed – and the Fox sisters held the keys to the door separating the living from the dead. Their paranormal abilities were an antidote to science's cold rationality and for many an open rebuke to Leviticus' stern warning in the Old Testament 'not to turn to mediums or seek out spiritists, for you will be defiled by them'.

Maggie and Kate began touring the country performing to packed theatres. Séances became a nightly ritual in dining rooms and parlours throughout the United States and Europe. Queen Victoria, grieving the death of her husband, Prince Albert, became consumed with the occult after a thirteen-year-old medium passed on a message in which he referred to her by her pet name known only to her husband. A new class of mediums and spiritists quickly emerged to act as paying guides for these evening sojourns into the afterlife. People grew comfortable with the idea of inanimate objects springing to life. Table tipping became a worldwide phenomenon. A crowd gathered around a table in a suitably darkened room. They would then be asked to place their hands on the table, palms down, and concentrate. More often than not the table would soon begin moving on its own, tilting, shaking and even, in some instances, pinning participants against nearby walls.

Scientists like England's Michael Faraday, the discoverer of electromagnetic induction, conducted experiments that proved this table movement (and the upturned glass making the rounds of a Ouija board) were due to the 'ideomotor response' – muscle movement independent of deliberate thought. But few were listening by then and even fewer cared. To many, science's insights into electricity and magnetism were little more than grand examples of alchemy. Perhaps electricity and magnetic attraction were simply physical manifestations of matter from another dimension – that same one inhabited by the deceased.

By the 1860s the crude knockings and tappings associated with the Fox sisters had been superseded by increasingly sophisticated methods of communication with the afterlife. There were voice mediums, who spoke with the accents of the dead. There were automatic writers, who channelled spirits through pen and paper. One of the most famous of these would be a Chicago woman, Pearl Curran, who wrote several novels and hundreds of verses while 'collaborating' with the spirit of a seventeenth century woman she knew as Patience Worth.

But by far the most acclaimed was a man many believed had the ability to defy Isaac Newton's theory of gravitation. Daniel Dunglas Home, it was said, was like the spirits who spoke to, and through, him. He was a man who could float and leave the earth behind.

—

He was tall and slim with piercing blue eyes and a head of unruly red hair. Like Newton, he had been a sickly child who had not been expected to live for long following his birth in 1833 to Elizabeth Home, a Scottish woman rumoured to have been blessed, or cursed, with second sight. He was soon adopted by Elizabeth's childless sister, who took him to the United States at the age of nine. Daniel Home (he adopted the middle name 'Dunglas' later in a nod to a well-known Scottish castle) began claiming he was experiencing visions during his teenage years.

Home's aunt, aware of the strange rappings reported by the Fox sisters just a few years earlier, believed her adopted son was possessed by the Devil and organised for an exorcism to be conducted by Congregationalist, Baptist and Methodist ministers. When he continued reporting visions she ordered him out of the house and Home (pronounced 'Hume') embarked on a life roaming the world as a performing medium.

By the 1860s his fame had spread throughout the Western world. Emperor Napoleon III summoned him to the French imperial residence, Tuileries Palace, where Home staged a séance in which the Empress felt the touch of a hand that suddenly materialised out of thin air. She claimed it belonged to her late father because she recognised a defect in one of the fingers. The King of Naples became a client, along with the German emperor and the queen of Holland.

Home married into Russian aristocracy and the great writer Aleksey Tolstoy acted as one of his groomsmen.

Home travelled widely and became friends with Kate Fox. But his real fame lay in his reputation for levitating. In 1852 Home staged a séance at the house of a silk manufacturer in Manchester, Connecticut, when he allegedly began rising from the ground several times and, according to those present, at one point reached the ceiling. In 1868 three witnesses claimed to have watched him not only levitate but fly out of the third storey window of a room, only to float back in through the window of an adjoining room. When questioned, all admitted it had been dark, none had seen him moving from one window to the other or had noticed the wide window ledge outside, or that only a four-foot gap existed between the two balconies.

Frank Podmore, a founding member of the British socialist organisation the Fabian Society, claimed to have watched Home perform a low-level levitation. 'We all saw him rise from the ground slowly to a height of about six inches, remain there for about ten seconds, and then slowly descend,' Podmore would recall.

Podmore, a spiritualism sceptic, was aware of many of the methods employed by mediums – draping themselves in muslin cloth beneath their clothing so that, in a darkened room and with the audience's expectations already heightened, they could quickly appear as a spirit. Many employed small mirrors to generate reflections on walls. Some favoured 'false limbs' that could suddenly appear as 'spirit hands', while others were discovered using telescopic rods that were quietly extended in darkened rooms and used to tap nearby walls.

But Podmore was flummoxed when it came to Home's talents. He was unaware of a trick commonly employed by magicians in the twentieth century known as the 'Balducci Levitation', where the illusionist positions himself facing away from a crowd. The audience can see the rear portion of one foot and most of the other foot – apart from its front half and toes. The illusionist, who builds the expectations of his audience by searching for the right 'moment' and 'place' to perform his levitation, trembles and pretends his body is straining against the force of gravity. He then uses that partly hidden portion of the foot to lift himself and hold his balance for several seconds. To those watching from behind, he appears to be levitating.

Home was eventually caught out. The poet Robert Browning reportedly grabbed a 'luminous object' floating near the table during a séance conducted by Home in the 1850s, which turned out to be Home's foot.

Yet his reputation as one of the only genuine mediums in the world would continue to grow long after his death in 1886. It seemed to underline the one resounding truth that lay at the heart of the spiritualist movement: people only ever saw or heard what they wanted to.

There was no better example of this than the confession made by one of the Fox sisters in 1888, two years after the body of Daniel Dunglas Home finally stopped defying gravity and was laid to rest in a Parisian cemetery.

It turned out that spiritualism, like many things, began with an apple.

—

On a Sunday afternoon in September 1888, a reporter for the *New York Herald* sat in an apartment on West Forty-Fourth Street watching a woman with a face etched with 'sorrow and world-wide experience' pace nervously back and forth in front of him. Maggie Fox was agitated. She could not stand still. She spoke quickly, but covered her mouth with a cupped hand. Without warning she would leap to a nearby piano and begin playing 'wild incoherent tunes'.

Maggie was seething with resentment. She was also nearing the bottom of a long and deep descent into alcoholism. She had never recovered from the death of her lover and intended husband, the celebrated Arctic explorer, Elisha Kane, thirty years earlier. While they had never officially married, she had adopted his surname and insisted on referring to herself as his wife. She and her younger sister, Kate, were also at war with Leah, the older sister who had once managed their careers. They now believed Leah had manipulated them and left them penniless. Leah, in turn, had accused the younger Kate – now a widow with two children – of being an unfit mother because of her own repeated drinking sprees. Kate and Maggie had also fallen out with other leaders of the spiritualism movement.

Maggie wanted revenge. She informed the reporter she would give a public lecture the following month when the truth about the Fox sisters' abilities would finally be revealed.

'When Spiritualism first began Katie and I were little children, and this old woman, my other sister [Leah], made us her tools,' she told the reporter. 'Mother was a silly woman. She was a fanatic. I call her that because she . . . believed in those things.

'We were but innocent little children. What did we know? Aah, we grew to know too much. Our sister used us in her exhibitions, and we made money for her. Now she turns upon us because she's the wife of a rich man, and she opposes us both wherever she can.

'Oh, I am after her! You can kill sometimes without using weapons, you know.'

Maggie gave the reporter an exhibition of her ability to communicate with the dead. He heard rapping sounds on the apartment door, some from beneath a table and others that reverberated across the floor. He asked her how she did it and while she told him she would keep the explanation for her lecture, she made it clear they were not created by spirits.

'Why, I have explored the unknown as far as human will can. I have gone to the dead so that I might get from them some little token. Nothing came of it. Nothing. Nothing.'

Maggie's lecture was booked for the evening of 21 October at the New York Academy of Music, a poorly designed 4000-seat hall that had once served as the city's opera house but which had, ironically, turned to vaudeville acts to pay the bills. On the morning of Maggie's much anticipated stage appearance, the *New York World* splashed an interview with the Fox sisters across an entire page.

Maggie told the newspaper she and Kate had been young and mischievous children who enjoyed terrifying their mother 'when this horrible deception began'.

All those mysterious sounds and brief glimpses of ethereal beings that had raised the hopes of so many grieving and desperate people? All those promises of life continuing in a tranquil spiritual realm long after the physical body had decayed and turned to dust?

It had all started with an apple, Maggie explained.

'At night when we went to bed we used to tie an apple on a string and move the string up and down, causing the apple to bump on the floor, or we would drop the apple on the floor, making a strange noise every time it would rebound.'

But the girls could use the apple only when the room was dark and they were alone. It had been Kate who discovered she could create rapping noises by manipulating the joints of her fingers. The girls practiced until they could replicate the effect with their toes and ankle joints as well.

'The rappings are simply the result of a perfect control of the muscles of the leg below the knee which govern the tendons of the foot and allow action of the toe and ankle bones that are not commonly known,' Maggie said.

'And that is the way we began. First as a mere trick to frighten mother, and then, when so many people came to see us children, we were frightened ourselves and kept it up.'

That night the Academy of Music was packed with a raucous crowd, including a large section of committed spiritualists determined to criticise Maggie's denunciation of the movement. They sat impatiently, hooting and jeering as the nervous promoter of the event, Dr C. M. Richmond, a rotund New York dentist, budding magician and part-time investigator of the paranormal, served as the warm-up act by explaining some of the tricks employed by mediums.

'The doctor . . . labored under the disadvantage of not being accustomed to public speaking,' noted one report. 'The unfriendly or wholly indifferent elements in his audience had considerable amusement at his expense.'

Finally, Maggie – 'a little compact woman, dark-eyed and dark-haired' – stepped on to the stage.

'When she stepped before the footlights [she] found herself before a wearied and non-sympathetic audience,' the *New York World* informed its readers the following morning. 'It was evident that she was suffering from intense nervous excitement and was not in the best condition for making a public declaration of repentance for her life-long share in an infamous imposition and swindle upon the public.'

But the same reporter noted that if Maggie's 'tongue had lost its power her preternatural toe joints had not. Discovering that she was not in proper condition for a public address, her companions on the stage invited her to give a public demonstration of her ability to produce raps without further delay.'

The hall suddenly fell silent. Soon a series of short and sharp raps were heard – 'those mysterious sounds which have for more than thirty years frightened and bewildered hundreds of thousands of people in this country and Europe'.

A group of doctors took to the stage, examined Maggie's foot and announced the sounds had been generated by the clicking of the first joint on her big toe. The boisterous spiritualists in the audience went quiet.

'Only the most hopelessly prejudiced and bigoted fanatics of Spiritualism could withstand the irresistible force of this commonplace explanation and exhibition of how spirit rappings are produced,' concluded the *New York World*. 'The demonstration was perfect and complete, and if spirit rappings find any credence hereafter it would seem a wise precaution on the part of the authorities to begin the enlargement of the State's insane asylums without any delay.'

Maggie would recant her confession a year later but by then few were listening. She died in 1893 – penniless, 'worn and dissipated' and broken-hearted.

A year earlier – the same year Sidney Dickinson and his wife Marion found themselves trapped in a haunted house on the other side of the world – Kate Fox had died after embarking on another frenzied drinking spree.

Spiritualism might have been damaged by their disclosures. But even though science had regained the ascendancy in the battle to explain the mysteries of the universe, the movement still boasted millions of followers around the world. It would continue to flourish well into the first half of the twentieth century as its faithful continued to hear the knockings and rappings of the deceased.

But not all the dead insisted on staying in touch with the living. Maggie and Kate Fox were buried together in a Brooklyn cemetery, joined in death just as they had been in life.

Worn out by all their endless troubles in the physical world, they were never heard from again.

—

Sidney Dickinson continued working long after the death of his wife Marion in 1906. In February 1919 he was visiting Professor Raymond Stetson in Oberlin, a small city southwest of Cleveland, Ohio, when he was struck by an electric street car and suffered a fractured skull. He died three days later without regaining consciousness. He was sixty-seven. His book, *True Tales of The Weird – a Record of Personal Experiences of the Supernatural*, was published the following year.

Simeon Solomon, the art dealer who purchased Deeming's canary for three pounds and who was assaulted by Deeming during the coronial inquest, died a month after Deeming's execution. Hemmed between two passing trams, he suffered an epileptic seizure and passed away soon after. In the hours following his death a family member dropped the canary's cage while cleaning it. The cage door sprang open and the canary escaped, only to be devoured by the family cat, according to *The Bendigo Independent* (25 June 1892, p.3).

Detective Bill Considine was forty-nine when he died in 1895. He resigned from the police force a year after Deeming's capture.

Detective Henry Cawsey died at the age of eighty-four in 1935. Both men received rewards of twenty-five pounds for their work on the case.

Marshall Lyle continued to practise as a lawyer and later stood unsuccessfully for a seat in the Victorian parliament. He gave lectures on prison reform and instinctive criminality throughout the 1890s and maintained a keen interest in the colony's art and theatre scene. He became consul-general for Colombia for several years and died in 1944 at the age of eighty-two.

Alfred Deakin served three terms as Australian Prime Minister. He was an influential member of the committee that drafted the new nation's constitution and his lobbying campaigning in London is considered to have played a key role in convincing the British government to allow the Australian colonies to become a federation. He died in 1919 after suffering chronic hypertension and a neurological condition marked by severe memory loss.

—

Frederick Deeming, who adopted more than twenty aliases during his travels around the world, has been as elusive in death as he was in life.

Despite his and Marshall Lyle's consent, the Victorian government refused a request by the Victorian branch of the British Medical Association to examine his brain. That decision, and another ruling two years later in a similar case in New South Wales, drew the ire of the anthropologist Cesare Lombroso, who said: 'If they feel it necessary in the interests of society to kill a man, I am unable to understand why in the interests of society they should object to have his body examined.'

A plaster cast of Deeming's shaven head was made in the hours following his execution and, over the following century, was displayed at the Crime Museum of Scotland Yard and to tourists visiting the Old Melbourne Gaol.

Among those who examined it shortly after Deeming's execution was a Hobart specialist, Alfred Taylor. Like many scientists of the era,

Taylor was a believer in phrenology, a pseudo-science based on the theories of the Viennese physician Franz Gall.

A month after Deeming's execution, Taylor told the *Tasmanian News*: 'The greatest circumference of the head is 21 and ¾ inch, the smallness being due to a notable deficiency in the region of faculties that give a love of children, friends, etc . . . The largest bulk of brain lies in the region of destructiveness, secretiveness, acquisitiveness, and constructiveness . . . Spirituality, wonder and veneration – three faculties necessary to the manifestation of religious emotions – are also small. The relative development of the reasoning and perceptive faculties would indicate a character likely to reason falsely and to base conclusions upon unsound data. The features are very striking – the hawk-like (attacking) nose, high cheek bones, square jaw, broad chin, prominent ears, sensitive nostrils, muscular neck and firm mouth, indicating great vital energy and tenacity of purpose . . . to gain possession of whatever he wished for he removed obstacles that stood in the way without hesitation. His deficient caution and love of display led to his ultimate self-betrayal and ignominious death on the scaffold.'

After the plaster cast was made – a common procedure for executed criminals in the nineteenth century – Deeming was buried in quicklime near the bushranger Ned Kelly in an unmarked grave in the gaol's burial yard. When the Old Melbourne Gaol was closed in 1929, construction workers carrying out excavation work exposed a number of graves, including one believed to belong to Kelly. 'As soon as this gruesome discovery was made a crowd of boys who had been standing round expectantly while eating their luncheons rushed forward and seized the bones,' reported *The Argus* (13 April 1929). 'The workmen intervened, but in the scramble portions of the skeleton were carried off, including even the teeth.'

The confusion that followed would result in almost a century of false leads and claims about the location and identity of the bones belonging to Deeming and Kelly, Australia's most notorious killers of the nineteenth century.

In the aftermath of the 1929 gaol imbroglio, a decision was made to exhume and relocate all those buried within the grounds of the gaol. Many of these exhumations were carried out in a haphazard manner, the bones belonging to many bodies mixed together and thrown into bags. At least four skulls and body parts – two of which were believed to be those of Kelly and Deeming – were then given to the Director of the Institute of Anatomy in Canberra, Sir Colin MacKenzie.

Sir Colin delivered a lecture before the Anthropological Society of New South Wales in 1934 based on what he said were casts of Deeming's skull and thigh bone. He said Deeming had either been the victim of a brain disease or an atrocious villain and 'instinctive criminal'. 'A comparison of his skull with others, however, showed that he was of a decidedly primitive type, who could not be called sane or be classed as insane,' reported *The Sydney Morning Herald* in its coverage of Sir Colin's lecture. 'His slouching walk had the anatomical basis of a primitive creature. His was a case of arrested development.'

Sir Colin gave the skulls to the National Trust in 1971 and one of them was put on display at the Melbourne Gaol as belonging to Ned Kelly. It was stolen in 1978 and after it was returned DNA testing proved it did not belong to Kelly, but was believed to be that of Deeming. In 2014 the grave of one of Frederick's younger brothers, Thomas, who died in 1911, was exhumed. Using DNA samples provided by Thomas' great-great-granddaughter in England, a team of molecular biologists at the Victorian Institute of Forensic Medicine concluded that the skull was not Deeming's, either.

Frederick Bailey Deeming would be pleased. One hundred and thirty years after his execution, his whereabouts remain unknown.

APPENDIX

The following is the final will signed by Frederick Deeming. It replaced a previous will written a week earlier which had bequeathed a portion of the proceeds from the projected sale of his autobiography to Kate Rounsefell. The final chapters of that autobiography were seized by gaol authorities and, despite an injunction sought by Marshall Lyle, were destroyed by order of the Colonial Secretary's office.

This is the last will and testament of me, Frederick Bailey Deeming – known here as Albert Oliver Williams, also known as Baron Swanston – made this eighteenth day of May, in the year of our Lord one thousand eight hundred and ninety-two. I give and bequeath to my dear brother, Edward Deeming, of London, one 18-carat gold curb Albert watch chain and three gold coins attached to the same, and I appoint Marshall Lyle, my solicitor, to address and post the same to him.

I give and bequeath to Robert Garn, of Miller's Point, Sydney, one leather bound photo album; also one calendar watch, in red morocco case. I give and bequeath to Mr Shegog, governor of the gaol, one silver spirit flask, marked F.B.D. I give to William Mercer, warder, one pair of gold sleeve links and two gold studs, now in the gaol. I give and bequeath to Thomas B. Longbottom, warder, one silver match box, marked B.S. I give and bequeath to John H. Turner, warder, one blue coat overcoat, now in the gaol. I give and bequeath to George Taylor, warder, one silver pen holder, now in the gaol. I give and bequeath to Kate Rounsevell [sic] my will, made on the 9th day of May 1892, in return for her kindness to me, and in token of the lie she told in court. I give and bequeath to Marshall Lyle all my property now in the hands of the Melbourne police and also what is in the gaol, except what is mentioned in this, my will. I also give, devise and bequeath to the said Marshall Lyle all right, title or interest to any landed or personal property, all moneys, jewellery or any description of property or interest except what is mentioned in this will. I give, devise and bequeath to Mr J. Shegog, the governor of the Melbourne gaol, in return for his extreme kindness to me while in his charge, one piece of land, 52 x 150 feet, block No. 26, in section 14, in the town of Lismore, border of New South Wales and Queensland, the deeds of which are banked with the Joint Stock Banking Company, of Sydney; and I give, divide and bequeath to Marshall Lyle one block of land, No. 27, in the same section, the deeds being placed as above. I also give and bequeath to the said Marshall Lyle all writings written by me in the Melbourne Gaol in any way pertaining to my biography; also poetry, and all letters left by me, including three letters written [by] Kate Rounsevell, also including paper of instruction, with drawing to enable him to secure money buried in Lamer, East Africa, the money to be disposed as stated in instructions, with the exception of what is mentioned for Kate Rounsevell, and that part to go to Marshall Lyle, and nothing to the said Kate Rounsevell. I also give and bequeath to Marshall Lyle for publication the last statement written by me before my death, and not one word to be kept from the press. I give and bequeath to Mr H. Scott, gaol chaplain, one large Bible, now in the keeping of Mr Shegog. I give and bequeath to John H. Turner, warder, one gold sovereign purse, marked F.B.D., now with the police. I give and bequeath to Maria Pickering [Emily's sister], of Rainhill, England, one silver sandwich box marked Emily on lid; also all lady's clothing found with my effects, including the box and its contents found at Bairnsdale station. I give and bequeath to Mrs Robert Garn, of Miller's Point, Sydney, one boat shaped ring, now in the hands of police. I hereby declare that the only debts owed by me *are as follows: – Mrs Snell, of Snell's hotel, 2 pounds, Southern Cross, Western Australia; and the sum of 8s. [eight shillings] to Mr Manderson, storekeeper; and these two accounts I asked Mr Marshall Lyle to pay, and as I have now completed my last will and testament, I appoint Mr H. Scott, chaplain, as executor for the safe carrying out of the same; and I appoint Marshall Lyle to be solicitor for the same; and it is my last desire that every word of the contents of my will be published in the Melbourne papers, and for the executor's word that such should be done he hereto subscribed his name – Henry F. Scott.*

FREDERICK B. DEEMING, otherwise ALBERT O. WILLIAMS, otherwise, BARON SWANSTON.

Signed by the testator in the presence of us, being present at the same time, who, at his request in his presence and in the presence of each other, have hereto subscribed our name as attesting witnesses – (1.) L. STEWART (2.) JOHN HENRY TURNER (3.) JAMES KELLY

—

Frederick Deeming's personal effects were put up for sale on Thursday 2 November 1893 in the Melbourne auction room of Baylee and Co, acting under instructions from an administrator appointed by the Supreme Court of Victoria. The axe and knife Deeming was believed to have used to murder Emily were sold for four pounds fifteen shillings. The overcoat he wore during the final days of his criminal trial was sold for one pound, while other pieces of clothing fetched between one and five shillings each. Two magnifying glasses and a cheque signed 'H. Dawson' went for ten shillings while a gold curb chain sold for six pounds, fifteen shillings. Six pairs of 'partially worn socks' fetched one shilling. The entire collection of 136 lots sold for close to 100 pounds. Collectors who purchased items over two pounds received a certificate from Marshall Lyle certifying they were genuine articles owned by Deeming and seized by the Crown.

SOURCE NOTES

PART I

Most of what has been written about Frederick Deeming over the past 130 years has either overlooked or ignored Sidney Dickinson's book *True Tales of The Weird – a Record of Personal Experiences of the Supernatural*, presumably because of its heavy focus on the long-discredited spiritualist movement. I used it as a source not just because Sidney's susceptibility to Marion's beliefs is highly entertaining, but because it also highlights the desires and beliefs of so many in the nineteenth century who looked to spiritualism as an alternative to traditional religion. The book is online at https://www.gutenberg.org/files/46647/46647-h/46647-h.htm. Frederick Deeming may not have been exceptionally small for his time. Some researchers have estimated the average height for a man in the 1870s was around five feet and five inches. Various reports of the era have suggested Deeming stood anywhere between 5'3" and 5'6". But his short stature and 'sloping shoulders' were frequently referred to by witnesses and journalists.

Celia Thaxter's relationship with Marion Dickinson is well documented in the hundreds of Thaxter letters held by the Boston Public Library (https://www.digitalcommonwealth.org/collections/commonwealth:qb98nm50n), along with other Thaxter correspondence with the novelists Sarah Orne Jewett (http://www.public.coe.

edu/~theller/soj/let/Corresp/1885.html) and Annie Fields (https://www.digitalcommonwealth.org/search/commonwealth:qb98p457v).

Jane Clark, the senior research curator at the Museum of Old and New Art in Hobart, graciously provided me with many of her notes and background material on Sidney Dickinson's life and lectures around the world with his stereopticon. Her chapter on Dickinson in the book *The Magic Lantern at Work* was an invaluable source. Reviews of Dickinson's lectures throughout Australia can be found in the National Library of Australia's world-leading digitised newspaper resource, Trove (https://trove.nla.gov.au/) and the National Library of New Zealand's Papers Past (https://paperspast.natlib.govt.nz/).

I also relied on Dickinson's work for *The New York Times* and the *Boston Journal*, as well as articles written by him for *Scribner's* and *Scientific American*. One of his final pieces of work, a 1915 short story called 'The Golden-Haired Maiden', was published in *The Crisis*, the official magazine of the National Association for the Advancement of Colored People. It can be found here (https://www.marxists.org/history/usa/workers/civil-rights/crisis/0600-crisis-v10n02-w056.pdf). The description of Sidney's meeting with Wilkie Collins relies on his own account in *True Tales of The Weird*. Biographical information on Collins was sourced from the books *Wilkie Collins – An Illustrated Guide* and *Wilkie Collins – A Life of Sensation*.

Dickinson's article about Australia appeared in a *Scientific American* supplement on 20 October 1900. Additional Dickinson material was sourced from https://ramblesinhistory.blog/2017/10/02/a-mothers-letter-from-northampton-ma-1882/. Reports about his NZ and Australian speaking tours were sourced from *The Age, The Argus, The Sydney Morning Herald, The Evening News, The Ballarat Courier* and *The Launceston Examiner*. He also published a lengthy article on hunting for platypus, which was published in *Scribner's Magazine* in 1893 and can be found here: https://www.unz.com/print/Scribners-1893jun-00791/.

PART II

The sale of Deeming's pet lion was reported by the *Liverpool Mercury* on Saturday 19 March 1892. William Cross's disputed ownership of the lion with Wombwell and Bailey's Travelling Menagerie featured in a story in *The Lancashire Evening Post* on 30 March 1892. An insightful summary of Cross and his place in the exotic animal trade was written by Alexander Scott in the *Journal of Victorian Culture*, Vol 25, January 2020 pp.1–20. Several Australian newspapers also reported the escape of his 300 pythons, including the *Portland Guardian* on Friday 16 October 1891.

The early history of the Deeming family is scant, but it is clear many worked in Lancashire's coal pits during the first half of the nineteenth century. The tragic history of one of those Deeming clans appeared in *The Leicester Chronicle* on 8 March 1856. Extracts of The Children's Employment Commission Report into the working conditions in collieries of children can be found at https://www.nationalarchives. gov.uk/education/resources/victorian-lives/children-mines/.

Thomas Deeming's mental health problems were first raised by his eldest child, Edward, and Edward's wife, Mary Jane, in comments to English reporters and then in a sworn affidavit made on 29 April 1892 at the London offices of solicitors Wilson and Wallis. Another sworn statement by Edward was read during the appeal to the Privy Council four days before Frederick's execution. It was published in full by London's *Evening Mail* on page 7 on Friday 20 May 1892. Edward also said Frederick worked for a short time at the Laird Brothers shipyard, a detail Frederick also mentioned to the Perth lawyer, Richard Haynes. Census data about the family of Ann and Thomas Deeming and their movements during the second half of the nineteenth century, along with the registered deaths of both parents, appear in Mike Covell's exhaustively researched self-published book, *Frederick Bailey Deeming – Jack the Ripper or Something Worse?*

An in-depth summary of Deeming's medical history and mental health was published in *The British Medical Journal* on 27 August

1892 and included a 'certified true extract' by Dr Alexander Crombie, Surgeon-Superintendent, relating to Deeming's stay in the Presidency General Hospital in Calcutta. It stated: 'On March 28th, 1878, Frederick Deeming, steward of the steamer *Malcolm*, was admitted for tonsillitis, with a history of ague [malaria]; that he remained in the hospital for 83 days, suffering from epilepsy from April 17th until his discharge on June 18th, when he was sent home to England. During those two months he had over 50 epileptiform attacks, sometimes as many as 14 in a day; in some there were localised twitchings of the right arm and leg for about a week, there was paresis of the right arm and leg with partial anaesthesia; at another time he remained unconscious most of the day.'

Deeming's theft of eight gas burners was recorded by the *New South Wales Police Gazette and Weekly Record of Crime* (8 March 1882, p.91). His sentence of six weeks' hard labour was reported by several newspapers, including *The Sydney Daily Telegraph* (7 April 1882). A record of Marie Deeming's arrival in Australia on the *Samuel Plimsoll* in 1882 is held by the NSW State Archives (Assisted Immigrants Index 1839–1896, Reels 2142, 2493). Deeming's court case in Rockhampton was reported in the *Morning Bulletin* (21 November 1883, p.3).

The statement of John McKewen, Deeming's former apprentice in Sydney, was first made to the editor of *The Hay Standard* (2 April 1892, p.1). Deeming's financial difficulties, his insolvency hearing and subsequent gaoling for fourteen days in 1887 were covered by several newspapers at the time, including *The Sydney Morning Herald* and the *Evening News*. Records relating to his insolvency are held by the NSW State Archives (Insolvency Index 1842–1887, File No: 22657).

His time in South Africa remains a frustratingly confusing period for those trying to track his movements because of the lack of archival material and the often speculative reporting about his time there. But there is no doubt he arrived there in the first quarter of 1888. *The South Australian Advertiser* (31 January 1888, p.4) listed 'Mrs and Mrs Ward and two children' and 'Messrs H. Howe and

D. S. Howe' as the only passengers on board *Barossa* bound for St Helena, while reports in *The Advertiser* (21 March 1892, p.5) and the *South Australian Register* (23 March 1892, p.6) provide details of that voyage. It is clear that after arriving in Cape Town he spent time in the Kimberley region as well as Johannesburg. But the full extent of his crimes in South Africa will never be known. Some of the claims of murder and fraud were later denied by South African police. It also seems unlikely, given his poor spelling and grammar, that he would have had the capacity to swindle a major bank of tens of thousands of pounds. But it is almost certain, given the efforts made to track his later movements in England, that he pulled off several scams and by the time he arrived back in Birkenhead in 1889 to rejoin Marie he had with him a substantial amount of cash. Deeming's account of his time in South Africa given to Richard Haynes was reported in the *Western Mail* (28 May 1892, p.3). The extensive account by a private detective named Joseph Ellis who was hired to trace Deeming after his arrival back in England appeared in Liverpool's *The Weekly Courier* (26 March 1892, p.5).

The daunting task of examining the Jack the Ripper case and Deeming's potential involvement was made much easier thanks to the advice and assistance of Baltimore-based historian, poet and world-renowned Ripperologist, Christopher T. George. A curated list of Ripper-related titles and material can be found in the bibliography.

Deeming's time in Antwerp, Hull and subsequent voyage to Montevideo was pieced together from many sources. Harry Webster gave several interviews about his experiences with Deeming, including *The Argus* (9 August 1924, p.8) and *The Age* (2 April 1892, p.8). I also relied in part on reports in *The Londonderry Sentinel* (19 April 1892, p.3), the *Lancashire Evening Post* (29 March 1892, p.4), the *Western Chronicle* (25 March 1892, p.8), *Aberdeen Press and Journal* (22 March 1892, p.6), *The Beverley Guardian* (13 September 1890), *The Hull Daily News* (15 September 1890) and the *Hull Daily Mail* (26 September 1890, p.4, and 11 July 1890, p.3). As well, an extensive list of trial-related matter from the Hull City Archives

(CQB 396/1328 CR (A) 1890) appears in *Frederick Bailey Deeming – Jack the Ripper or Something Worse?*.

PART III

The journey of the *Kaiser Wilhelm II* from England to Australia in November–December 1891 and the experiences of Albert and Emily Williams on board were reconstructed using reports in *The Age*, *The Argus* and *The Herald* along with witnesses' depositions in the coronial inquiry into Emily's death and testimony in Deeming's subsequent murder trial. Many of these can be found in the Deeming case files held by the Public Records Office of Victoria including: VPRS 1100/PO Capital Sentences Files; VPRS 1087/PO Despatches from the secretary of State to the Governor; VPRS 30/PO Criminal Trial Briefs; VPRS 264/PO Capital Case Files; VPRS 515/PO Central Register of Male Prisoners; VPRS 3524/PO Criminal Trial Brief Register II.

Other depositions can be found in the National Library of Australia in the Papers of Alfred Deakin (MS 1540-Papers of Alfred Deakin/Series6/Subseries 6 3/Item 191).

The marriage of Albert Williams and Emily Mather was reported in London's *The Standard* (September 1891, p.1). Emily's letters to her mother were extensively reported and, among several sources, I relied on the *Croydon Chronicle and East Surrey Advertiser* (26 March 1892, p.7).

Information on the *Kaiser Wilhelm II* – which should not be confused with a German battleship of the same name that was launched in 1897 – was sourced from contemporary shipping lists, the website www.norwayheritage.com and the Glenwick-Gjonvik Archives (https://www.gjenvick.com/SteamshipLines/NorthGerman Lloyd/1889-KaiserWilhelmII.html).

The assault of Sidney Dickinson and the subsequent court hearing was detailed in *The Argus* (10 October 1891, p.12); *The Herald* (9 October 1891, p.1) and *The Age* (10 October 1891, p.10). The Dickinsons' search for a new home in Melbourne is related in *True Tales of the Weird*.

PART IV

Sidney Dickinson's account of the smell lingering over Melbourne in the early 1890s comes from his article in *The New York Times* (21 May 1893, p.20). Construction of the city's sewerage system began in May 1892 following a series of recommendations by a Royal Commission four years earlier.

Superintendent Douglas Kennedy's career was detailed in *The Weekly Times* (30 December 1893, p.31). Corruption in the ranks of the Victorian police force was uncovered by the 1881 Royal Commission on the Police Force of Victoria (https://digitised-collections.unimelb.edu.au/bitstream/handle/11343/21370/268762_UDS2010417-3.pdf?sequence=1&isAllowed=y).

Evidence that Kennedy's detective branch was filled with preening egos spilled into the public several weeks before the discovery of Emily Williams's body. Kennedy had been summoned to appear before an inquiry into a man's wrongful arrest and conviction by one of his detectives, Sergeant Edward O'Donnell. The inquiry had already revealed the rivalries and constant feuding inside the elite new detective unit. It had been told these feuds sometimes erupted into brawling in the muster room. O'Donnell was disliked by many of his colleagues and some refused to work with him. Superintendent Kennedy, it seemed, shared their distrust, acknowledging at the inquiry there was a 'healthy rivalry' among his detectives. Kennedy shared his men's dislike for O'Donnell, saying, 'He has a nasty, disagreeable temper at times, and that makes men not like him . . . A man who cannot agree with his comrades ought not to be in the police force.'

The formation of Kennedy's detective branch is detailed in *The People's Force* (Haldane, Robert. Melbourne University Press, third edition, 2017) while the origin of the science of fingerprinting can be found in Francis Galton's work, *Finger Prints* (Macmillan, 1893).

Dr Robert Scott's reminiscences of Frederick Deeming were made in a statement to *The Age* (10 March 1892, p.5). Other events detailed in this section were reconstructed using evidence at the inquest and murder trial and from contemporary Australian newspaper accounts.

Samuel Lowe's extensive account of his interview with Dove Mather and his subsequent investigation that led to the discovery of the bodies of Marie Deeming and her four children appeared in *The Argus* (17 August 1895, p.4) and was reprinted in newspapers around the world.

PART V

Descriptions of the mining township of Southern Cross and Deeming's time working at Fraser's Mine and his subsequent arrest came from contemporary newspaper reports and the books *Glint of Gold* (Uren, Malcolm. Robertson and Mullens Ltd, 1948) and *They Wished Upon a Star: A History of Southern Cross and Yilgarn* (McMahon, P. T. Pan, 1999). Biographical detail about Constable Evan Williams was gleaned from several sources including a report in the *Pingelly-Brookton Leader* (7 August 1947, p.4), while an account of Jim Fairclough's life can be found in *The Albany Advertiser* (18 January 1940, p.5). Deeming's encounters with Ambrose Lamandé were widely reported in the 1890s, including the *National Advocate* (10 June 1892, p.4), along with Lamandé's own account which appeared as a letter in *The Argus* (29 June 1898, p.7).

The State Records Office of Western Australia also holds documents relating to the arrest of Baron Swanston at Southern Cross, including the original warrant issued for his arrest (1892/0413).

The inquest into the deaths of Marie Deeming and her children was widely reported across England. I have drawn from many of those reports including those in the *Liverpool Echo*, the *Manchester Times*, *The Manchester Evening News*, the *Liverpool Mercury*, the *Leicester Chronicle*, *The Penny Illustrated Paper*, *London Daily News* and the *Liverpool Weekly Courier*.

For Deeming's court appearances in Perth I relied on contemporary newspaper accounts. His conversations with his lawyer, Richard Haynes, and his extensive recollections about his life were reported in the *Western Mail* (28 May 1892, pp.3–4).

Davison Symmons was one of Australia's most highly regarded journalists and a decent profile of his career can be found in *The Worker* (16 April 1908, p.17).

PART VI

Marshall Lyle continued to correspond with Cesare Lombroso throughout the 1890s. Several of Lyle's letters can be found at The Lombroso Project, a digital catalogue of Lombroso's unpublished work at http://www.lombrosoproject.it/eng/index.php. Reports of Lyle's defence of William Colston appeared in Melbourne newspapers throughout 1891. I have also referenced an obituary of Lyle in *The Herald* (19 August 1944, p.5) and mentions of him in Chapter 10 of the book *Literature as Translation*, edited by Christopher Conti and James Gourley, Cambridge Scholars Publishing, 2014.

Lombroso's major work, *Criminal Man*, can be accessed at https://www.gutenberg.org/files/29895/29895-h/29895-h.htm.

Edward Thunderbolt was one of the most colourful characters in Melbourne in the 1890s. In June 1892 Thunderbolt organised for the body of Emily Williams to be disinterred from its grave in the paupers' burial area of the Melbourne cemetery and reburied in the Church of England section. This was in accordance with the wishes of her mother, Dove, who wrote to Thunderbolt saying: 'She was always a member of the Church of England, and if it can be done I should like her body to be placed in that portion of the cemetery belonging to the Episcopal Church.' One of Thunderbolt's inventions – a servomotor used to regulate the racing of a ship's engine when encountering heavy seas – was granted a patent by the United States Patent Office in August 1895. The following year *The Age* (9 March 1896, p.6) reported that his wife, Marion Thunderbolt, had charged him with 'leaving her without means of support' and alleged he had fathered a child with a young woman with whom he was having an affair. He later moved to England in an attempt to commercialise his inventions but according to *The Leader* (15 April 1905, p.33), he was sacked by the directors of the company he had formed – Thunderbolt Patent Governor Company Limited – for alleged 'misconduct, disobedience and incapacity'.

Alfred Deakin's early years and heavy involvement in spirituality have been explored in several books including Judith Brett's *The Enigmatic Mr Deakin* (Text Publishing, 2017) and Alfred Gabay's *The Mystic Life of Alfred Deakin* (Cambridge University Press, 1992). I have also referenced the National Library of Australia's extensive collection of *The Papers of Alfred Deakin*, particularly 'Series 5. Religion and spiritualism, 1874–1913' and 'Series 6. Law Practice, 1854–1898', which includes records of the Deeming case, a draft of Deakin's address to the jury and affidavits of witnesses from previous hearings. His wife Pattie's role as a medium in many séances has been extensively reported and a good summary of her involvement in the spiritualist movement can be found at https://www.sea.museum/2018/09/06/seeking-the-lost-browne-boys-spiritualism-and-grief. Deakin and Lyle continued their relationship for many years. In 1907 Deakin was president of The Victorian Land Settlement Division of the Immigration League of Australia, and Lyle served as its secretary.

To reconstruct Deeming's murder trial I drew from hundreds of contemporary Australian and English newspaper accounts, reports filed by Sidney Dickinson for *The New York Times* and from documents held by the Public Records Office of Victoria.

The letter from 'Signor D'atorz' raising the possibility that Deeming, after marrying Marie, did not travel straight to Australia but instead went first to Canada and the United States and committed several crimes is held by the Public Records Office of Victoria (PROV, VPRS 937/PO Inward Registered Correspondence, unit 511, Deeming Case).

A final word of thanks to publisher Alison Urquhart for her unwavering support, and to Michael Epis and Patrick Mangan, two committed and passionate editors who waded patiently through my drafts and improved this story immeasurably.

BIBLIOGRAPHY

Abbott, Karen, *The Fox Sisters and the Rap on Spiritualism*, Smithsonian Magazine, October 2012

Abrahamsen, David, *Murder and Madness: The Secret Life of Jack the Ripper*, Donald Fine, 1992

Anderson, Steven, *A History of Capital Punishment in the Australian Colonies, 1788 to 1900*, Springer Nature Switzerland, 2020

Anonymous, *Frederick Bailey Deeming: A Romance of Crime*, Port Melbourne Tribune Printing and Publishing Company, 1892

Anonymous, *The Complete History of the Windsor Tragedy, Embracing the Career of Frederick Bailey Deeming*, Mason, Firth and McCutcheon, 1892

Anonymous, *The Criminal of the Century: A Complete History of the Career of Frederick Bailey Deeming, Alias Baron Swanston, Alias Albert Williams & C., The Perpetrator of the Windsor and Rainhill Murders*, Australian Mining Standards Office, 1892

Anonymous, *The Life and History of A. O. Williams (Frederick Bayley Deeming), The Supposed Rainhill Murderer, By One Who Knew Him*, Poppin's Court, Fleet Street, 1892

Anonymous, *The Life of Deeming: Murderer of Women and Children*, John F. Williams, 1892

Begg, Paul and Bennett, John, *Jack the Ripper*, Carlton Books, 2017

Begg, Paul, Fido, Martin, Skinner, Keith, *The Complete Jack the Ripper A–Z*, John Blake, 2015

Birmingham, John, *Leviathan: The Unauthorised Biography of Sydney*, Penguin, 2000

Bloomfield, Jeffrey, 'Deeming and the Privy Council: A Comedy of Terrors'. *Ripperologist*, Number 51, January 2004

Booth, Charles, Ed, *Life and Labour of the People in London*, MacMillan and Co, 1895

Brett, Judith, *The Enigmatic Mr Deakin*, Text Publishing, 2017

Brown-May, Andrew, *Melbourne Street Life: The Itinerary of our Days*, Australian Scholarly Publishing, 1998

Castieau, John Buckley (edited by Finnane, Mark), *The Difficulties of My Position: The Diaries of Prison Governor John Buckley Castieau, 1855–1884*, National Library of Australia, 2004

Clune, Frank, *The Demon Killer: The Career of Deeming, Satanic Murderer*, Invincible Press, 1948

Collard, Ian, *Cammell Laird: Volume Two, The Naval Ships*, The History Press, 2006

Collard, Ian, *Ships of the Mersey: A Photographic History*, Amberley Publishing, 2013

Cornwell, Patricia, *Portrait of a Killer: Jack the Ripper – Case Closed*, Berkley, 2002

Covell, Mike, *Frederick Bailey Deeming: 'Jack the Ripper' or something worse?*, Creativia, 2014

Curtis, L. Perry, *Jack the Ripper and the London Press*, Yale University Press, 2001

Davenport, Reuben Briggs, *The Death Blow to Spiritualism; Being the True Story of the Fox Sisters, as Revealed by Authority of Margaret Fox Kane and Catherine Fox Jencken*, G. W. Dillingham Co. 1888

Davies, Alan, *Coal Mining in Lancashire and Cheshire*, Amberley Publishing, 2010

Davison, Graeme, *The Rise and Fall of Marvellous Melbourne*, Melbourne University Press, 1978

Dickinson, Sidney, *True Tales of the Weird: A Record of Personal Experiences of the Supernatural*, Duffield and Company, 1920

Docker, John, *The Nervous Nineties: Australian Cultural Life in the 1890s*, Oxford University Press, 1991

Duxbury, Stephen, *The Brief History of Lancashire*, The History Press, 2017

Ellis, Havelock, *The Criminal*, Walter Scott, 1890

Evans, Stewart, Skinner, Keith, *Jack the Ripper: Letters from Hell*, History Press, 1997

Fido, Martin, *The Crimes, Detection and Death of Jack the Ripper*, Weidenfeld and Nicolson, 1987

Fishbourne, J. Y., and Springthorpe, J. W., 'An Account of the Mental Condition and Trial of the Rainhill and Windsor Murderer (Deeming alias Williams)', *The British Medical Journal*, 9 July 1892

Franks-Buckley, Tony, *The History of Birkenhead and Bidston: The Wirral Peninsula*, Createspace, 2012

Gabay, Alfred J., *Messages from Beyond: Spiritualism and Spiritualists in Melbourne's Golden Age*, Melbourne University Press, 2001

Gabay, Al, *The Mystic Life of Alfred Deakin*, Cambridge University Press, 1992

Galton, Francis, *Finger Prints*, Macmillan, 1892

Gasson, Andrew, *Wilkie Collins – An Illustrated Guide*, Oxford University Press, 1998

Gilchrist, Catie, *Murder, Misadventure and Miserable Ends: Tales from a Colonial Coroner's Court*, HarperCollins, 2019

Godl, John, 'The Skull of Jack the Ripper?', *Ripperana: The True Crime Mystery Magazine*, Number 23, January 1998

Goodman, David, *Foul Deeds and Suspicious Deaths around Hull*, Wharncliffe Books, 2005

Gurvich, Maurice and Wray, Christopher, *The Scarlet Thread: Australia's Jack the Ripper, a True Crime Story*, Fairfax Books, 2007

Haldane, Robert, *The People's Force: A History of Victoria Police*, Melbourne University Press, 2017

Home, Daniel Dunglas, *Incidents In My Life*, Cosimo Classics, 2005

Honeycombe, Gordon, *Murders of the Black Museum – The Dark Secrets Behind A Hundred Years of the Most Notorious Crimes in England*, Kings Road Publishing, 2011

Innes, Brian, *Serial Killers: Shocking, Gripping True Crime Stories of the Most Evil Murders*, Quercus, 2017

Jolly, Martyn and DeCourcy, Elisa (Edited by), *The Magic Lantern at Work: Witnessing, Persuading, Experiencing and Connecting*, Routledge, 2020

Jones, Barry O., 'Deeming, Frederick Bailey (1853–1892)', *Australian Dictionary of Biography*, Volume 8, Melbourne University Press, 1981

Kelly, Lorraine and King, Norma, *Goldfields Stories: Early Days in Western Australia,* Lorraine Kelly, 2018

Kidd, Paul B, *Australia's Serial Killers: The Definitive History of Serial Multicide in Australia*, Macmillan, 2000

Knepper, Paul, *The Cesare Lombroso Handbook*, Routledge, 2014

La Nauze, J. A., *Alfred Deakin: A Biography*, Melbourne University Press, 1965

Lombroso-Ferrero, Gina, *Criminal Man: According to the Classification of Cesare Lombroso*, G. P. Putnam's Sons, 1911

London, Jack, *People of the Abyss*, Creative Media Partners, LLC, 2017 (originally published in 1903)

Low, Patrick, Rutherford, Helen, Sandford-Couch, Clare (Eds.), *Execution Culture in Nineteenth Century Britain*, Routledge, 2020

Lycett, Andrew, *Wilkie Collins: A Life of Sensation*, Hutchinson, 2013

Meredith, Martin, *Diamonds, Gold and War: The British, the Boers and the Making of South Africa*, Public Affairs, 2008

Martin, Beth, *Albany's Brush with a Mass Murderer: A man of many faces, Frederick Bailey Deeming*, Albany Historical Society, 1998

Mazzarello, Paolo, 'Cesare Lombroso: an anthropologist between evolution and degeneration', *Functional Neurology*, April-June, pp.97–101, 2011

McMahon, P. T., *They Wished Upon A Star: A History of Southern Cross and Yilgarn*, Pan, 1999

Nadel, G., *Australia's Colonial Culture*, Angus and Robertson, Sydney, 1957

Nelson, G. K., *Spiritualism and Society*, Routledge & Kegan Paul, 1969

Newnham, W. H., *Melbourne: The Biography of a City*, F. W. Cheshire, 1956

Oppenheim, Janet, *The Other World: Spiritualism and Psychical Research in England, 1850–1914*, Cambridge University Press, 1988

O'Sullivan, J. S., *A Most Unique Ruffian: The Trial of F. B. Deeming, Melbourne, 1892*, Invincible Press, 1968

Owen, Alex, *The Darkened Room: Women, Power and Spiritualism in Late Victorian England*, Virago Press, London, 1989

Peel, Mark and Twomey, Christina, *A History of Australia*, Red Globe Press, 2017

Plimmer, John, *Whitechapel Murders Solved*, House of Stratus, 2003

Privy Council, *Judgement of the Lords of the Judicial Committee of the Privy Council on the Petition for special leave to Appeal of Frederick Deeming, from the Colony of Victoria; delivered 19 May, 1892* https://www.casemine.com/judgement/uk/5b4dc23f2c94e07cccd2332e

Rubenhold, Hallie, *The Five – The Untold Lives of the Women Killed by Jack the Ripper*, Doubleday, 2019

Rumbelow, Donald, *The Complete Jack the Ripper*, Penguin, 2004

Scott, Alexander, 'The "Missing Link" Between Science and Show Business: Exhibiting Gorillas and Chimpanzees in Victorian Liverpool', *Journal of Victorian Culture*, Vol. 25, Issue 1, January 2020, pp.1–20

Serle, Geoffrey, *The Rush to be Rich: A History of the Colony of Victoria 1883–1889*, Melbourne University Press, 1971

Sharpe, Elizabeth M., *In The Shadow of the Dam: The Aftermath of the Mill River Flood of 1874*, Free Press, 2014

Shepherd, Jade, '"One of the best fathers until He Went Out of His Mind": Paternal Child-Murder, 1864–1900', *Journal of Victorian Culture*, Vol. 18, Issue 1, March 2013

Singer, Kurt, *My Strangest Case: By Police Chiefs of the World*, W. H. Allen, 1957

Sugden, Philip, *The Complete History of Jack the Ripper*, W. H. Allen, 1975

Taylor, Langdon, *A Handy Guide to Palmistry*, Roxburghe Press, 1806

Thaxter, Rosamond, *Sandpiper: The Life and Letters of Celia Thaxter*, Peter E. Randall, 1999

Thompson, Erin, *Deconstructing 'Jack': How Jack the Ripper Became More Fiction Than Fact*, Augsburg Honors Review, Vol. 11, 2018

Tulloch, Alexander, *The Story of Liverpool*, The History Press, 2008

Uren, Malcolm, *Glint of Gold: A story of the goldfields of Western Australia and the men who found them*, Robertson and Mullens Ltd, 1948

Waldron, David, 'Playing the Ghost: Ghost hoaxing and supernaturalism in late nineteenth-century Victoria', *Provenance*, Issue 13, pp.34–43, 2014

Weaver, Rachael, *The Criminal of the Century*, Australian Scholarly Publishing, 2006

Weisberg, Barbara, *Talking to the Dead: Kate and Maggie Fox and the Rise of Spiritualism*, HarperCollins, 2004

Westcott, Tom, *The Bank Holiday Murders: The True Story of the First Whitechapel Murders*, Crime Confidential Press, 2013

White, Edward, 'In the Joints of Their Toes: The ruse that gave rise to the spiritualist movement', *The Paris Review*, 4 November 2016

Discover a
new favourite